Teach Yourself VISUALLY™

Microsoft®
Access® 2013

NF

Visual™

by Paul McFedries

WILEY

John Wiley & Sons, Inc.

Teach Yourself VISUALLY™ Access® 2013

Published by
John Wiley & Sons, Inc.
10475 Crosspoint Boulevard
Indianapolis, IN 46256

www.wiley.com

Published simultaneously in Canada

Library of Congress Control Number: 2013932930

ISBN: 978-1-118-51770-3

Manufactured in the United States of America

10 9 8 7 6 5 4 3 2 1

Trademark Acknowledgments

Contact Us

For general information on our other products and services please contact our Customer Care Department within the United States at (877)762-2974, outside the United States at (317)572-3993 or fax (317)572-4002.

For technical support, please visit www.wiley.com/techsupport.

WILEY   Sales | Contact Wiley at (877) 762-2974 or fax (317) 572-4002.

Credits

Executive Editor
Jody Lefevere

Project Editor
Dana Rhodes Lesh

Technical Editor
Vince Averello

Copy Editor
Dana Rhodes Lesh

Editorial Director
Robyn Siesky

Business Manager
Amy Knies

Senior Marketing Manager
Sandy Smith

**Vice President and Executive
Group Publisher**
Richard Swadley

**Vice President and Executive
Publisher**
Barry Pruett

Project Coordinator
Katie Crocker

Graphics and Production Specialists
Ana Carrillo
Joyce Haughey
Andrea Hornberger
Jennifer Mayberry

Quality Control Technician
Lauren Mandelbaum

Proofreading and Indexing
Cynthia Fields
BIM Indexing & Proofreading Services

About the Author

Paul McFedries is a full-time technical writer. Paul has been authoring computer books since 1991 and has more than 80 books to his credit. His books have sold more than four million copies worldwide. These books include the Wiley titles *Teach Yourself VISUALLY Microsoft Excel 2013*, *Teach Yourself VISUALLY Microsoft Windows 8*, *Windows 8 Visual Quick Tips*, *iPhone 5 Portable Genius*, and *iPad 4th Generation and iPad mini Portable Genius*. Paul is also the proprietor of Word Spy (www.wordspy.com), a website that tracks new words and phrases as they enter the language. Paul invites you to drop by his personal website at www.mcfedries.com or follow him on Twitter at @paulmcf and @wordspy.

Author's Acknowledgments

It goes without saying that writers focus on text, and I certainly enjoyed focusing on the text that you will read in this book. However, this book is more than just the usual collection of words and phrases. A quick thumb through the pages will show you that this book is also chock-full of images, including sharp screenshots. Those colorful images make for a beautiful book, and that beauty comes from a lot of hard work by Wiley's immensely talented group of designers and layout artists. They are all listed in the Credits section on the previous page, and I thank them for creating another gem. Of course, what you read in this book must also be accurate, logically presented, and free of errors. Ensuring all of this was an excellent group of editors that included project editor and copy editor Dana Lesh and technical editor Vince Averello. Thanks for your exceptional competence and hard work. Thanks, as well, to Wiley executive editor Jody Lefevere for asking me to write this book.

How to Use This Book

Whom This Book Is For

This book is for the reader who has never used Microsoft Access. It is also for readers who want to expand their knowledge of Access and learn about the features of the latest version.

The Conventions in This Book

① Steps

This book uses a step-by-step format to guide you easily through each task. **Numbered steps** are actions you must perform; **bulleted steps** clarify a point, step, or optional feature; and **indented steps** give you the result.

② Notes

Notes give additional information — special conditions that may occur during an operation, a situation that you want to avoid, or a cross-reference to a related area of the book.

③ Icons and Buttons

Icons and buttons show you exactly what you need to click to perform a step.

④ Tips

Tips offer additional information, including warnings and shortcuts.

⑤ Bold

Bold type shows command names or options that you must click and text or numbers you must type.

⑥ Italics

Italic type introduces and defines a new term.

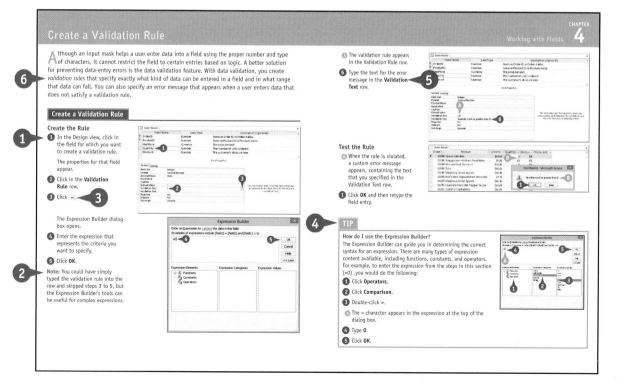

Table of Contents

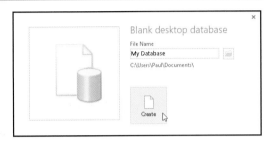

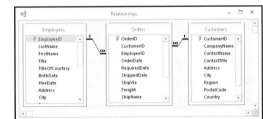

Chapter 3 — Entering and Editing Data

Chapter 4 — Working with Fields

Table of Contents

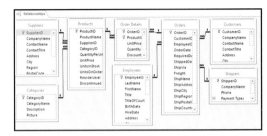

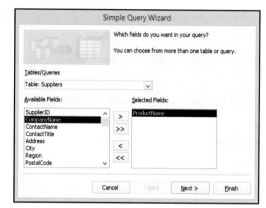

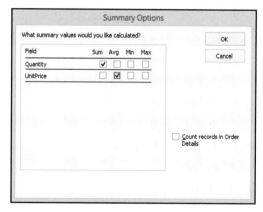

Table of Contents

Chapter 11 | Creating Reports

Chapter 12 | Grouping and Sorting Data

Table of Contents

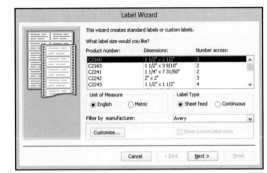

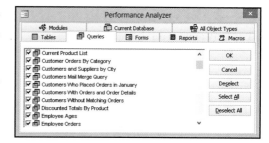

CHAPTER 1

Getting Started with Access

Are you new to Microsoft Access or upgrading to the latest version of the program? This chapter introduces you to Access and to some useful database concepts. You also learn how to create and open a database as well as how to navigate through the Access interface.

An Introduction to Access

Microsoft Access is a program for creating and working with special files called *databases,* which are designed to store collections of related information. For example, one database might store business data such as customers, invoices, and inventory, whereas another might store personal data such as contacts, movies, and household items. You can use Access to create, retrieve, and manage large or small collections of information.

To get the most out of Access, you need to understand basic concepts such as tables, records, and fields; database objects such as datasheets and forms; and database tools such as filters, queries, and reports.

Tables, Records, and Fields

In Access, data is stored in *tables,* and each individual entry in a table is called a *record.* For example, in a Customers table, the information about each customer is a separate record. Each record is composed of one or more *fields* that contain individual pieces of data. In this example, customer fields may include Name, Address, City, State, and Zip Code.

City	Country	Postal Code	Region	Phone	Fax	Click to Add
⊞ México D.F.	Mexico	05023		(5) 555-3932		
⊞ London	UK	WA1 1DP		(171) 555-7788	(171) 555-6750	
⊞ Luleå	Sweden	S-958 22		0921-12 34 65	0921-12 34 67	
⊞ Mannheim	Germany	68306		0621-08460	0621-08924	
⊞ Strasbourg	France	67000		88.60.15.31	88.60.15.32	
⊞ Madrid	Spain	28023		(91) 555 22 82	(91) 555 91 99	
⊞ Marseille	France	13008		91.24.45.40	91.24.45.41	
⊞ Tsawassen	Canada	T2F 8M4	BC	(604) 555-4729	(604) 555-3745	
⊞ London	UK	EC2 5NT		(171) 555-1212		
⊞ Buenos Aires	Argentina	1010		(1) 135-5555	(1) 135-4892	
⊞ México D.F.	Mexico	05022		(5) 555-3392	(5) 555-7293	
⊞ Bern	Switzerland	3012		0452-076545		
⊞ São Paulo	Brazil	05432-043	SP	(11) 555-7647		

Record: ◄ ◄ 15 of 91 ► ►► ►* No Filter Search

Datasheets and Forms

By default, each table appears as a spreadsheet grid called a *datasheet.* You can type directly into a datasheet. To make data entry more convenient, some people choose to create on-screen *forms,* which are like dialog boxes that prompt for field entries. An attractively formatted form is easier and more pleasant to use to enter new records than a plain datasheet.

Customers

Customer ID	ALFKI	City	Berlin	
Company Name	Alfreds Futterkiste	Region		
Contact Name	Maria Anders	Postal Code	12209	
Contact Title	Sales Representative	Country	Germany	
Address	Obere Str. 57	Phone	030-0074321	
		Fax	030-0076545	

Record: ◄ ◄ 1 of 91 ► ►► ►* No Filter Search

Filters and Queries

It is often useful to display a filtered view of a table. You can filter a table to show only certain records, only certain fields, or both. You can run a one-time filter, or you can create a *query*, which is like a saved filter. Queries also enable you to combine data from multiple related tables into a single datasheet of results.

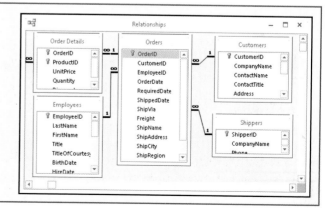

Reports

Tables and query results appear in plain datasheets, which are not very attractive when printed. Reports present data from tables and queries in an attractive, customizable format — complete with titles, headers and footers, and even logos and graphics.

Relational Databases

Microsoft Access creates *relational databases* — that is, databases that can contain multiple tables with links between them. For example, a business may have a Customers table for storing customer contact information and an Orders table for storing information about orders placed. Each customer in the Customers table has a unique ID, and each order in the Orders table references a specific customer ID.

Start and Exit Access

Before you can create or open a database file, you must first start Access. This brings the Access window onto the Windows desktop so that you can then begin using the program.

How you start Access depends on which version of Windows you are using. In this section, you learn how to start Access 2013 in Windows 8 and in Windows 7. When you are finished working with Access, you should exit the program.

Start and Exit Access

Start Access in Windows 8

 On the Windows 8 Start screen, click **Access 2013**.

The Microsoft Access window appears on the desktop.

Start Access in Windows 7

1 Click **Start**.

2 Click **All Programs**.

3 Click **Microsoft Office 2013**.

4 Click **Access 2013**.

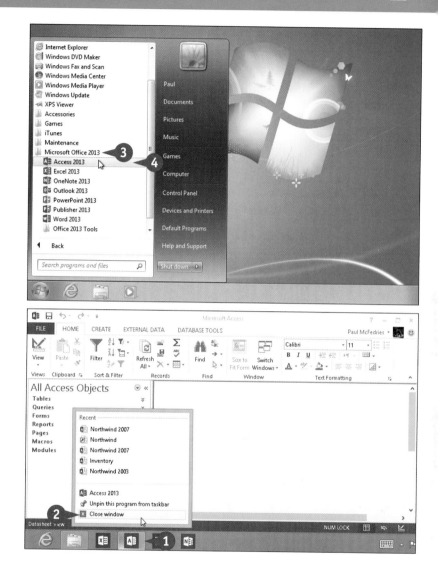

The Microsoft Access window appears on the desktop.

Exit Access

1 Right-click the Access taskbar button ().

2 Click **Close window**.

Note: If you have two or more database files open, click **Close all windows** instead.

Access closes, returning you to your desktop view.

TIP

Are there faster methods that I can use to start Access?

Yes. After you have used Access a few times in Windows 7, it should appear on the main Start menu in the list of your most-used programs. If so, you can click that icon to start the program. You can also force the Access icon onto the Start menu by following steps **1** to **3** in the "Start Access in Windows 7" subsection, right-clicking the **Microsoft Access 2013** icon, and then clicking **Pin to Start Menu**. If you are using Windows 8, you can right-click the **Access 2013** tile and then click **Pin to Taskbar** to add the Access icon to the desktop taskbar.

Create a Blank Database

The simplest way to get started with Microsoft Access is to create a blank database. A blank database contains only a single, empty table and no other database objects, such as queries, forms, or reports. A blank database provides the freedom to create exactly the objects that you want for your project.

If another person or your company has provided you with a database file, you should open that file instead; see the section "Open a Database."

Create a Blank Database

1 Click **File**.

Note: If you have just started Access, skip to step **3**.

The File options appear.

2 Click **New**.

The New options appear.

3 Click **Blank desktop database**.

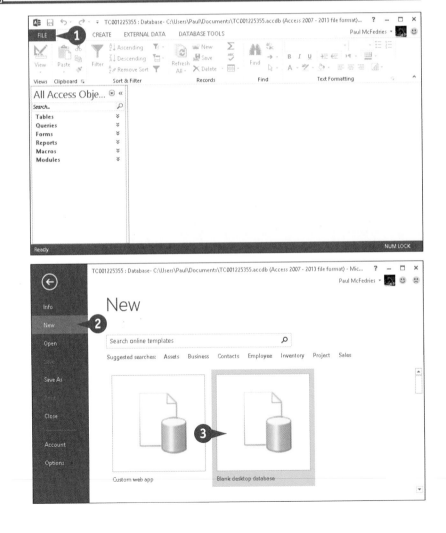

The Blank Desktop Database dialog box appears.

④ Type a filename for the database.

⑤ Click **Create**.

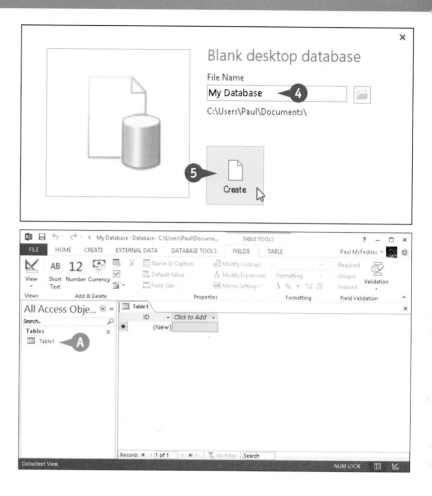

Ⓐ A new database opens, with a new blank table started.

TIP

Are there shortcuts that I can use to create a blank database?
Yes, Access offers a couple of techniques that you can use to shorten the process of creating a blank database. First, you can quickly display the New tab by pressing Ctrl + N. Second, if you prefer to use your mouse to begin the process of creating a blank database, you can add the New command to the Quick Access Toolbar. After you have done this, you can click **New** on the Quick Access Toolbar to go directly to the New tab. See the section "Customize the Quick Access Toolbar" to learn how to add commands to this toolbar.

Create a Database by Using a Template

Rather than start from scratch with a blank database, you can get your database project off the ground easier and faster by creating a new database based on a template.

A *template* is a special file that includes prefabricated database objects that you can use right away. For example, a contact management template might include a table with fields such as Name, Address, and Phone, as well as a form for entering data and a report that organizes the contacts into an address book. With a template, all you do is fill in the data, and Access does the rest.

Create a Database by Using a Template

1 Start Microsoft Access.

Note: If Access is already running, click **File** and then click **New** instead.

2 Type a word that describes the type of database you want to create.

Ⓐ You can also click any of these suggested template search terms.

Ⓑ You can also click one of these Microsoft-supplied templates that are stored on your computer and then skip to step **5**.

3 Press Enter.

The search results appear.

4 Click the template that best matches your needs.

A dialog box for that template appears.

 Type a name for the database file.

6 Click **Create**.

If you chose an online template, it is downloaded from the Internet.

The database opens. Its appearance depends on the template that you chose.

TIPS

When I create a database using a template, why do I sometimes see a security warning at the top of the database?

The Security Warning information bar tells you that the template includes extra programming tools called *macros* that provide some of the template's functionality. Macros can be dangerous if you download a template or database file from an unknown location. However, the templates available through Office Online are safe, so you should click **Enable Content** in the information bar to enable the template's macros.

What do I do if a Welcome or Getting Started tab or window appears in the new database?

Some templates offer extra features that make the template easier to use. For example, depending on the template, there may be instructions to read, a video to play, or web links to explore. Just follow the prompts that appear. Note that you might not see this extra content until you click **Enable Content** in the information bar.

Open a Database

If you have created multiple databases, you can open a database that you previously created to continue developing its structure, type data in it, or analyze its data.

Your database files will most often be stored on your computer's hard drive. However, it is also possible to open databases from your network or from the online SkyDrive storage area associated with your Microsoft account.

Open a Database

1 Start Microsoft Access.

2 Click **Open Other Files**.

Note: If Access is already running and you have another database open, click **File** instead.

The File options appear.

3 Click **Open**.

The Open options appear.

Ⓐ If you opened the database recently, you can also click **Recent** and then click the database. In this case, you can skip the rest of the steps in this section.

4 Click **Computer**.

5 Click **Browse**.

The Open dialog box appears.

Ⓑ If necessary, you can navigate to a different location.

6 Click the database that you want to open.

7 Click **Open**.

Access opens the database.

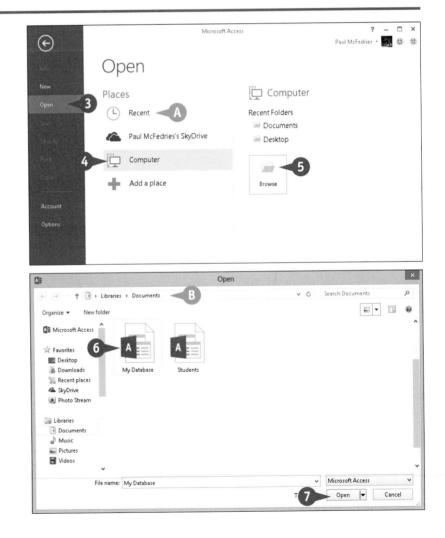

12

Close a Database

When you have finished your work with an Access database, you should close the file. You can have multiple databases open at once, each in its own copy of the application, but closing a database when you are finished with it frees up your computer's memory.

When you close a database, Access checks to see whether any open objects have unsaved changes. If Access detects an object that has unsaved changes, it prompts you to save it. This is a very important step because it prevents you from losing work, so be sure to save your changes when and if Access prompts you.

Close a Database

1 Click **File**.

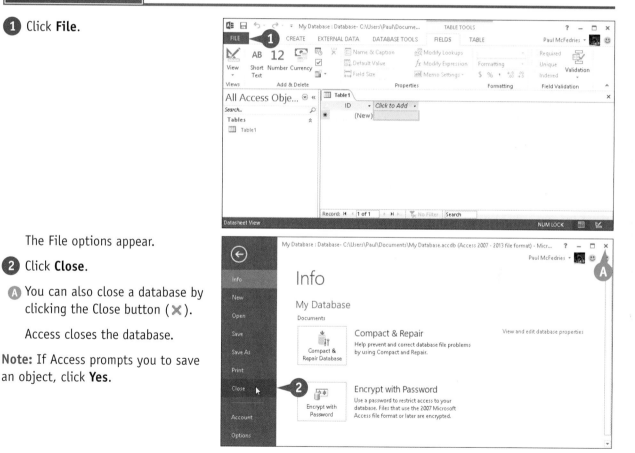

The File options appear.

2 Click **Close**.

A You can also close a database by clicking the Close button (✕).

Access closes the database.

Note: If Access prompts you to save an object, click **Yes**.

Understanding the Access Interface

A ccess 2013 has a user interface consistent with those of other Office 2013 applications, including Word and Excel. It contains tabs, a multiple-tabbed Ribbon, and a status bar.

A File

Displays a menu of file commands.

B Quick Access Toolbar

Provides shortcuts to commonly used features. This toolbar is customizable.

C Tabs

Contain buttons and other controls for working with data.

D Ribbon

Displays and organizes tabs.

E Dialog box launcher

Clicking this icon ( ) opens a dialog box related to the group.

F Groups

Organize controls into sections within tabs.

Ⓐ Object tabs

Provide access to all open database objects, such as tables, reports, and forms.

Ⓑ Scroll bars

Enable you to scroll through a datasheet.

Ⓒ View buttons

Switch between various views of the selected object. The buttons are different depending on what type of object is active. Hover over a button to find out which view each button represents.

Ⓓ Record selector

Displays the current record number and enables you to navigate to other records.

Ⓔ Status bar

Displays information about the current object or view.

Ⓕ The Navigation pane

Lists all available database objects.

Customize the Quick Access Toolbar

You can make Access easier to use by customizing the Quick Access Toolbar to include the Access commands that you use most often. You run Quick Access Toolbar commands with a single click, so adding your favorite commands saves time because you no longer have to search for and click a command on the Ribbon.

By default, the Quick Access Toolbar contains three buttons: Save, Undo, and Redo. You can add common commands such as New and Open to the Quick Access Toolbar, as well as hundreds of other Access commands.

Customize the Quick Access Toolbar

1 Click the Customize Quick Access Toolbar button (＝).

A If you see the command that you want, click it and skip the rest of the steps in this section.

2 Click **More Commands**.

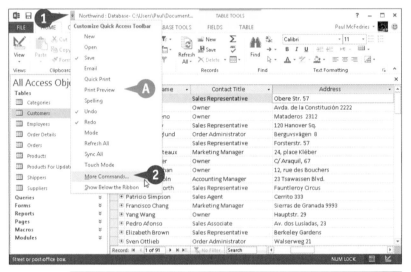

The Access Options dialog box appears.

B Access automatically displays the Quick Access Toolbar tab.

3 Click the **Choose commands from** ☑.

4 Click the command category that you want to use.

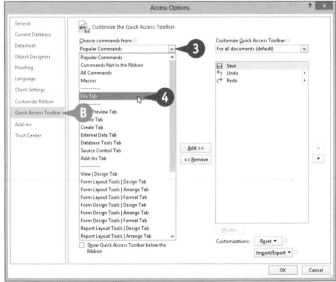

5 Click the command that you want to add.

6 Click **Add**.

C Access adds the command.

D To remove a command, click it and then click **Remove**.

7 Click **OK**.

Access tells you to close and reopen the database for the change to take effect.

8 Click **OK**.

E Access adds a button for the command to the Quick Access Toolbar.

Note: You do not need to close and then reopen the database.

Note: Another way to remove a command is to right-click the command and then click **Remove from Quick Access Toolbar**.

TIPS

Can I get more room on the Quick Access Toolbar to show more buttons?

Yes, you can increase the space available to the Quick Access Toolbar by moving it below the Ribbon. This gives the toolbar the full width of the Access window, so you can add many more buttons. Click the Customize Quick Access Toolbar button (⤓) and then click **Show Below the Ribbon**.

Is there a faster way to add buttons to the Quick Access Toolbar?

Yes. If the command that you want to add appears on the Ribbon, you can add a button for the command directly from the Ribbon. Click the Ribbon tab that contains the command, right-click the command, and then click **Add to Quick Access Toolbar**. Access inserts a button for the command on the Quick Access Toolbar.

Customize the Ribbon

Yᵒu can improve your Access productivity by customizing the Ribbon with extra commands that you use frequently. The Ribbon is a handy tool because it enables you to run Access commands with just a few clicks of the mouse. However, the Ribbon does not include every Access command. If there is a command that you use often, you should add it to the Ribbon for easy access.

To add a new command to the Ribbon, you must first create a new tab or a new group within an existing tab and then add the command to the new tab or group.

Customize the Ribbon

Display the Customize Ribbon Tab

1 Right-click any part of the Ribbon.

2 Click **Customize the Ribbon**.

The Access Options dialog box appears.

Ⓐ Access automatically displays the Customize Ribbon tab.

Add a New Tab or Group

3 Click the tab that you want to customize.

Ⓑ You can also click **New Tab** to create a custom tab.

4 Click **New Group**.

Ⓒ Access adds the group.

5 Click **Rename**.

The Rename dialog box appears.

6 Type a name for the group.

7 Click **OK**.

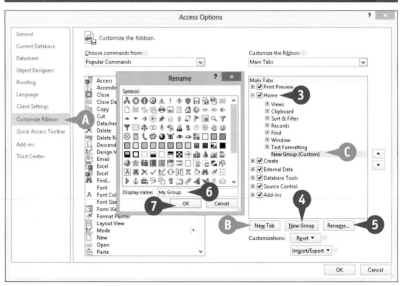

18

Add a Command

8 Click the **Choose commands from** ▾.

9 Click the command category that you want to use.

10 Click the command that you want to add.

11 Click the custom group or tab that you want to use.

12 Click **Add**.

D Access adds the command.

E To remove a custom command, click it and then click **Remove**.

13 Click **OK**.

Access tells you to close and reopen the database for the change to take effect.

14 Click **OK**.

F Access adds the new group and command to the Ribbon.

Note: You do not need to close and then reopen the database.

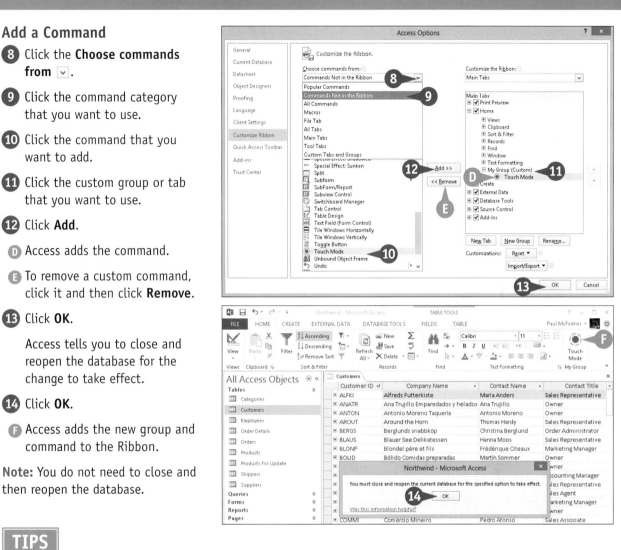

TIPS

Can I customize the tabs that appear only when I select an Access object?

Yes. Access calls these *tool tabs*, and you can add custom groups and commands to any tool tab. Right-click any part of the Ribbon and then click **Customize the Ribbon** to display the Access Options dialog box with the Customize Ribbon tab displayed. Click the **Customize the Ribbon** ▾ and then click **Tool Tabs**. Click the tab that you want and then follow the steps in this section to customize it.

How do I restore the Ribbon to its default configuration?

Right-click any part of the Ribbon and then click **Customize the Ribbon** to display the Access Options dialog box with the Customize Ribbon tab displayed. To restore a tab, click the tab, click **Reset**, and then click **Restore only selected Ribbon tab**. To remove all customizations, click **Reset** and then click **Restore all customizations**.

Change the Navigation Pane View

The Navigation pane on the left side of the database window presents a list of all the objects in the database, including its tables, queries, forms, and reports. This is an important element of the Access interface because it enables you to view and manage the objects, so you should set up the Navigation pane to suit the way that you work.

If you need more horizontal room to work on a table or form, you can hide the Navigation pane. You can also adjust the width of the Navigation pane as well as change the way it sorts and lists objects.

Change the Navigation Pane View

Hide the Navigation Pane

1 If the Navigation pane is displayed, click ≪.

Access hides the Navigation pane.

Display the Navigation Pane

1 If the Navigation pane is hidden, click ≫.

Access displays the Navigation pane.

Adjust the Navigation Pane Size

1 Drag the border to the left or right (↳ changes to ⟷).

A A black line shows the new position for the border.

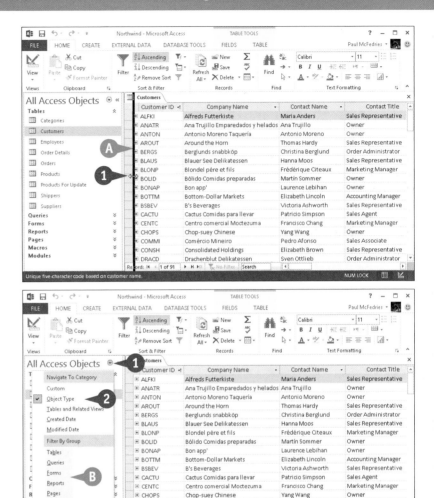

Change the Way Objects Are Displayed

1 Click ⊙.

A menu of object options opens.

2 Click the way that you want to view the object list.

B You can also filter the list to show only a certain type of object.

C You can choose **All Access Objects** to return to the full list after filtering.

TIPS

What are some other ways to display and hide the Navigation pane?

Pressing F11 toggles the Navigation pane on and off. You can also click **Navigation Pane** along the left edge of the window when it is hidden to display it. Another way to hide it is to double-click the divider line between the Navigation pane and the main window when it is displayed.

What is the purpose of the ⥥ and ⥣ arrows in the Navigation pane?

You use these arrows to expand or collapse a Navigation bar category. To expand a category and see its contents, click ⥥. To collapse a category and hide its contents, click ⥣.

Open and Close an Object

You perform work in Microsoft Access by manipulating database objects such as tables, queries, and forms. Before you can work on an object, you must open it. You can open any available database object from the Navigation pane. The object appears in the main window to the right of the Navigation pane; from there, you can work with the object's content. You can open multiple objects at the same time and then switch among them.

When you no longer need to work with an object, you should close it to reduce clutter in the main database window.

Open and Close an Object

Open an Object

1 If necessary, click the category's ˅ icon to expand it.

2 Double-click the object.

A The object appears in the database window.

B Access displays a tab for the object.

C To switch among open objects, click the tab of the object that you want.

Close an Object

1 Click the tab of the object that you want to close.

2 Click ✕.

Note: You can also right-click the object's tab and then click **Close**.

The object closes.

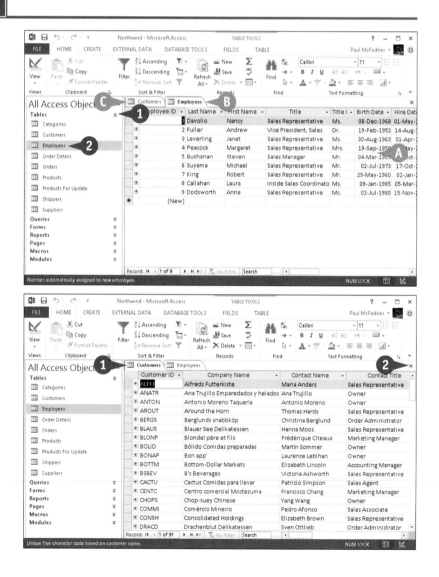

Change an Object's View

Access offers you multiple ways to interact with each database object. For example, with a table, you can work either with the data, including adding, editing, and deleting records, or you can work with the table structure, including adding, editing, and deleting fields. To switch between these different ways of interacting with a database object, you change the object's view.

The available views depend on the object type but usually include a view for using the object, such as the Datasheet view, and a view for modifying the object, such as the Design view.

Change an Object's View

Select a View from the Ribbon

1 Click the **Home** tab.

2 Click the **View** ⏷.

3 Click the view that you want to use.

Note: You can also right-click an object's tab and then click the view that you want from the shortcut menu.

Select a View by Using the View Buttons

1 In the status bar, click the button for the view that you want.

Note: The buttons that are available change depending on the object type.

A To determine which view a button represents, move over the button to see a screen tip.

CHAPTER 2

Working with Tables

After you create a blank database, you cannot enter data until you create at least one table. Therefore, tables are the foundation of any database. A table's structure defines the fields and their properties and specifies how data should be entered. In this chapter, you learn how to create and manage tables.

Plan Effective Tables

As a database designer, you have the opportunity to create tables in your database that match your storage needs. You can create tables based on templates that Access provides, or you can create your own tables. Before creating the tables, however, you should spend some time thinking about what type of data each table should contain.

This involves thinking about what purpose your tables will serve, how your tables will be related to each other, which fields you'll need in each table, and how you will differentiate between each record in a table.

Choose One Purpose per Table

Each table should have a single, well-defined purpose. For example, a table may store customer contact information, product inventory, or personnel records. Do not worry that the information you need to work with is stored in different tables because you can easily create queries and reports that summarize and combine data from any number of tables.

Avoid Redundant Data Entry

Combining multiple purposes in a single table results in needless duplication and increases the chance of data-entry error. For example, suppose that your Orders table also contained fields for the customer's shipping address. Every time a repeat customer placed an order, you would need to re-enter the shipping address. By placing customer shipping information in a separate Customers table, you eliminate the duplication.

Plan for Relationships

Think about how tables will be related. For example, the Orders and Customers tables may be related to display a list of all the orders placed by a certain customer. You could also relate the Employees and Orders tables to display a list of orders taken by certain employees. It may be helpful to draw a diagram to envision the relationships needed.

Decide on the Fields to Use

If you think that you may need to sort or filter by a certain type of information, make it a separate field. For example, to sort an Employees table by last name, you need separate fields for First Name and Last Name. And if you ever plan on addressing your employees with Mr., Ms., or Miss, you need a field that contains that salutation.

Field Name	Data Type	Description (Optional)
LastName	Short Text	Employee's last name.
FirstName	Short Text	Employee's first name.
Title	Short Text	Employee's title.
TitleOfCourtesy	Short Text	Title used in salutations.
BirthDate	Date/Time	Employee's date of birth.
HireDate	Date/Time	Employee's date of hire.
Address	Short Text	Employee's street or post-office box.
City	Short Text	Employee's city.
Region	Short Text	Employee's state or province.
PostalCode	Short Text	Employee's ZIP or postal code.
Country	Short Text	Employee's country of residence.

Field Properties

Plan to Differentiate between Records

In most tables, at least one field should be unique to each record to differentiate between them. For example, the Customers table may have a unique Customer ID field. You could then use the value to refer to that customer in relationship to other tables. For example,

Customer ID	Company Name	Contact Name	Contact Title
ALFKI	Alfreds Futterkiste	Maria Anders	Sales Representativ
ANATR	Ana Trujillo Emparedados y helados	Ana Trujillo	Owner
ANTON	Antonio Moreno Taquería	Antonio Moreno	Owner
AROUT	Around the Horn	Thomas Hardy	Sales Representativ
BERGS	Berglunds snabbköp	Christina Berglund	Order Administrato
BLAUS	Blauer See Delikatessen	Hanna Moos	Sales Representativ
BLONP	Blondel père et fils	Frédérique Citeaux	Marketing Manager
BOLID	Bólido Comidas preparadas	Martín Sommer	Owner
BONAP	Bon app'	Laurence Lebihan	Owner
BOTTM	Bottom-Dollar Markets	Elizabeth Lincoln	Accounting Manage
BSBEV	B's Beverages	Victoria Ashworth	Sales Representativ

each order could be positively matched with a particular customer by using the customer ID.

Create a Table in the Datasheet View

Access offers two methods for creating a table: the Datasheet view and Design view. The easiest of these methods is the Datasheet view, which enables you to add new fields simply by typing the field names into the column-heading placeholders. This method works well when you need a quick table consisting of just a few fields.

The Datasheet view does not offer many options for setting up your table fields, so if you need more control over your table creation, you must use the Design view method, as described in the "Create a Table in the Design View" section.

Create a Table in the Datasheet View

1 Click the **Create** tab.

2 Click **Table**.

A new datasheet opens with an ID field and a Click to Add placeholder.

3 Click the **Click to Add** placeholder.

A menu of field types appears.

4 Click the field type that you want.

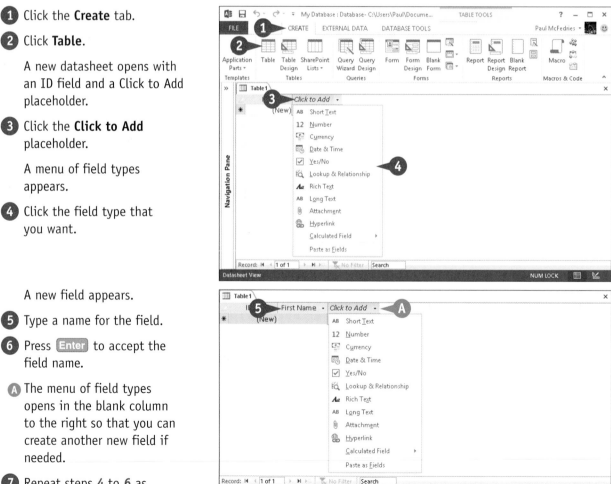

A new field appears.

5 Type a name for the field.

6 Press Enter to accept the field name.

Ⓐ The menu of field types opens in the blank column to the right so that you can create another new field if needed.

7 Repeat steps **4** to **6** as needed to finish entering field names.

Your table is created.

Save a Table

A fter creating a new table, you must save the table to make it a permanent part of the database. When you save a table, Access prompts you to give the table a name. Choose a name that is descriptive enough that it will help you remember the table's purpose. However, for technical reasons, it is best to avoid using spaces and non-alphanumeric characters. If you would like to use two or more words in the name, either separate them with the underscore character (_) or combine the words and use uppercase for the first letter of each word (for example, CustomerOrderDetails).

Save a Table

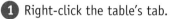

1️⃣ Right-click the table's tab.

2️⃣ Click **Save**.

Ⓐ You can also click the Save button (🔲) on the Quick Access Toolbar.

The Save As dialog box opens.

3️⃣ Type a name for the table.

Note: Access allows table names to include spaces, but you should avoid using spaces to make the names easier to refer to in some types of queries. Use an underscore symbol instead.

4️⃣ Click **OK**.

Ⓑ The table remains open, and its new name appears on its tab.

You can either leave the table open to work with it, or you can close it. To close the table, right-click its tab and then click **Close**.

Create a Table in the Design View

As shown in the section "Create a Table in the Datasheet View," you can build a small table easily and quickly using a datasheet. However, if you want more control over the structure of your table or if you are creating a table with many fields, you should construct the table in the Design view.

This gives you access to the full range of table-creation tools that enable you to get the exact fields that you want. In the Design view, you can create and arrange fields, specify field types and properties, and enter field descriptions. Chapter 4, "Working with Fields," covers modifying a table in the Design view in more detail.

Create a Table in the Design View

1 Click the **Create** tab.

2 Click **Table Design**.

The Design view opens with a new table started.

3 Click in the first empty cell beneath **Field Name** and type a field name.

Note: It is a good design practice to begin with an ID field that will contain a unique value for each record.

4 Click the **Data Type** ⌄ and select a data type for the field.

For a detailed explanation of data types, see the section "Understanding Data Types."

Ⓐ You can click in the **Description** column to type a description for the field.

Note: Descriptions are only necessary if the purpose of the field is not obvious from its name.

⑤ Repeat steps **3** and **4** to create additional fields as needed.

⑥ Save your changes to the table, as described in the "Save a Table" section. If Access prompts you for a primary key, click **No**.

Note: See the section "Set the Primary or Composite Key" to set up the primary key for the table.

Field Name	Data Type	Description (Optional)
OrderID	AutoNumber	Unique order number. Ⓐ

Field Properties

Field Name	Data Type	Description (Optional)
OrderID	AutoNumber	Unique order number.
CustomerID	Short Text	ID of customer who placed the order.
EmployeeID	Number	ID of employee who took the order.
OrderDate	Date/Time	The date the order was placed.
RequiredDate	Date/Time	The date the customer requires the order.
ShippedDate	Date/Time	The date the order was shipped.
ShipVia	Number	The ID of the shipping company.
Freight	Currency	The shipping cost.

Field Properties

TIPS

Is it always necessary to start with an ID field?
You should have one field that contains unique data for each record, but it does not have to be named *ID*. If you have your own numbering scheme for this unique field, set the data type to accommodate it. But if you do not already have a scheme, use AutoNumber to save some time.

Why can I not use spaces in the field names?
You can use spaces if you want, but it makes it harder to refer to the fields when you create functions and write complex query specifications. It is better to get into the habit of not using spaces. You can simulate spaces by using the underscore character. You can also specify a caption for the field, as explained in Chapter 4.

Open a Table in the Design View

After you have created and saved a table, you might find that you need to make changes to it. For example, you might think of one or more fields to add, or you might want to change a field's data type, add descriptions, or even delete fields. To perform these and other table design tasks, you must open the table in the Design view.

If you do not already have the table open, you can go directly into the Design view from the Navigation pane. If the table is already open in another view, you can switch to the Design view.

Open a Table in the Design View

When the Table Is Not Open

1 In the Navigation pane, right-click the table.

2 Click **Design View**.

The table opens in the Design view.

When the Table Is Open in Another View

1 Click the **Home** tab.

2 Click the **View** ▼.

3 Click **Design View**.

The table opens in the Design view.

Ⓐ You can also click the Design View icon (✍) in the status bar.

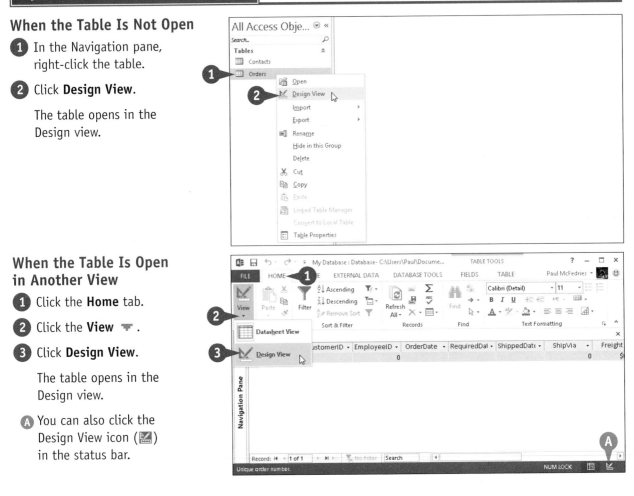

Rearrange Fields

When you first build a table, the order in which the fields appear in the datasheet is the order in which you added the fields. That is, the field order in the Design view from top to bottom corresponds to the order in a datasheet from left to right. Field order also determines the default positioning of fields on forms and reports. However, this order is not set in stone. If the current field order is not logical or efficient, you can change the order in which the fields appear.

Rearrange Fields

1 Click the selector to the left of the field name.

Note: To move multiple adjacent fields, click the first one, press and hold Shift, and then click the last one.

2 With ☐ on the selector, drag up or down to move the field.

A A horizontal line shows where the field is going.

3 When the field is where you want it, release the mouse button.

4 Repeat steps **1** to **3** to move other fields as needed.

Orders		
Field Name	Data Type	Description (Optional)
OrderID	AutoNumber	Unique order number.
CustomerID	Short Text	ID of customer who placed the order.
EmployeeID	Number	ID of employee who took the order.
OrderDate	Date/Time	The date the order was placed.
RequiredDate	Date/Time	The date the customer requires the order.
ShippedDate	Date/Time	The date the order was shipped.
ShipVia	Number	The ID of the shipping company.
Freight	Currency	The shipping cost.

Orders		
Field Name	Data Type	Description (Optional)
OrderID	AutoNumber	Unique order number.
CustomerID	Short Text	ID of customer who placed the order.
EmployeeID	Number	ID of employee who took the order.
OrderDate	Date/Time	The date the order was placed.
RequiredDate	Date/Time	The date the customer requires the order.
ShippedDate	Date/Time	The date the order was shipped.
ShipVia	Number	The ID of the shipping company.
Freight	Currency	The shipping cost.

Insert and Delete Fields

After you have created your table, you might realize that you missed a field, or a user might request that another field be included. Whatever the scenario, you can insert new fields into the field list. You can add a field at the bottom of the list and then move it to the position that you want. However, it is easier to insert the new field directly where you want it in the field list.

If you added a field by accident or if you realize that you do not need a particular field in your table, you can also remove existing fields.

Insert and Delete Fields

Insert a Field

1 Click the field that the new field should appear above.

2 Click the **Design** tab.

3 Click **Insert Rows**.

A A new row appears in the grid — above the one that you selected.

4 Type a field name and choose a field type as you would normally.

Delete a Field

1 Click the field that you want to delete.

Note: To delete multiple contiguous fields, click the first one, press and hold Shift, and then click the last one.

2 Click the **Design** tab.

3 Click **Delete Rows**.

The row is deleted, along with any data that the fields contained.

B If you make a mistake, immediately click ↺ or press Ctrl + Z to undo the deletion.

Understanding Data Types

Each field has a data type that defines what you can store in it. Data entry is restricted to valid entries for the type that you choose, which helps to prevent data-entry errors. For example, you cannot enter letters in a field set to Number, and you must enter valid dates or times in a Date/Time field.

Data Type	Used For	Notes
Short Text	Text and numbers	This is a general-purpose field containing any data. It has a limit of 255 characters and cannot be used for numeric calculation. Use this type for numeric entries that will not have calculations performed on them, such as telephone numbers and zip codes.
Long Text	Text and numbers	This type has a limit of 63,999 characters. In the Access 2007 and later file format, it can hold rich text with formatting. There are some limitations on usage in formulas and functions.
Number	Numbers only	This type offers a flexible field size of 1, 2, 4, 8, or 16 bytes. It can also hold symbols used as helpers for numbers, such as decimal points and commas.
Date/Time	Numbers representing dates or times	This type stores dates and times as 8-byte numbers. It stores only numbers representing valid dates and times.
Currency	Numbers representing currency values	This type stores currency values as 8-byte numbers. Even though the field might show only two decimal places depending on formatting, it keeps track of up to four places to prevent rounding off.
AutoNumber	Automatically generated numbering for each record	This type stores Access-generated values as 4-byte numbers.
Yes/No	Boolean data	The value -1 represents Yes, and the value 0 represents No, but the field can be formatted to display values as True/False, On/Off, or Yes/No.
OLE Object	Embedded OLE objects	Use this type when you need to attach external documents in a backward-compatible database or when you need OLE linkage.
Hyperlink	A text address representing an external source	You can link to websites, e-mail addresses, files on your computer, files on a LAN, or virtually any other location.
Attachment	Any supported file type	This type works only in Access 2007 and later. You can attach data files from word-processing programs, spreadsheets, graphic-editing programs, and so on.
Calculated	The result of a calculation performed on one or more other fields	You can use this field type to create calculated fields directly in a table; in earlier versions, you could create calculated fields only in queries.
Lookup Wizard	Varies	Depending on the usage, this type creates either a lookup list from data that you specify or a lookup list from the values in another table. It can also be used to set up multivalued lists.

Change a Field's Data Type

You can change a field's data type to better represent what you plan to store in it. It is easiest to set field types before you enter data into the table, but you can change the field type at any time.

To avoid losing data, you should change the data type to one that is compatible with the existing data, such as changing Short Text to Long Text. Any existing data that violates the rules of the new data type is deleted, but Access warns you before deleting it.

Change a Field's Data Type

1 In the Design view, click the **Data Type** ☑ for the field.

2 Click the new type.

The type changes in the Data Type column.

3 Click 🖫 on the Quick Access Toolbar to save the changes to the table.

You can also press **Ctrl** + **S**.

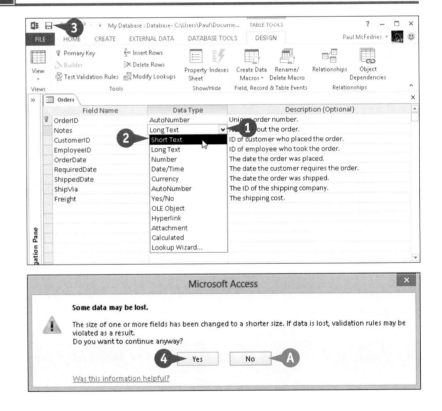

If the existing data violates the rules of the new data type, a warning message appears.

Note: Even though the warning may say that records were deleted, they have not actually been deleted at this point; you can still change your mind.

4 Click **Yes** to allow the deletion of records that violate the new field type's rules.

A You can click **No** to abandon the change.

Understanding Primary and Composite Keys

In many tables, it is advantageous to be able to uniquely identify each record. For example, if you have a Contacts table that has multiple entries for people named John Smith, how do you easily differentiate between them? In Access, you do this by designating a *primary key*, which is the field by which each record will be uniquely identified and by which relationships between tables can be created. A table usually has only one primary key. When a unique combination of two or more fields' values forms the primary key, it is called a *composite key*.

Which Field?

Traditionally, the first field in the table is the primary key. Using this convention makes it easy to browse and sort records by this field. However, you may use any field that you like for it. You can use an

Field Name	Data Type	Description
ContactID	AutoNumber	The unique contact ID
Salutation	Short Text	The contact's title of courtesy
First Name	Short Text	The contact's first name

AutoNumber field to allow Access to assign numbering for you, or you can use a Number or Text field. The only limitation is that the field must contain a unique value for each record. The primary key field cannot be left blank, and it cannot duplicate the value of another record.

Composite Keys

In rare cases, a single field may not uniquely identify each record. For example, suppose you have a table that records which students have taken which classes. It contains two fields: StudentID and ClassID.

Field Name	Data Type	Description
ClassID	Number	The class number.
StudentID	Number	The student number
ClassName	Short Text	The name of the class.

Neither of those fields is unique for each record, but the combination of the two is unique for each record. In those situations, you may need to set a multifield primary key (also called a *composite key*), in which each record must have a unique combination of entries in those fields.

Set the Primary or Composite Key

I f you try to save a new table without a primary key, Access displays a dialog box asking whether you want to create a primary key now. If you click **Yes,** Access either adds an AutoNumber field as the primary key or sets an existing AutoNumber field as the primary key.

If you click **No** and later decide that your table should have either a primary key or a composite key, you can set it yourself in the Design view. Remember that although having a primary or composite key is not required for every table, it is highly recommended.

Set the Primary or Composite Key

Set a Primary Key

1 In the Design view, click in the row for the field that you want to set as the primary key.

2 Click the **Design** tab.

3 Click **Primary Key**.

A The Primary Key symbol ( ) appears to the left of the field.

Note: The Primary Key symbol is an on/off toggle; you can click it to remove it.

Set a Composite Key

1 In the Design view, click to the left of the first field that you want to include.

2 Hold down Ctrl and then click to the left of additional fields that you want to include.

3 Click the **Design** tab.

4 Click **Primary Key**.

B appears to the left of each of the chosen fields.

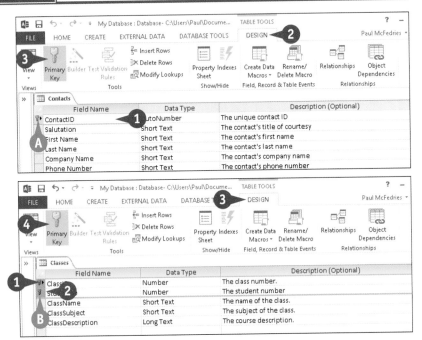

38

Rename a Table

When you save a new table, Access prompts you to provide a name for the table. If you later decide that the name you chose is inappropriate or does not reflect the content of the table, you can rename it. Access automatically updates all references to the table throughout the database, so any forms, reports, or queries based on that table continue to work.

Note, however, that you cannot rename a table when it is open in either the Datasheet view or Design view. The table must be closed before you can rename it.

Rename a Table

1 In the Navigation pane, right-click the table.

2 Click **Rename**.

The table name appears in Edit mode.

3 Edit the name as needed.

You can use the `Backspace` and `Delete` keys to delete one character to the left or right of the insertion point, respectively.

4 Press `Enter` or click away from the table name to accept the new name.

The new name appears on the table.

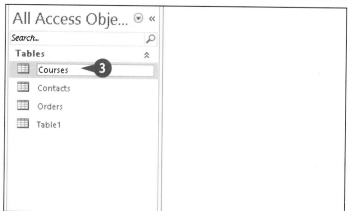

39

Delete a Table

Tables normally store important or useful information, so the person responsible for the database takes steps to keep that data safe. For example, you learn how to back up a database in Chapter 16, "Maintaining a Database." However, some tables become expendable over time because the data is now out-of-date, inaccurate, or redundant. In such cases, you can delete any table from your database — even tables that contain records.

Be careful not to delete anything that you need to keep because it is not possible to undo a table deletion.

Delete a Table

1 In the Navigation pane, right-click the table name.

2 Click **Delete**.

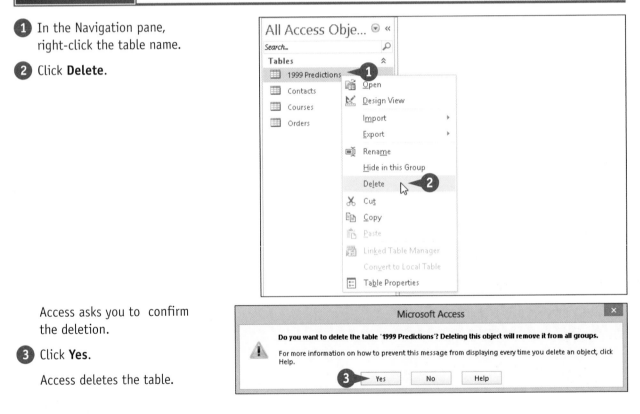

Access asks you to confirm the deletion.

3 Click **Yes**.

Access deletes the table.

Copy a Table

One of the secrets of Access productivity is to not reinvent the wheel when it comes to your tables. For example, you might have a Contacts table that has fields to store first names, last names, addresses, and so on. If you then decide to create a Customers table, it will likely have many of the same fields. Rather than create the new table from scratch, you can save time by making a copy of the existing table. After creating the copy, you can make any minor changes needed to differentiate it from the original.

Copy a Table

1 In the Navigation pane, right-click the original table.

2 Click **Copy**.

3 Right-click an empty area of the Navigation pane.

4 Click **Paste**.

The Paste Table As dialog box opens.

5 Type a name for the copy.

6 Choose how you want the original data pasted:

A If you want to include only the fields from the original table, click **Structure Only** (○ changes to ●).

B If you want to include the fields and the records from the original table, click **Structure and Data** (○ changes to ●).

7 Click **OK**.

Access creates the new table based on the paste options that you selected.

CHAPTER 3

Entering and Editing Data

Entering text, numbers, dates, and other information into a database is one of the most common activities that you will perform when using Access. This chapter explains how to enter data into existing database tables and how to edit, sort, and view the data that you have entered.

Enter New Records

To populate a table within your database, you add a new record to the table, fill that record's fields with data, and then repeat as needed.

You can enter records into a table either by using a datasheet or a form. A *datasheet* — which offers a row-and-column grid format with the records as the rows and the fields as the columns — enables you to see records that have already been entered. A *form* — which is a window that shows only the fields for a single record — enables you to concentrate on one record at a time.

Enter New Records

Enter a Record into a Datasheet

1. In the Navigation pane, double-click the table.

   The table opens in the Datasheet view.

2. If there is already data in the table, click the New Record button (▶).

   The insertion point moves to the first field in the new row.

3. If the first field contains **(New)**, press Tab to move past it.

Note: A field that contains **(New)** is an AutoNumber field, which means that Access will fill it in automatically.

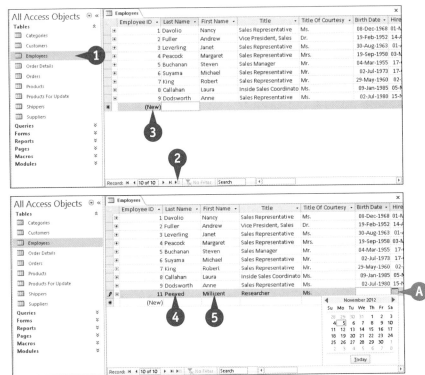

4. Type an entry in the selected field.

5. Press Tab to move to the next field.

Ⓐ Some fields have special selectors that you can use to make an entry, such as a calendar.

6. Repeat steps 4 and 5 until all fields have been filled in for that record.

Note: The next row in the datasheet becomes active when you press Tab at the last (rightmost) field in a row.

Enter a Record into a Form

1 In the Navigation pane, double-click the form.

The form opens.

2 If an existing record appears in the form, click ▶▦ .

The form clears and is now ready for a new record.

3 If the first field contains **(New)**, press `Tab` to move past it.

4 Type an entry in the selected field.

5 Press `Tab` to move to the next field.

6 Repeat steps 4 and 5 until all fields have been filled in for that record.

The form clears, and a new record begins when you press `Tab` at the last field on the form.

Can I skip certain fields?
Yes. Just press `Tab` to move past a field without entering anything in it. If the field is set up to require an entry, however, Access does not let you continue past it without typing something. In Chapter 4, "Working with Fields," you learn how to specify whether a field is required.

Do I have to complete the fields in the given order?
No. You can click to move the insertion point to any field. You may want to do that to skip several fields. You can also start a new record early, without moving through all the fields, by clicking ▶▦ . In a datasheet, you can also press ⬇ to move down to the next row to start a new record.

Navigate between Records

After you have entered two or more records into a table, you need to know how to navigate between the records. For example, you may want to revisit a record to make changes to the data, to add data to any fields you skipped previously, or to review the data that you have entered.

Note that although this section points out the table navigation controls using a datasheet, the same controls also appear when you add and enter data using a form.

Ⓐ Click the First Record button (◄) to jump to the first record.

Ⓑ Click the Previous Record button (◄) to go to the previous record or press ⬆ once.

Ⓒ Type a record number here to jump to that record.

Ⓓ Click the Next Record button (▶) to go to the next record or press ⬇ once.

Ⓔ Click the Last Record button (▶|) to jump to the last record.

Ⓕ Click the New Record button (▶) to start a new record.

Ⓖ Use the scroll bars to see other fields or records.

Edit Records

After you add a record to a database, the information you entered is not set in stone. For example, if you missed entering a field because you lacked the data, you can edit the record to add data to that field. Similarly, if you made an error when entering the original data, you can edit the record to correct the error.

You can edit database records from either a datasheet or a form. After redisplaying the record that you want, you can move the insertion point to the field to be edited and make a change or delete the field entry entirely.

Edit Records

Edit the Content of a Field

1 Click in the field where you want the insertion point to be placed.

2 Edit the existing text:

You can press **Delete** to remove a single character to the right of the insertion point.

You can press **Backspace** to remove a single character to the left of the insertion point.

3 Type your new text.

A Access displays the icon to indicate that your table has unsaved data.

4 Click this bar to save your work.

Delete the Existing Entry in a Field

1 Drag across an entry to select it.

Alternatively, you can press **Tab** to move to the next field and select its content.

2 Press **Delete**.

The selected text is deleted.

Employees

Employees

Employee ID	13
Last Name	Sellars
First Name	P
Title	IT Specialist
Title Of Courtesy	Mr.
Birth Date	23-Aug-1959
Hire Date	27-Oct-2012
Address	28 Gwelp Avenue

City	Galt
Region	Indiana
Postal Code	46290
Country	USA
Home Phone	317-555-2837
Extension	
Notes	
Reports To	Fuller, Andrew

Record: 10 of 10   No Filter   Search

Employees

Employees

Employee ID	13
Last Name	Sellars
First Name	Paul
Title	IT Specialist
Title Of Courtesy	Mr.
Birth Date	23-Aug-1959
Hire Date	27-Oct-2012
Address	28 Gwelp Avenue

City	Galt
Region	Indiana
Postal Code	46290
Country	USA
Home Phone	317-555-2837
Extension	
Notes	
Reports To	Fuller, Andrew

Record: 10 of 10   No Filter   Search

Attach Files to a Record

If you have content that is related to a particular record but exists as a file from another program, you do not need to enter that content directly into your table. Instead, you can associate — that is, *attach* — the file to the record.

In Access, you use a special type of field called an *attachment field* to attach files from other programs to individual records. For example, you may store an employee's résumé with his or her personnel record. A single record can have multiple attached files.

Attach Files to a Record

1 Navigate to the record to which you want to attach a file.

2 Double-click an attachment field.

Note: Attachments can be placed only in attachment fields. To learn how to set a field's type to Attachment, see Chapter 4.

 In a datasheet, an attachment field is indicated by a paper clip (🔗(0)). The number in parentheses is the current number of attachments that the field holds.

The Attachments dialog box opens.

3 Click **Add**.

| Employees | | | | | | ×
|---|---|---|---|---|---|
| Extensic ▾ | Photo ▾ | Notes ▾ | Reports To ▾ | 🔗 | Clic |
| ⊞ 5467 | EmpID1.bmp | Education includes a BA in psychology from Co | Fuller, Andrew | 🔗(0) | |
| ⊞ 3457 | EmpID2.bmp | Andrew received his BTS commercial and a Ph. | | 🔗(0) | |
| ⊞ 3355 | EmpID3.bmp | Janet has a BS degree in chemistry from Bostor | Fuller, Andrew |) | |
| ⊞ 5176 | EmpID4.bmp | Margaret holds a BA in English literature from (| Fuller, Andrew |) | |
| ⊞ 3453 | EmpID5.bmp | Steven Buchanan graduated from St. Andrews | Fuller, Andrew | 🔗(0) | |
| ⊞ 428 | EmpID6.bmp | Michael is a graduate of Sussex University (MA | Buchanan, Steven | 🔗(0) | |
| ⊞ 465 | EmpID7.bmp | Robert King served in the Peace Corps and trav | Buchanan, Steven | 🔗(0) | |
| ⊞ 2344 | EmpID8.bmp | Laura received a BA in psychology from the Un | Fuller, Andrew | 🔗(0) | |
| ⊞ 452 | EmpID9.bmp | Anne has a BA degree in English from St. Lawre | Buchanan, Steven | 🔗(0) | |
| ⊞ 475 | | Paul has a BSc degree in computer science fror | Fuller, Andrew | 🔗(0) | |
| * | | | | 🔗(0) | |

Record: ◄ ◄ 1 of 10 ► ►I ►⊞ 🔽 No Filter Search

Attachments ×

Attachments (Double-click to open)

3 Add...

Remove

Open

Save As...

Save All...

OK   Cancel

The Choose File dialog box opens.

④ Navigate to the folder or drive where the file is stored.

Note: Windows 8 is shown here, and Windows 7 and Vista look very similar. If you have Windows XP, the dialog box uses Windows XP–style navigation controls instead.

⑤ Click the name of the file that you want to attach.

⑥ Click **Open**.

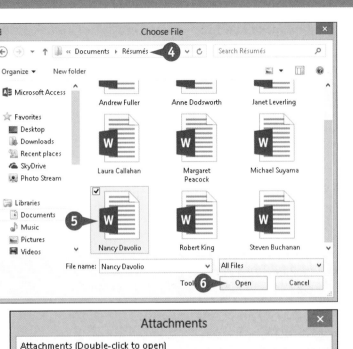

Ⓑ The file is added to the list of files in the Attachments dialog box.

Ⓒ You can repeat steps **3** to **6** to attach more files if necessary.

⑦ Click **OK**.

The file is attached to the record, and a (1) appears on the attachment icon.

TIP

Can I attach files using a form instead of a datasheet?

Yes. In the form, navigate to the record to which you want to add an attachment, click the attachment field, and then click the Manage Attachments icon (Ⓐ) to open the Attachments dialog box. You can also double-click the attachment field. Then follow steps **4** to **7** in this section to attach a file to the record.

Open, Save, and Remove File Attachments

The purpose of attaching a file to a record is to avoid having to enter all the data contained in the attachment. However, you will still need to work with that information, so after you have attached a file to a record, you can open that file and review and work with its contents at any time.

Access also gives you several other tools for working with attached files. For example, you can save an attached file as a separate file outside of Access, which is useful if you no longer have the original file. You can also remove an attached file from a record.

Open, Save, and Remove File Attachments

Open an Attached File in Its Native Program

1 Double-click the attachment field that contains the attachment.

The Attachments dialog box opens.

2 Double-click the attachment.

The attachment opens in its native program.

A Alternatively, you can click the attachment and then click **Open**.

Save an Attachment Outside Access

1 Double-click the attachment field that contains the attachment.

The Attachments dialog box opens.

2 Click the attachment.

3 Click **Save As**.

The Save Attachment dialog box opens.

④ Navigate to the folder or drive in which you want to store the file.

Ⓑ You can change the name in the **File name** field.

⑤ Click **Save**.

Access saves the file to the location that you chose.

You are returned to the Attachments dialog box.

⑥ Click **OK**.

Remove an Attachment

① Double-click the attachment field that contains the attachment.

The Attachments dialog box opens.

② Click the attachment.

③ Click **Remove**.

Access removes the attachment from the record.

④ Click **OK**.

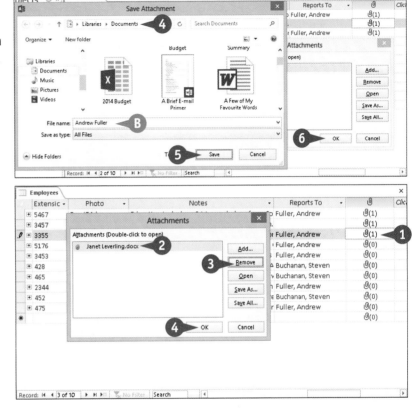

TIPS

Are there any disadvantages to using attachments?
Yes. An attachment is embedded in the Access database, so each one increases the size of the Access file. Access compresses attachment files when possible, but they still greatly add to the file size.

What are my options if I do not want to use attachments?
Instead of attaching related documents, you can hyperlink to them. Set up a field's type as Hyperlink (see Chapter 4) and then create a link to the original file rather than embed the whole file into the database. The main disadvantage of this method is that if the original file is moved, you must update the link in Access. In addition, if you send the Access database to someone else, you must also make sure that you send the hyperlinked files.

Insert an OLE Object

You can use the object linking and embedding (OLE) field type to store data files of various types. An OLE field has one advantage over an attachment field: It can maintain a dynamic link to the original file so that the version in Access updates automatically whenever the original file changes.

To insert an object into a database field, you must set up the field to use the OLE Object data type; you learn how to do this in Chapter 4.

Insert an OLE Object

1 Right-click the field that has the OLE data type.

2 Click **Insert Object**.

A dialog box opens.

3 Click **Create from File** (○ changes to ◉).

4 Click **Browse**.

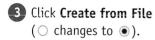

The Browse dialog box opens.

5 Navigate to the folder or drive containing the file that you want to embed.

6 Click the file.

7 Click **OK**.

The Browse dialog box closes.

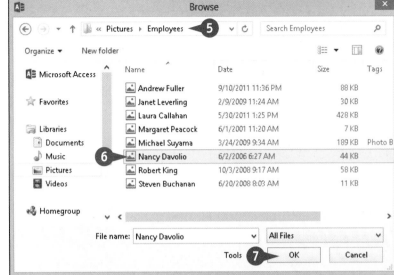

A If you want to create a link, click **Link** (☐ changes to ☑).

Note: If you create a link, the copy in Access is updated when the original updates; otherwise, no link is maintained between the copies.

8 Click **OK**.

The field shows the type of file that you chose.

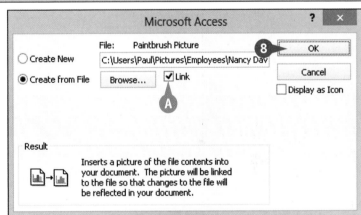

TIPS

What does the Create New option do?
Create New lets you create a new embedded object by using virtually any program on your computer. After you click **Create New** (○ changes to ◉), a list of object types appears. Click the type that you want and then click **OK**.

Why would I want to use the Display As Icon option?
That option is primarily for use in other programs, not Access. In Access, in the Datasheet view, the OLE content appears with the text name of the file type, regardless of whether this check box is selected.

Open, Edit, and Remove OLE Objects

After inserting a file into an OLE field, you can open it for viewing or editing. If you inserted the original file as a linked object, the original file opens; otherwise, Access opens the copy that is embedded in the database. You can then view and edit the file.

If you no longer require the embedded OLE object, you can also remove the object from the OLE field. This deletes the embedded copy in Access but does not delete the original file.

Open, Edit, and Remove OLE Objects

Open and Edit a File in an OLE Field

1. Double-click the field containing the OLE object.

A The object opens in the application that is associated with its type.

2. Make any changes needed to the file.

3. Click the Save button (🖫).

4. Click the Close button in the OLE object's application window to close it.

The object closes.

Remove an OLE Object from a Field

1. Click the field containing the object.

2. Click the **Home** tab.

3. Click **Delete**.

You can also press the Delete key on the keyboard.

Access removes the OLE object from the record.

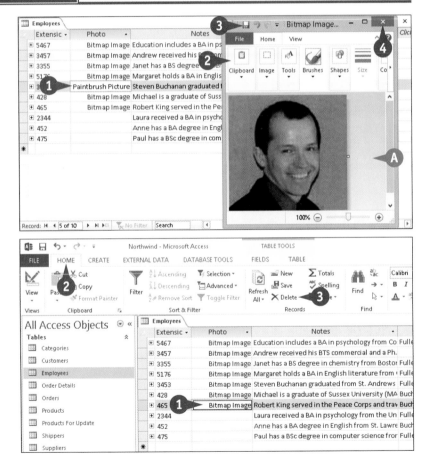

Enter Data in a Multivalued Field

Although most table fields require just a single value, there may be situations in which a field requires two or more values. For example, a company might accept multiple payment types, such as cash, check, and credit cards. In such cases, you can store multiple values in a single field. Instead of typing in the field, you open a list and then click a check box next to each value that you want to include.

To enter multiple values, the field must be set up with the Lookup Wizard to accept multiple values; you learn how to do this in Chapter 5, "Working with Relationships."

Enter Data in a Multivalued Field

① Click in the field that supports multiple values.

② Click the ⌄ that appears in the field.

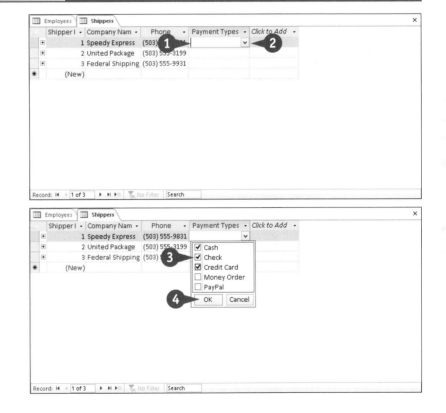

Access displays a list of check boxes for each possible value.

③ Click the check box next to each value that you want to select (☐ changes to ☑).

④ Click **OK**.

Access displays the selected items in the field.

Select Records

When you are working with a table, you will come across situations in which you will need to work with an entire record. For example, you might need to copy a record's data, so before that you must select the record. Similarly, if you need to delete a record (see the section "Delete Records" on the facing page), Access requires that you select the entire record in advance.

Whatever the situation, Access offers techniques that enable you to select a single record or to select multiple adjacent records.

Select Records

Select a Single Record

1 Move ⌖ over the record selector box of the record that you want to select.

⌖ changes to ➡.

2 Click the record selector box.

A Access selects the entire record.

Select Multiple Records

1 Move ⌖ over the record selector box of the first record that you want to select.

⌖ changes to ➡.

2 Drag ➡ over the record selector box of each record that you want to select.

B As you drag, Access selects each record.

Note: You can also select the first record, hold the Shift key, and then click the record selector box of the last record that you want to include in the selection.

Delete Records

A table is only as useful as it is accurate and up to date. You can ensure both the correctness and the timeliness of your data by being vigilant about editing your records and by adding new records as needed, but also by removing records that are no longer useful or relevant. In an Access database, you rid a table of unneeded records by deleting them.

You can delete records either individually or in groups. Either way, it is important to note that deleted records are gone permanently; there is no retrieving them, so delete with care.

Delete Records

1 Select the record or records that you want to delete.

Note: See the section "Select Records" to learn how to select one or more records.

2 Click the **Home** tab.

3 Click ✕.

You can also press Delete on the keyboard.

Access displays a dialog box asking you to confirm the deletion.

4 Click **Yes**.

Access deletes the record or records.

Sort Records

You can make a table easier to navigate and records within that table easier to find by sorting the data based on the values in a particular field. If that field contains many duplicate items, you can specify additional sort fields.

You can sort the data in either ascending or descending order. An ascending sort arranges the values alphabetically from A to Z, or numerically from 0 to 9; a descending sort arranges the values alphabetically from Z to A, or numerically from 9 to 0.

Sort Records

By a Single Field Using the Ribbon Method

1 Click anywhere in the field by which you want to sort.

2 Click the **Home** tab.

3 Click **Ascending** (↑) to sort in ascending order.

A Alternatively, you can sort in descending order by clicking **Descending** (↓).

Access sorts the table records.

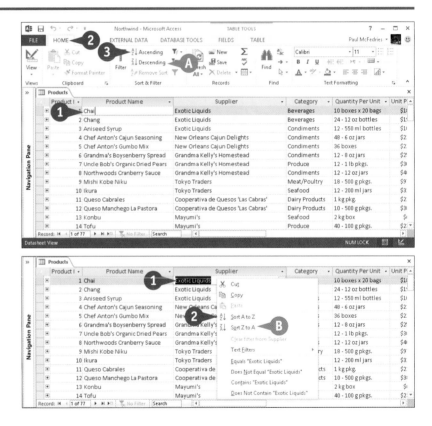

By a Single Field Using the Right-Click Method

1 Right-click anywhere in the field by which you want to sort.

2 Click **Sort A to Z** to sort in ascending order.

B Alternatively, you can sort in descending order by clicking **Sort Z to A**.

Access sorts the table records.

Note: Depending on the field type, the sort options may be different. For example, for a Date/Time field, the commands are Sort Oldest to Newest and Sort Newest to Oldest.

By Multiple Fields

1 Click the **Home** tab.

2 Click **Advanced** ( ).

3 Click **Advanced Filter/Sort**.

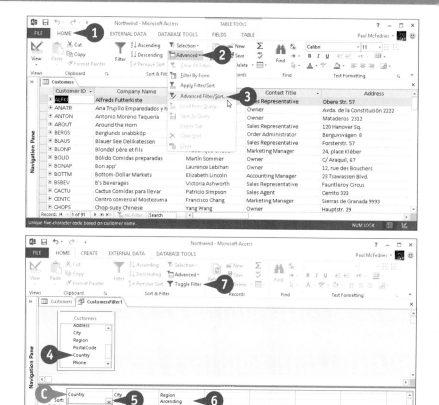

A query grid appears.

4 Double-click the field that you want to use for the sort.

C Access adds the field to the grid.

5 Click the field's **Sort** ▼ and then click **Ascending** or **Descending**.

6 Repeat steps 4 and 5 to add more fields, in the order by which you want to apply them.

7 Click **Toggle Filter**.

Access sorts the table by the fields that you specified.

TIPS

How do I sort records in a form?
All the same techniques for sorting a datasheet also work in a form, even though most forms show only one record at a time. The sort affects the order in which records appear when you move among them by using the Next Record and Previous Record buttons. The record number for each record stays the same.

How do I remove a sort?
If the sort was the most recent action that you performed on the table, click the Undo button ( ) or press Ctrl + Z to undo it. If you have performed other actions since the sort, it is not possible to remove the sort without also losing this work. If you have not saved the table since the sort and you do not mind losing any work you have performed since the sort, close the table without saving your changes.

Resize Datasheet Columns and Rows

When you create a table, Access provides each field with a standard width. This often means that when you display the table in the Datasheet view, some of the fields might have names or data that appear truncated because the columns are not wide enough to display the data. In such cases, you can adjust the widths of the columns in the datasheet to better display the data.

Similarly, if a particular record contains data that does not fit within the displayed fields, you can adjust the row height to create more space to display the data.

Resize Datasheet Columns and Rows

Change a Column's Width

1 Position ⌖ in the heading area, to the right of the column that you want to adjust.

2 Drag to the left or right to adjust the width of the column.

Ⓐ A vertical line appears, showing what the new width will be.

3 Release the mouse button when the column is at the width that you want.

Change the Height for All Rows

1 Position ⌖ to the left of the records — on the divider between any two rows.

Note: All rows will be changed equally; you cannot adjust one row separately from the others.

2 Drag up or down to adjust the row height.

Ⓑ A horizontal line appears, showing what the new height will be.

3 Release the mouse button when the row is at the height that you want.

60

Print a Datasheet or Form

When you need a hard copy of a datasheet or form, either for your files or to distribute to someone else, you can send the data to your printer. This section assumes that you have a printer connected to your computer and that the printer is turned on. Also, before printing, you should check that your printer has enough paper to complete the print job.

Printed datasheets and forms are not formatted for printing. They are useful for examining data, but you will probably want to create reports for more attractive printouts to distribute to others.

Print a Datasheet or Form

1 To print only certain records, select them.

Note: See the section "Select Records" to learn how to select one or more records.

2 Press Ctrl + P.

The Print dialog box opens.

Ⓐ You can click here to select a different printer.

Ⓑ You can click here to enter a page range to print only certain pages (○ changes to ●).

Ⓒ You can click here to print only the selected record(s) (○ changes to ●).

Ⓓ You can type a number here to print multiple copies.

3 Click **OK**.

Access prints the datasheet or form.

CHAPTER 4

Working with Fields

Each table consists of one or more fields. In this chapter, you learn about field properties and how to set properties such as the field size, caption, format, and default value. You also learn how to create input masks and validation rules to help reduce data-entry errors.

Understanding Field Properties

When you create a table, you define each field with data such as the field name, data type, and an optional description. These are examples of the field's *properties,* which are a collection of data that defines the field and controls how it works. Each field has several other properties, including its size, the caption that appears as the field's datasheet heading, and the format that the field uses to display its data. Other properties define rules for making entries, such as specifying whether an entry is required or restricting an entry to certain values.

Ⓐ Properties pane

When a field is selected in the Design view, its properties appear in the lower pane.

Ⓑ General tab

The General tab contains most of the properties that you will work with.

Ⓒ Lookup tab

The Lookup tab is primarily for setting up lookup lists.

Ⓓ Drop-down lists

Some properties have drop-down lists from which you can make a selection; click ⌄ to open the list. Other fields have builder buttons (⋯), which open a dialog box that guides you through the process of building an entry.

Orders			✕
Field Name	Data Type	Description (Optional)	
OrderID	AutoNumber	Unique order number.	
CustomerID	Short Text	ID of customer who placed the order.	
EmployeeID	Number	ID of employee who took the order.	
OrderDate	Date/Time	The date the order was placed.	
RequiredDate	Date/Time	The date the customer requires the order.	
ShippedDate	Date/Time	The date the order was shipped.	
ShipVia	Number	The ID of the shipping company.	
Freight	Currency	The shipping cost.	
Notes	Long Text	Notes about the order.	

Field Properties

General | Lookup

Field Size	255
Format	
Input Mask	
Caption	
Default Value	
Validation Rule	
Validation Text	
Required	No
Allow Zero Length	Yes
Indexed	Yes (Duplicates OK)
Unicode Compression	Yes
IME Mode	No Control
IME Sentence Mode	None
Text Align	General

The display layout for the field. Select a pre-defined format or enter a custom format. Press F1 for help on formats.

Ⓔ Property information

When the insertion point is in a property's box, information about that property appears here.

Ⓕ Yes/No properties

Some properties represent yes/no questions; these are typically already filled in with default values.

Understanding Field Sizes

Each field has a size that limits the amount of data you can store in it. There are different ways of expressing the field size depending on the type of field.

The following table lists the specifications for the data types for which Field Size is a configurable setting. Many field types do not allow you to set a field size. For a numeric field, the advantage of choosing a field size that takes up fewer bytes is that it results in a smaller database file. The file size difference becomes more apparent the more records the table contains.

Field Type	Default Size	Notes
Text	255 characters	You can specify any number of characters from 0 to 255. Each character occupies 1 byte of disk space.
Number	Long Integer	The choice of number format determines the number of bytes used to store it: **Byte:** Integers from 0 to 255 (1 byte). **Integer:** Integers from -32,767 to +32,767 (2 bytes). **Long Integer:** Integers from -2,147,483,648 to +2,147,483,647 (4 bytes). **Single:** Integers from -3.4×10^{38} to $+3.4 \times 10^{38}$ and up to 7 significant digits (4 bytes). **Double:** Floating-point numbers from -1.797×10^{308} to $+1.797 \times 10^{308}$ and up to 15 significant digits (8 bytes). **Replication ID:** A globally unique identifier (GUID), such as a randomly generated ID number (16 bytes). **Decimal:** Integers with a defined decimal precision with values between -10^{28} and $+10^{28}$. The default precision is zero, and the default number of decimal places displayed is 18.
AutoNumber	Long Integer	The same as Number, except there are only two choices: Long Integer or Replication ID.

Change a Field Size

If you are working with a field that offers a configurable field size, it is best to set the field's size to as small a value as possible, while still being large enough to accommodate all possible entries. This is the most efficient course because it keeps the database file size to a minimum.

If your table will contain just a few entries, its field sizes will not make that much difference. However, the difference in file size becomes more pronounced as more records are stored in the table.

Change a Field Size

For the Text Data Type

1 In the Design view, click in the field that you want to change.

The properties for that field appear.

2 Click in the **Field Size** row on the **General** tab.

3 Type a new field size.

Note: The field size for a text field is expressed as a number of characters.

Access changes the field size.

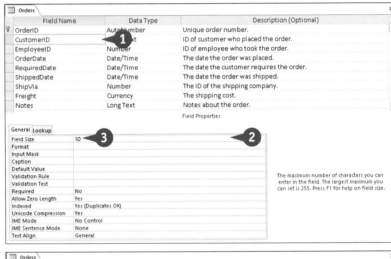

For the Number Data Type

1 In the Design view, click in the field that you want to change.

The properties for that field appear.

2 Click in the **Field Size** row.

3 Click the **Field Size** ☑ and then click the field size that you want.

Note: For a numeric field, size is expressed as a number type. See the section "Understanding Field Properties" for details.

Access changes the field size.

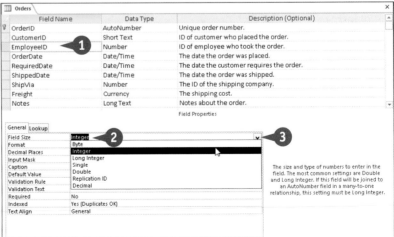

Set a Field Caption

A field's *caption* is the text that appears as the field's heading in the Datasheet view, and the default caption is the field name. For example, if you name a field OrderDate, the text "OrderDate" appears as the field's datasheet heading. You can specify captions for fields that are different from their actual names.

For example, if you have a field called LastName, you can set up its caption to appear as "Last Name" with a space between the words, which is easier to read. Captions appear not only in datasheet headings, but also on labels in forms and reports.

Set a Field Caption

1 In the Design view, click in the field for which you want to set a caption.

The properties for that field appear.

2 Click here and type a caption.

Note: The caption can include spaces and symbols and can have up to 255 characters.

Orders		
Field Name	Data Type	Description (Optional)
⚷ OrderID	AutoNumber	Unique order number.
CustomerID	Short Text	Same entry as in Customers table.
EmployeeID	Number	Same entry as in Employees table.
OrderDate ← **1**	Date/Time	
RequiredDate	Date/Time	
ShippedDate	Date/Time	

Field Properties

General | Lookup

Format	dd-mmm-yyyy
Input Mask	
Caption	Order Date ← **2**
Default Value	
Validation Rule	
Validation Text	
Required	No
Indexed	Yes (Duplicates OK)
IME Mode	No Control
IME Sentence Mode	None
Text Align	General
Show Date Picker	For dates

A field name can be up to 64 characters long, including spaces. Press F1 for help on field names.

A When you display the table's datasheet, the field's caption appears as its column heading.

Note: To check the caption in a datasheet, click the Save button (🖫) to save it and then switch to the Datasheet view.

Orders						
Order I ▾	Customer ▾	Employee ▾	Order Date ▾	Required Dat ▾	Shipped Dat ▾	Ship V ▲
⊞ 10248	Wilman Kala	Buchanan, Steven	04-Nov-2011	01-Aug-2011	16-Nov-2011	Federal St
⊞ 10249	Tradição Hipermercados	Suyama, Michael	05-Jul-2011	16-Aug-2011	10-Jul-2011	Speedy Ex
⊞ 10250	Hanari Carnes	Peacock, Margaret	08-Jul-2011	05-Aug-2011	12-Jul-2011	United Pa
⊞ 10251	Victuailles en stock	Leverling, Janet	08-Jul-2011	05-Aug-2011	15-Jul-2011	Speedy Ex
⊞ 10252	Suprêmes délices	Peacock, Margaret	09-Jul-2011	06-Aug-2011	11-Jul-2011	United Pa
⊞ 10253	Hanari Carnes	Leverling, Janet	10-Jul-2011	24-Jul-2011	16-Jul-2011	United Pa
⊞ 10254	Chop-suey Chinese	Buchanan, Steven	11-Jul-2011	08-Aug-2011	23-Jul-2011	United Pa
⊞ 10255	Richter Supermarkt	Dodsworth, Anne	12-Jul-2011	09-Aug-2011	15-Jul-2011	Federal St
⊞ 10256	Wellington Importadora	Leverling, Janet	15-Jul-2011	12-Aug-2011	17-Jul-2011	United Pa
⊞ 10257	HILARIÓN-Abastos	Peacock, Margaret	16-Jul-2011	13-Aug-2011	22-Jul-2011	Federal St
⊞ 10258	Ernst Handel	Davolio, Nancy	17-Jul-2011	14-Aug-2011	23-Jul-2011	Speedy Ex
⊞ 10259	Centro comercial Moctezuma	Peacock, Margaret	18-Jul-2011	15-Aug-2011	25-Jul-2011	Federal St
⊞ 10260	Old World Delicatessen	Peacock, Margaret	19-Jul-2011	16-Aug-2011	29-Jul-2011	Speedy Ex
⊞ 10261	Que Delícia	Peacock, Margaret	19-Jul-2011	16-Aug-2011	30-Jul-2011	United Pa
⊞ 10262	Rattlesnake Canyon Grocery	Callahan, Laura	22-Jul-2011	19-Aug-2011	25-Jul-2011	Federal St
⊞ 10263	Ernst Handel	Dodsworth, Anne	23-Jul-2011	20-Aug-2011	31-Jul-2011	Federal St
⊞ 10264	Folk och fä HB	Suyama, Michael	24-Jul-2011	21-Aug-2011	23-Aug-2011	Federal St
⊞ 10265	Blondel père et fils	Fuller, Andrew	25-Jul-2011	22-Aug-2011	12-Aug-2011	Speedy Ex ▾

Record: ◄ ◄ 1 of 830 ► ►I ►⊞ No Filter | Search

Set a Field's Format

A field's format determines how Access displays the field's data. In a field that contains dates, for example, you could display the dates using the format 12/25/2013, 25-Dec-13, or Wednesday, December 25, 2013. You can change a field's format to update its appearance in datasheets, forms, and reports.

The field format is most significant for fields that store data numerically, such as Number, Currency, and Yes/No. For example, if you have a field that contains sales tax values, you might prefer to display those numbers as percentages, such as 5%, rather than decimal values, such as 0.05.

Set a Field's Format

1 In the Design view, click in the field that you want to change.

The properties for that field appear.

2 Click the **Format** and then click the format that you want to apply to the field.

Ⓐ For a Number or AutoNumber field, the choices represent different number types, such as General, Currency, and Percent.

Ⓑ For Date/Time data types, the choices appear as date/ time formats.

C For Yes/No fields, the choices appear as ways of expressing yes or no.

D For a Calculated field, all the choices from all the other field types are available because Access cannot automatically determine what type of data it will hold.

Why is the Format list blank for some fields?
Many of the Access data types have no preset formats, so the Format list for those fields is blank. Data types that show a blank Format list are Short Text, Long Text, and Hyperlink. Other data types have no data format at all, so those fields do not even display the Format list. Data types that do not display the Format list are OLE Object and Attachment.

Set a Default Value

You can speed up data entry for fields that usually contain the same value by making that value the default. For example, suppose that you have a table that includes a PaymentType field, which can take values such as Cash, Check, and Credit Card. If most of your clients pay by credit card, you can make Credit Card the default value in the PaymentType field.

When you have specified a default value for a field, each time you start a new record, Access automatically fills in the field with that value.

Set a Default Value

1 In the Design view, click in the field for which you want to set a default value.

The properties for that field appear.

2 Click here and type a default value.

Note: When you move away from the text box, Access automatically adds quotation marks around what you typed if the field type is Text.

A When you display the table's datasheet, the default value appears in new records.

Note: The default value does not automatically populate existing records.

Make a Field Required

In many tables, one or more fields must be filled in for each record. For example, in a Customers table, the CompanyName field should be filled in for each record. To ensure that a particular field is always filled in with data, you can configure the table to make the field required. When a field is required, Access does not enable users to skip it during data entry.

The primary key field is always required for each record in a database, but you can also make other fields required without changing the primary key setting.

Make a Field Required

1 In the Design view, click in the field that you want to make required.

The properties for that field appear.

2 Click the **Required** ✓ and then click **Yes**.

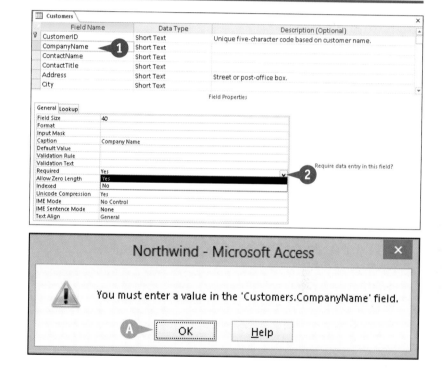

When you enter a new record in the table, a warning appears if you do not enter a value in that field.

A Click **OK** to clear the error and then type a value in the required field.

Index a Field

When you perform searches on a database that contains many records, a delay can occur as Access searches. To minimize searching delays, you can set a field to be automatically *indexed*, which means that Access gathers extra data about the field that enables it to locate data in the field extremely fast. Searches based on that field will take place more quickly.

The two types of indexing are Yes (Duplicates OK) and Yes (No Duplicates). The latter has the side effect of forcing each record to have a unique value for that field, as with the primary key field.

Index a Field

1 In the Design view, click in the field that you want to index.

The properties for that field appear.

2 Click the **Indexed** ☑ and then click **Yes (Duplicates OK)**.

This sets the field to be indexed without forcing entries in it to be unique.

Ⓐ You can choose **Yes (No Duplicates)** if you prefer that records have unique entries for that field.

If you chose **Yes (No Duplicates)** and you then try to enter an identical value for two records, an error message appears.

Ⓑ Click **OK** to clear the message and then correct the error.

Align Data within a Field

You can make your tables easier to read by aligning text and numbers within a field. By default, Access uses the General alignment, which means that it aligns numbers with the right side of the field and text with the left side of the field. For any field, you can choose the Left or Right alignment, or you can choose Center, which aligns data with the center of the field.

Excel also offers a Distribute alignment, which adds space between each character so that the field data is aligned with both the left and right side of the field.

Align Data within a Field

1 In the Design view, click in the field whose data you want to align.

The properties for that field appear.

2 Click the **Text Align** ⌄ and then click the alignment that you want.

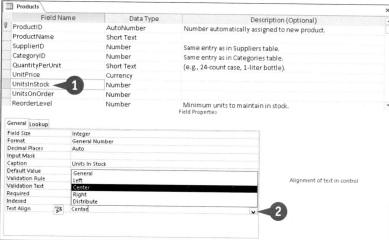

A The next time that you display the datasheet, Access applies the selected alignment to the field.

Create an Input Mask

A major database problem is data entered inconsistently, such as phone numbers entered as (123)555-6783 and 123-555-6783. You can help prevent such inconsistencies by applying an input mask to the field. An *input mask* is a kind of template that shows users how to enter the data and prevents them from entering incorrect characters, such as a letter where a number is required.

For example, here is an input mask for a phone number: (___)___-____. Each underscore (_) acts as a placeholder for (in this case) a digit, and the parentheses and dash appear automatically as the user enters the number.

Create an Input Mask

1 Click in the field for which you want to create an input mask.

The properties for that field appear.

2 Click in the **Input Mask** row.

3 Click the Build icon (⋯).

The Input Mask Wizard opens.

4 Click the type of input mask that you want.

Ⓐ To try the mask, you can click in the **Try It** box and then type a sample entry.

5 Click **Next** to customize the mask.

Ⓑ If you do not want to customize the mask, click **Finish**.

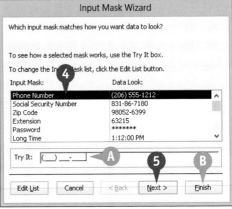

6 Modify the input mask's code if you want to.

7 Click the **Placeholder character** ∨ to select a different placeholder character if necessary.

C To try the mask, you can click in the **Try It** box and then type a sample entry.

8 Click **Next**.

Input Mask Wizard

Do you want to change the input mask?

Input Mask Name: Phone Number

Input Mask: !(999) 000-0000 ◄ **6**

What placeholder character do you want the field to display?

Placeholders are replaced as you enter data into the field.

Placeholder character: _ ∨ ◄ **7**

Try It: (__) __-____ ◄ **C**   **8**

Cancel   < Back   Next >   Finish

9 Click how you want the data to be stored (○ changes to ●):

With the symbols in the mask: The extra symbols (such as the parentheses and dash in a phone number mask) are stored along with the data.

Without the symbols in the mask: The extra symbols are not stored with the data.

10 Click **Finish**.

The input mask code appears in the Input Mask row in the field's properties.

Input Mask Wizard

How do you want to store the data?

○ With the symbols in the mask, like this:

(264) 316-8517

● Without the symbols in the mask, like this: **9**

4442315281

10

Cancel   < Back   Next   Finish

TIP

What do the input mask characters mean?

Input masks use characters to represent the types of data that they will accept. The following table shows the most commonly used characters. For more characters, look up "Input Mask Character Reference" in Access Help.

Character	Use	Character	Use
0	Single digit, required	A	Single letter or number, required
9	Single digit, optional	a	Single letter or number, optional
#	A digit, space, plus sign, or minus sign	&	Any character or a space, required
L	Single letter, required	C	Any character or a space, optional
?	Single letter, optional		

Create a Validation Rule

Although an input mask helps a user enter data into a field using the proper number and type of characters, it cannot restrict the field to certain entries based on logic. A better solution for preventing data-entry errors is the data validation feature. With data validation, you create *validation rules* that specify exactly what kind of data can be entered in a field and in what range that data can fall. You can also specify an error message that appears when a user enters data that does not satisfy a validation rule.

Create a Validation Rule

Create the Rule

1 In the Design view, click in the field for which you want to create a validation rule.

The properties for that field appear.

2 Click in the **Validation Rule** row.

3 Click .

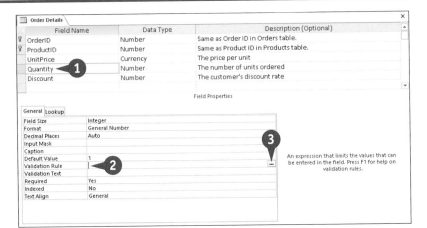

The Expression Builder dialog box opens.

4 Enter the expression that represents the criteria you want to specify.

5 Click **OK**.

Note: You could have simply typed the validation rule into the row and skipped steps **3** to **5**, but the Expression Builder's tools can be useful for complex expressions.

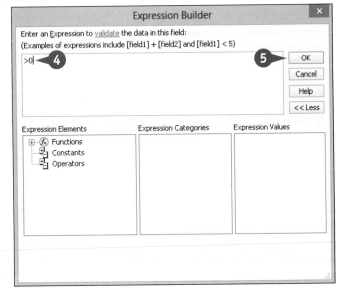

(A) The validation rule appears in the Validation Rule row.

(6) Type the text for the error message in the **Validation Text** row.

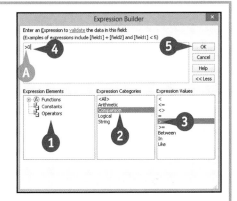

Order Details		
Field Name	Data Type	Description (Optional)
OrderID	Number	Same as Order ID in Orders table.
ProductID	Number	Same as Product ID in Products table.
UnitPrice	Currency	The price per unit
Quantity	Number	The number of units ordered
Discount	Number	The customer's discount rate

Field Properties

General | Lookup

Field Size	Integer
Format	General Number
Decimal Places	
Input Mask	
Caption	
Default Value	1
Validation Rule	>0
Validation Text	Quantity must be greater than 0
Required	Yes
Indexed	No
Text Align	General

The error message that appears when you enter a value prohibited by the validation rule. Press F1 for help on validation text.

Test the Rule

(B) When the rule is violated, a custom error message appears, containing the text that you specified in the Validation Text row.

(1) Click **OK** and then retype the field entry.

Order I	Product	Unit Pric	Quantity	Discou	Click to Add
10248	Queso Cabrales	$14.00	0	0%	
10248	Singaporean Hokkien Fried Mee	$9.80	10	0%	
10248	Mozzarella di Giovanni	$34.80		0%	
10249	Tofu	$18.60			
10249	Manjimup Dried Apples	$42.40			
10250	Jack's New England Clam Chowder	$7.70			
10250	Manjimup Dried Apples	$42.40			
10250	Louisiana Fiery Hot Pepper Sauce	$16.80			
10251	Gustaf's Knäckebröd	$16.80			

Northwind - Microsoft Access

! Quantity must be greater than 0

OK   Help

How do I use the Expression Builder?

The Expression Builder can guide you in determining the correct syntax for an expression. There are many types of expression content available, including functions, constants, and operators. For example, to enter the expression from the steps in this section (>0) ,you would do the following:

(1) Click **Operators**.

(2) Click **Comparison**.

(3) Double-click **>**.

(A) The > character appears in the expression at the top of the dialog box.

(4) Type **0**.

(5) Click **OK**.

Expression Builder

Enter an Expression to validate the data in this field:
(Examples of expressions include [field1] + [field2] and [field1] < 5)

>0|

OK
Cancel
Help
<< Less

Expression Elements	Expression Categories	Expression Values
Functions	<All>	<
Constants	Arithmetic	<=
Operators	Comparison	<>
	Logical	=
	String	>
		>=
		Between
		In
		Like

Create a Record-Level Validation Rule

Although most validation rules involve a single field in the table, you can create rules that involve two or more fields. For example, a rule might compare the value of one field with another. This is called a *record-level validation rule* because it involves multiple fields in each record.

For example, in an Orders table, you could set up a record-level validation rule that checks to make sure that the Order date is before (or the same as) the Shipped date because an order cannot be shipped before it is placed.

Create a Record-Level Validation Rule

1 In the Design view, click the **Design** tab.

2 Click **Property Sheet**.

The Property Sheet for the entire table appears.

3 Click in the **Validation Rule** box and type the expression.

4 Click here and type the error message text.

5 Click **Test Validation Rules**.

If the table contains data already, a warning appears that the data must be checked.

6 Click **Yes**.

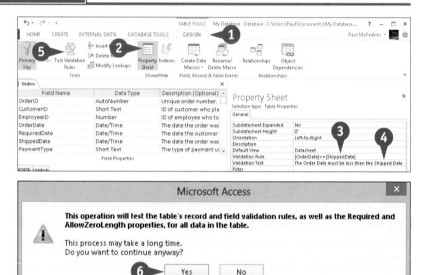

If the table has not been saved, a prompt appears to save it.

7 Click **Yes**.

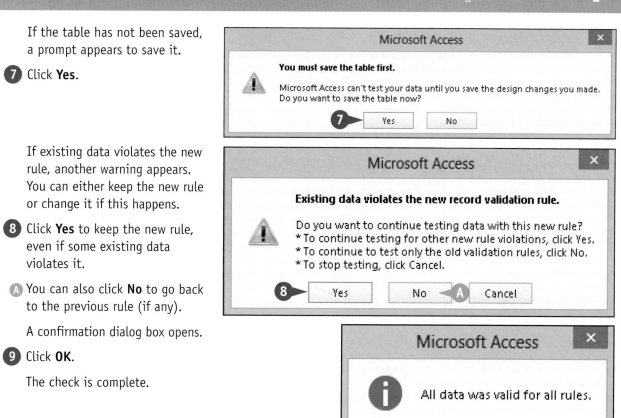

If existing data violates the new rule, another warning appears. You can either keep the new rule or change it if this happens.

8 Click **Yes** to keep the new rule, even if some existing data violates it.

A You can also click **No** to go back to the previous rule (if any).

A confirmation dialog box opens.

9 Click **OK**.

The check is complete.

TIPS

How do I construct a validation rule that contains field names?
You can either use the Expression Builder or type field names directly into the expression. To use the Expression Builder, click in the **Validation Rule** box and click ⋯ to open the Expression Builder. Click the table name in the **Expression Elements** list. Double-click each field to which you want to add to the expression in the **Expression Categories** list. Click **OK**. To enter field names directly into the **Validation Rule** box, enclose each one in square brackets: [OrderDate].

What happens to existing data that violates the validation rule?
Nothing happens to it; it is allowed to continue to exist. However, new records will not be permitted to violate the rule, and if you ever edit the record that violates the rule, you will not be able to save changes to it until you fix the violation.

CHAPTER 5

Working with Relationships

Relational databases are powerful because they can contain multiple related tables. You can create relationships between tables directly in the Relationships window, or you can create relationships by building lookups that populate a field in one table with values from another table.

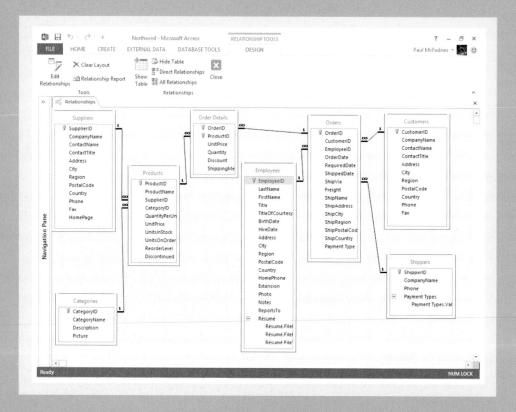

Understanding Relationships

M ost databases store information in multiple tables. Although most of these tables have nothing to do with each other (for example, tables of customer information and employee payroll data), it is likely that at least some of the tables do contain related information (such as tables of customer information and customer orders). You can connect such tables by creating *relationships* between them based on a common field that they share. These relationships make it possible to create forms, queries, and reports that include fields from multiple tables.

Common Fields

For a relationship to exist between two tables, they must have a common field. For example, the Customers table may have a CustomerID field, and the Orders table may also have a CustomerID field. The two tables could be joined, or *related,* by that field. The field type must be the same in both tables for a relationship to exist. One exception is that an AutoNumber field can be related to a Number field.

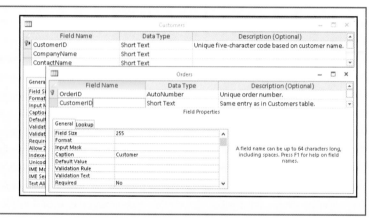

The Primary Key and Foreign Key

In most relationships, the primary key field in one table is related to a field in the other table that is *not* its primary key. In one table, the field contains unique values, whereas in the other table, it does not. The related field in the other table is called the *foreign key.* For example, in the Customers table, each record has a unique CustomerID field, but in the Orders table, two different orders may have the same CustomerID.

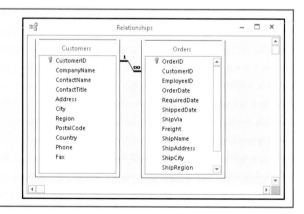

Referential Integrity

Relationships can optionally be set to *enforce referential integrity*. This prevents the foreign key field from containing values that do not appear in the primary key field. For example, in the Orders table, a CustomerID value could not be entered that had no valid corresponding entry in the Customers table. This would prevent users from entering orders for nonexistent customers.

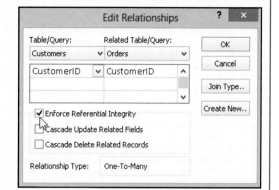

Cascade Update

When referential integrity is enabled, you can also enable Cascade Update and Cascade Delete. With Cascade Update, when a primary key entry changes, the foreign key entry in the related table also changes. For example, if a customer's CustomerID changes in the Customers table, all the orders in the Orders table will reflect the new ID number.

Cascade Delete

With Cascade Delete, when a record is deleted from the table containing the primary key part of the relationship, all corresponding records in the table containing the foreign key are deleted. For example, if a customer's record is deleted from the Customers table, then all that customer's orders are deleted from the Orders table. Use this feature with caution.

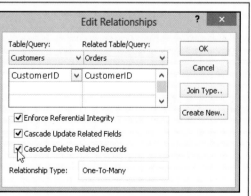

Create a Relationship between Two Tables

$\mathbf{B}$efore you can combine fields from two tables for use in queries, forms, and reports, you must first define a relationship between the two tables. You create and manage relationships using the Relationships window, which enables you to define a relationship by dragging a field from one table onto a field from another.

You can also specify the *join type*, which dictates what happens when there are records in one table that do not have a corresponding entry in the other table. The default join type is to include only records where the joined fields from both tables are equal.

Create a Relationship between Two Tables

Open the Relationships View

1. Click the **Database Tools** tab.

2. Click **Relationships**.

The Relationships window opens. If there are not any relationships yet in the database, the Show Table dialog box also opens.

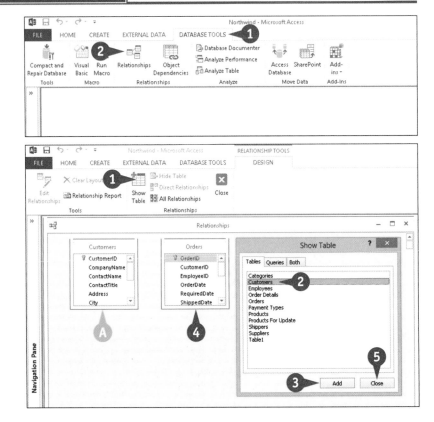

Add Tables to the Relationships Window

1. If the Show Table dialog box is not already open, click **Show Table**.

2. Click a table that you want to add to the Relationships window.

3. Click **Add**.

Note: You can double-click the table instead of following steps **2** and **3**.

Ⓐ The table appears in the Relationships window.

4. Repeat steps **2** and **3** as needed to add more tables.

5. Click **Close**.

Create a Relationship

1 Click the primary key field to be associated with a field in another table.

2 Drag the primary key field onto the associated field in the other table.

3 Click **Enforce Referential Integrity** if needed.

Ⓑ With referential integrity enabled, you can also click **Cascade Update Related Fields** and/or **Cascade Delete Related Records**.

4 Click **Create**.

A connector appears between the two fields.

Ⓒ On the "1" side, each record contains a unique entry for the joined field.

Ⓓ On the "Many" (∞) side, multiple records can have the same value for the joined field.

Note: If you did not enforce referential integrity, a plain line appears with no symbols on it.

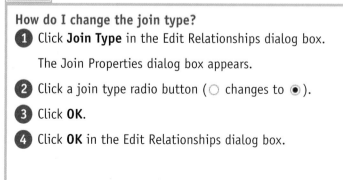

TIP

How do I change the join type?

1 Click **Join Type** in the Edit Relationships dialog box.

The Join Properties dialog box appears.

2 Click a join type radio button (○ changes to ⦿).

3 Click **OK**.

4 Click **OK** in the Edit Relationships dialog box.

Edit a Relationship

After you have created a relationship between two tables, that relationship is not set in stone, which means that you can edit the relationship as needed. For example, if you realize later that you associated an incorrect field in one of the tables, you can fix that problem. Similarly, you might change your mind about the nature of a relationship after creating it. For example, you may choose to change the referential integrity options or the join type.

Edit a Relationship

1. In the Relationships window, double-click the connector between two tables.

Note: Be sure to double-click the connector directly. If you miss it, you will see an empty Edit Relationships dialog box.

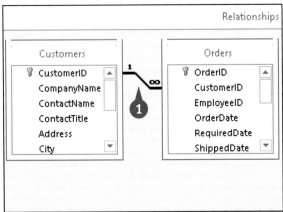

The Edit Relationships dialog box opens.

2. If you need to change the associated field in the related table, click ⌄ and then click the new field.

3. Click to select or deselect **Enforce Referential Integrity**.

4. If the referential integrity is enabled, you can do either or both of the following:

   Ⓐ Click to select or deselect **Cascade Update Related Fields**.

   Ⓑ Click to select or deselect **Cascade Delete Related Records**.

5. Click **OK**.

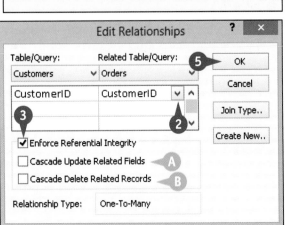

The relationship is changed according to the options that you chose.

Remove a Relationship

If you no longer require a particular relationship between two tables, you can remove that relationship. For example, if you want to change the data type of one of the fields, Access will not allow you to do that as long as the field is part of a relationship. You must remove the relationship before you can change the field's data type.

Before you proceed, bear in mind that you cannot undo a relationship deletion. After you have deleted a relationship, the only way to restore it is to re-create the relationship from scratch.

Remove a Relationship

1 In the Relationships window, right-click the line between the two tables.

2 Click **Delete**.

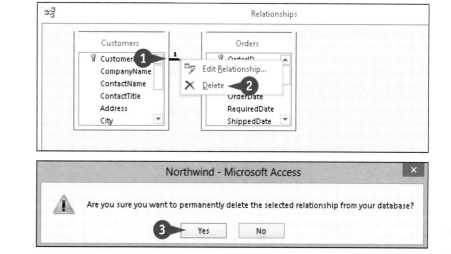

A confirmation dialog box opens.

3 Click **Yes**.

The relationship, and its indicator line, is removed.

Arrange the Relationships Window

You are free to create relationships between as many tables as your needs require and as the structure of your data dictates. This means that it is quite common to end up with a number of tables in the Relationships window, each with its own set of connector lines showing the relationships. As you create more relationships and larger databases, the connector lines between tables may be difficult to see because of overlap. You can move the tables around in the Relationships window, and you can also resize the window for each table.

Arrange the Relationships Window

Move a Table in the Relationships Window

1 Click and drag a table's title bar to a new location.

The relationship lines stay connected.

A If you need more room, you can use the scroll bars to scroll down or across.

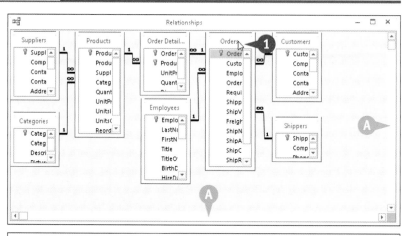

Resize a Table's Field List

1 Position ⇖ at the bottom of a table's field list and then click and drag up or down to shrink or enlarge the list box (⇖ changes to ↕).

You can also click and drag a field list's side border to expand the box horizontally or drag the lower-right corner to expand in both directions.

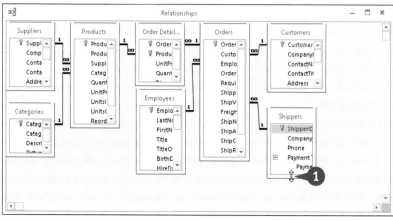

Print a Relationship Report

As you work on your database, you might find that as you add tables, the number of relationships between them increases to the point where it is difficult to remember and keep track of them all. Rather than constantly having to open or switch to the Relationships window, you might prefer to have a printed copy of the relationships as a reference. You can get a hard copy by creating and printing a relationship report.

Print a Relationship Report

1 Click the **Design** tab.

2 Click **Relationship Report**.

A printable version of the Relationships window appears in Print Preview.

3 Click **Print**.

The Print dialog box opens.

4 Set any printing options if needed:

Ⓐ You can click here to choose a different printer.

Ⓑ You can click here to increase the number of copies.

5 Click **OK**.

Access prints the relationship report.

View Object Dependencies

In Access, a table's *dependencies* are those database objects that rely on data from the table. For example, an Orders table might depend on data from a Customers table because you have set up a relationship between them. Similarly, there might also be queries or forms that depend on the table.

You can view an object's dependencies from the Object Dependencies task pane. This is easier than trying to decipher the relationships in the Relationships window in a very complex database. The Relationships window does not need to be open for you to view object dependencies.

View Object Dependencies

1 If you are in the Relationships window, click the **Design** tab.

2 Click **Close**.

3 If Access prompts you to save the layout, click **Yes**.

4 In the Navigation pane, click the object that you want to examine.

5 Click the **Database Tools** tab.

6 Click **Object Dependencies**.

7 If Access prompts you to turn on name AutoCorrect, click **OK**.

The Object Dependencies task pane opens.

8 Click a type of dependency to view (○ changes to ◉):

Ⓐ Click here to see objects that depend on the chosen object.

Ⓑ Click here to see objects that the chosen object depends on.

9 Click ▷ next to an object type to view the table's dependencies (▷ changes to ◢).

Object Dependencies ✕

Table: Customers   Refresh

◉ Objects that depend on me ——Ⓐ
○ Objects that I depend on ——Ⓑ ← **8**

◢ Tables
  ▷ ⊞ Orders
▷ Queries
  Forms
9 Reports
  ▷ Ignored Objects

Ⓒ The table's dependencies for that object type appear.

10 Click ▷ next to an object to view its own dependencies(▷ changes to ◢).

Ⓓ The object's dependencies appear.

11 Click ✕ to close the task pane when finished.

Object Dependencies **11** → ✕

Table: Customers   Refresh

◉ Objects that depend on me
○ Objects that I depend on

◢ Tables
  ▷ ⊞ Orders
◢ Queries
  ▷ 🔲 Customer Orders By Category
  ▷ 🔲 Customers Mail Merge Query ——Ⓒ
  ▷ 🔲 Customers With Orders and Order Details
  ▷ 🔲 Customers Without Matching Orders
  ▷ 🔲 Form Parameter Test
  ◢ 🔲 Invoices
    ▷ 🔲 Query: Invoices Filter
10 ▷ 🖻 Report: Customer Invoice ——Ⓓ
    ▷ 🖻 Report: Invoice

TIPS

Why would I need to view object dependencies?
In a complex database, almost every object depends on some other object. Very rarely would a table, for example, stand alone. Therefore, you should not delete an object until you understand what other objects will be affected by that deletion. For example, if you delete a table, a form that depends on it will be orphaned.

Is there a way to see all the dependencies for all the objects at once?
Yes. Access offers the Database Documenter feature, which among other things provides you with a list of all the object dependencies in your database. To learn how to use the Database Documenter, see the following section, "Document the Database."

Document the Database

As your database grows, it becomes increasingly difficult to keep track of all the objects that it contains as well as their relationships and dependencies. To help you get a handle on a large database, you can use the Database Documenter feature to generate a full report about the database, including all the details about each object and its relationships and dependencies.

This report is also useful to provide to another database designer to help him or her understand the structure of the database.

Document the Database

1 Click the **Database Tools** tab.

2 Click **Database Documenter**.

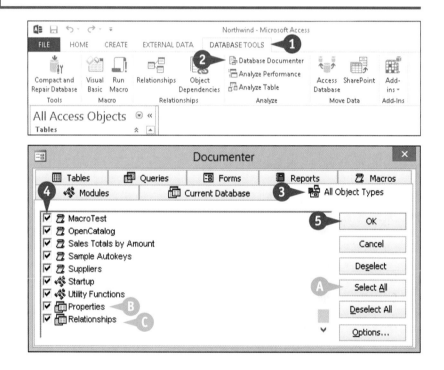

The Documenter dialog box opens.

3 Click the **All Object Types** tab.

4 Click the check boxes for each object that you want to include (☐ changes to ☑).

Ⓐ You can click **Select All** to select all the objects.

Ⓑ To include the database's properties, click here.

Ⓒ To include the Relationships diagram, click here.

5 Click **OK**.

The information appears in a report in Print Preview.

Note: If your database is quite large, it will take Access a few moments to generate the report.

6 To zoom in on the report, click it.

You can click again to zoom out.

D You can also click the **Zoom** ▼ and then click the zoom percentage that you prefer.

7 Click **Print**.

The Print dialog box opens.

8 Set any printing options if needed:

E Click here to choose a different printer.

F Click here to increase the number of copies.

9 Click **OK**.

Access prints the report.

10 Click **Close Print Preview**.

Access closes the report.

TIP

Can I export the report to another program instead of printing it?

Yes, Access offers several export options in the Print Preview tab's Data group. For example, you can export the report to an Excel workbook by clicking **Excel**. If you prefer to export the report to a PDF file, click **PDF or XPS** and then, in the Publish as PDF or XPS dialog box, make sure that **PDF** is selected in the **Save as type** list. To export the report as a plain text file, click **Text File**. Finally, you can also click **More** to see a list of other export formats, including Word and HTML Document.

Understanding Lookups

If a user has to type a customer name or product name from memory, that is a sure recipe for inconsistent and error-filled data. Fortunately, in many cases, you can avoid freeform text entry. If there are only a finite number of possible values for a field, you can eliminate this weak link in your data chain by giving users a list of items to choose from. This is called a *lookup*.

Access offers two methods for defining lookups: You can take the unique values for a field in an existing table or query, or you can type the list values yourself.

Relationships Based on Codes

Relationships between tables are often based on code values. For example, the CustomerID in the Customers table may be a code based on the customer name, so the related Customer field in the Orders table would also need to use the same codes. But when a user is entering a new order, he or she probably does not know the customer's ID code without looking it up.

Customers	
Customer ID ▾	Company Name ▾
⊞ ALFKI	Alfreds Futterkiste
⊞ ANATR	Ana Trujillo Emparedados y helados
⊞ ANTON	Antonio Moreno Taquería
⊞ AROUT	Around the Horn
⊞ BERGS	Berglunds snabbköp
⊞ BLAUS	Blauer See Delikatessen
⊞ BLONP	Blondel père et fils
⊞ BOLID	Bólido Comidas preparadas
⊞ BONAP	Bon app'

Lookups Match Numbers to Names

A lookup cross-references the related table and displays "friendly" fields that help users find the right record. For example, you could set up a lookup for the Customer field in the Orders table so that users could choose from a list of customer first and last names and be shielded from the customer ID numbers.

Customer	
	Alfreds Futterkiste
	Ana Trujillo Emparedados y helados
	Antonio Moreno Taquería
	Around the Horn
	Berglunds snabbköp
	Blauer See Delikatessen
	Blondel père et fils
	Bólido Comidas preparadas

Lookups Based on Tables

To set up a table lookup, change the data type for the field to Lookup and then use the Lookup Wizard to specify the source table. You do not need to set up the relationship between the tables beforehand.

Lookups Based on Existing Relationships

If you have an existing relationship established between the table containing the field and the table containing the lookup list, you may encounter an error in creating the lookup if the Lookup Wizard wants to create a different kind of relationship than what exists already. The quickest way to solve this problem is to delete the existing relationship and then allow the Lookup Wizard to re-create it.

Lookups Based on Lists That You Type

If the number of entries to appear in the drop-down list is small or if it will never or seldom change, it may be unnecessary to put the entries in a separate table. In such cases, you may prefer to create a lookup based on entries that you set up yourself. The Lookup Wizard can also create this type of lookup and can prompt you for the entries to use.

Create a Table for Use As a Field Lookup

I f you think the lookup values will change over time — either by adding new items or by editing or deleting existing items — you will find it easier to maintain the lookup by storing the values in a table. If the lookup values you want to use already exist in another table, you can use that table. If they do not, you need to construct a new table for the values. Lookup tables are typically very simple, consisting of only one or two fields.

Follow the steps in this section only if the data for the lookup does not exist already in another table.

Create a Table for Use As a Field Lookup

1. Click the **Create** tab.

2. Click **Table Design**.

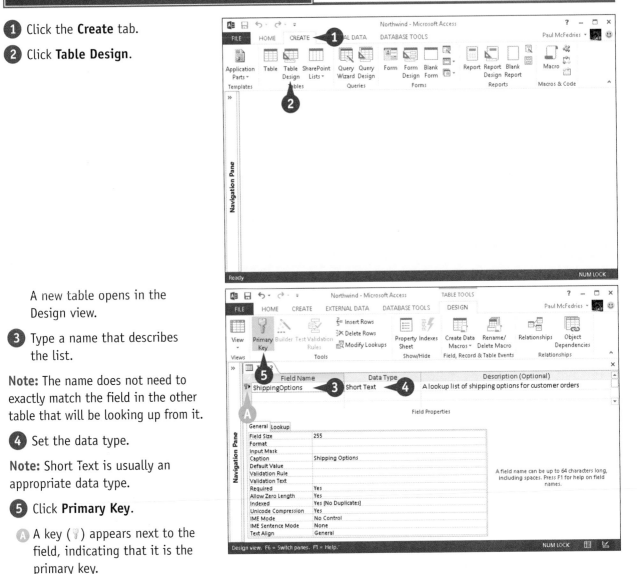

A new table opens in the Design view.

3. Type a name that describes the list.

Note: The name does not need to exactly match the field in the other table that will be looking up from it.

4. Set the data type.

Note: Short Text is usually an appropriate data type.

5. Click **Primary Key**.

A. A key ( ) appears next to the field, indicating that it is the primary key.

6 Click the Save button (🖫).

The Save As dialog box opens.

7 Type a name for the lookup table.

8 Click **OK**.

The Save As dialog box closes.

9 Click **View**.

The view switches to the Datasheet view.

10 Type the records into the table.

Note: It does not matter what order you enter them in because you can specify a sort order when you set up the lookup.

11 Click ✕.

Access closes the table.

TIPS

Why go to the trouble of creating a table?

A table makes editing the lookup list later much more convenient. With a lookup that consists of manually entered values, the only way to edit the values is through the field's properties in the Design view, which can be inconvenient. A lookup table can also be reused for multiple lookups in different tables.

Does the lookup table have to have a primary key defined?

No. That is not necessary. However, assigning a primary key for every table is considered a good housekeeping practice in a database. In addition, setting a field as a primary key is a good way to ensure that it contains no duplicate values.

Create a Field Lookup Based on a Table

You can create a lookup for a field whose values come from items stored in another table. When the user navigates to that field for data entry, Access does not display the standard text box. Instead, it displays a drop-down list containing the values from the lookup table.

One of the main advantages of using a lookup based on a table is that the lookup is easier to maintain. If you or another user changes the values in the other table, the values in the lookup also change.

Create a Field Lookup Based on a Table

① In the Design view, click the **Data Type** ⌄ for the field for which you want to use the lookup and then click **Lookup Wizard**.

Note: Make sure that you are working in the table and field that should use the lookup, not the table containing the lookup values.

The Lookup Wizard opens.

② Click **I want the lookup field to get the values from another table or query** (○ changes to ◉).

③ Click **Next**.

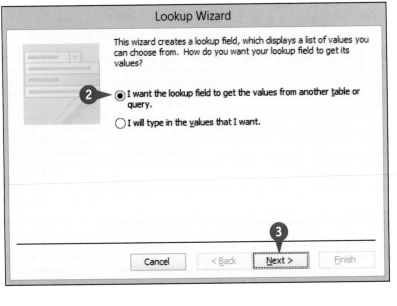

The table or query page of the wizard appears.

 4 Click the table that contains the lookup values.

 5 Click **Next**.

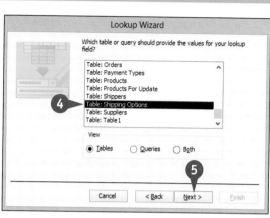

The select fields page appears.

6 Click the field containing the values.

7 Click the Add Field button (>).

The field moves to the Selected Fields list.

8 If there are other fields in the table that you want to appear in the lookup list, repeat steps **6** and **7** to add them.

Note: Access adds the primary key field automatically.

 9 Click **Next**.

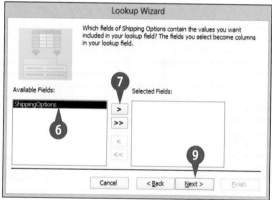

TIPS

Can I use a query instead of a table?
Yes. A *query* is a sorted or filtered version of a table or a combination of tables. When two or more tables have relationships between them, you can create queries that join the data from them into a single datasheet. That way, you can use data from multiple tables as if the data resided together in a single object. To select a query, click **Queries** (A) on the table or query page of the wizard (○ changes to ●).

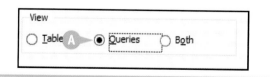

Can I create a lookup field without using the wizard?
Yes. You can use the Lookup tab in the field's Properties, placing a SQL (structured query language) statement in the Row Source box (B). You will probably not want to create lookups that way, but you might use the boxes on the Lookup tab to make minor changes to a lookup without having to completely re-create it.

continued ▶

Whe you are creating a lookup field, you can specify a sort order for the lookup values. It is almost always easier for users to locate values in a list that is sorted alphabetically or numerically. This can also be useful if you want the list items to appear in a different order in one usage than in another.

As part of the lookup field specification, you can also set the field width and type a label that serves as the name of the field.

Create a Field Lookup Based on a Table (continued)

The sort order page appears.

10 If you want to sort the list, click the **1** ⌄ and then click the field name.

Note: The default sort order is Ascending.

11 If you want to toggle the default sort order to Descending, click **Ascending**.

12 If there are other fields that you want to sort by, repeat steps **10** and **11**.

13 Click **Next**.

Lookup Wizard

What sort order do you want for the items in your list box?

You can sort records by up to four fields, in either ascending or descending order.

1 ShippingOptions **10** ⌄   Ascending **11**

2 ⌄   Ascending

3 ⌄   Ascending

4 ⌄   Ascending

13

Cancel   < Back   Next >   Finish

The column width page appears.

14 To change the column width for the lookup field, drag the right edge (⌕ changes to ↔).

You can also double-click the right edge to automatically fit the column to the current contents.

15 Click **Next**.

Lookup Wizard

How wide would you like the columns in your lookup field?

To adjust the width of a column, drag its right edge to the width you want, or double-click the right edge of the column heading to get the best fit.

Shipping Options ↔ **14**
International Expedited
International Standard
Next Day (Afternoon)
Next Day (Morning)
Super Saver
Two Days

15

Cancel   < Back   Next >   Finish

The label page appears.

16 Modify the label assigned to the field, if you want something different than the default label.

By default, the wizard uses the field name as the label.

17 Click **Finish**.

Lookup Wizard

What label would you like for your lookup field?

ShippingMethod ◀ **16**

Do you want to enable data integrity between these tables?

☐ Enable Data Integrity

○ Cascade Delete
● Restrict Delete

Do you want to store multiple values for this lookup?

☐ Allow Multiple Values

Those are all the answers the wizard needs to create your lookup field.

Cancel   < Back   Next >   **17** Finish

A prompt appears, asking you to save the table.

18 Click **Yes**.

The lookup is created. You can examine the lookup settings on the Lookup tab of the field's properties.

Lookup Wizard   ✕

⚠ The table must be saved before relationships can be created. Save now?

18 Yes   No

TIP

Can I make changes to the lookup?

Yes, although this depends on how extensive those changes are. To make small changes, click anywhere in the field using the Design view and then use the Lookup tab in the field's properties. If you need to re-create the lookup, Access at first does not allow you to do this because it has already set up a relationship between your data table and the table that contains the lookup values.

Before you can re-create the lookup field, you must first delete the relationship that the Lookup Wizard created. See the section "Remove a Relationship" to learn how to delete an existing relationship. Note that you will likely have to add the lookup table to the Relationships window. On the Design tab, click **Show Table**, click the lookup table, and then click **Add**.

Create a Field Lookup with Values That You Specify

If the list from which you want users to choose for a field lookup is fairly short and you do not expect that the values in the list will change frequently, you may prefer to create the lookup based on values that you type into the Lookup Wizard. This creates a makeshift lookup table that exists only in the Lookup properties for the field. If you need to edit the list, you can make the changes using the Lookup tab of the field's properties.

Create a Field Lookup with Values That You Specify

1 In the Design view, click the **Data Type** and then click **Lookup Wizard**.

Note: Make sure that you are working in the table and field that should use the lookup, not the table containing the lookup values.

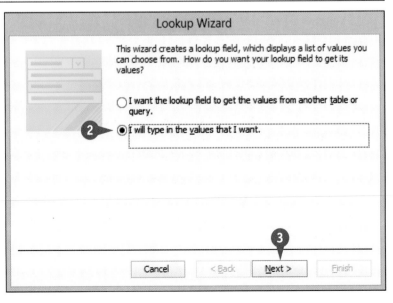

The Lookup Wizard opens.

2 Click **I will type in the values that I want** (○ changes to ⦿).

3 Click **Next**.

The values page of the wizard appears.

 Type the values that you want to display in the lookup list.

Note: It is common to use a single column. Use multiple columns only if a single column cannot adequately represent the values.

 Click **Next**.

The label page appears.

6 Modify the label assigned to the field, if needed.

By default, the wizard uses the field name as the label.

7 Click **Finish**.

Access completes the lookup field. You can examine the lookup settings on the Lookup tab of the field's properties.

Lookup Wizard

What values do you want to see in your lookup field? Enter the number of columns you want in the list, and then type the values you want in each cell.

To adjust the width of a column, drag its right edge to the width you want, or double-click the right edge of the column heading to get the best fit.

Number of columns: ☐ 1

Col1
Cash
Check
Credit Card
Money Order
PayPal
*

4

5

| Cancel | < Back | Next > | Finish |

Lookup Wizard

What label would you like for your lookup field?

PaymentType ◄ 6

Do you want to limit entries to the choices?

☐ Limit To List

Do you want to store multiple values for this lookup?

☐ Allow Multiple Values

Those are all the answers the wizard needs to create your lookup field.

7

| Cancel | < Back | Next > | Finish |

How can I change the values on the list?

On the Lookup tab of the field's properties, the Row Source box contains the values that you specified for the list, each one in quotation marks, separated by semicolons.

 If you need to modify the list, type your changes directly into the **Row Source** text box, making sure that you keep the correct syntax with the quotation marks and semicolons.

General	Lookup		
Display Control	List Box ◄ B		A
Row Source Type	Value List		
Row Source	"Cash";"Check";"Credit Card";"Money Order";"PayPal"		

Are users limited to only the values on my list?

No. The default display control is a combo box, which also enables users to enter their own values.

B If you want to restrict users to your values only, click the **Display Control** property's ⌄ and then click **List Box**.

Set Up a Multivalued Field

Most table fields are configured to store a single value. However, you might come across a situation in which you require a field to store multiple values. For example, if your company offers customers several different newsletters, each customer might want to subscribe to two or more of those publications. You can handle this in your table by creating a *multivalued* lookup field that can store multiple items from a lookup.

Creating a multivalued field is the same as creating any other lookup, except for the last option in the wizard.

Set Up a Multivalued Field

1 Follow steps **1** to **16** in the section "Create a Field Lookup Based on a Table."

Alternatively, you can follow steps **1** to **6** in the section "Create a Field Lookup with Values That You Specify."

2 Click **Allow Multiple Values** (☐ changes to ☑).

3 Click **Finish**.

If the field already contains data, a warning appears about changing the field to store multiple values.

4 Click **Yes**.

Lookup Wizard

What label would you like for your lookup field?

Newsletters

Do you want to enable data integrity between these tables?

☐ Enable Data Integrity

○ Cascade Delete

● Restrict Delete

Do you want to store multiple values for this lookup?

2 ☑ Allow Multiple Values

Those are all the answers the wizard needs to create your lookup field.

3 Cancel | < Back | Next > | Finish

Microsoft Access ✕

⚠ You have changed the 'Newsletters' lookup column to store multiple values. You will not be able to undo this change once you save the table.

Do you want to change 'Newsletters' to store multiple values?

4 → Yes | No

If you created a table-based lookup, a prompt appears, asking you to save the table.

⑤ Click **Yes**.

⑥ Click **View** to switch to the Datasheet view.

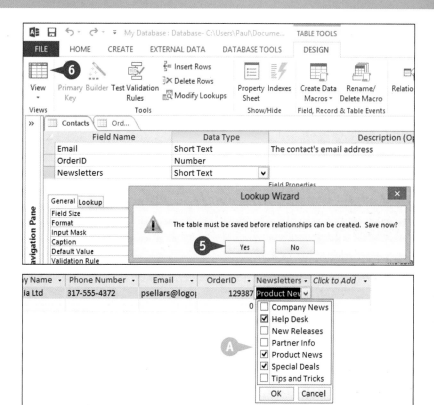

🅐 The lookup is created and is displayed with multiple values allowed in the chosen field.

Note: See Chapter 3, "Entering and Editing Data," for more on entering values into a multivalued field.

TIP

What are the drawbacks to using a multivalued field?
Multivalued fields are incompatible with Access versions 2003 and earlier. You cannot save a database in an earlier format if it includes multivalued fields, which may be an issue if you later need to share your data file with someone who only has the earlier version. Furthermore, you cannot convert a field from multivalue to single value; you have to delete it completely to make the database compatible, and you lose all the data that was stored in that field for the entire table.

CHAPTER 6

Finding and Filtering Data

Access provides many ways of locating individual data records within your database. In Chapter 3, you learn about sorting a datasheet — one of the simplest methods of looking something up. In this chapter, you learn about two other ways to search for data: using the Find feature to find a text string and using the Filter feature to show only records that match criteria you specify.

Understanding Find and Replace

Find and Replace is a single feature with two parts: one that enables you to locate text and another that enables you to replace found text with other text. Both features can save you tremendous amounts of time, particularly in large tables.

You use the Find tab to locate text within records. You can search for numbers, partial words, entire words, or phrases. You use the Replace tab to also locate text within a table, except that you can also replace the found text with some other text that you specify.

A Find What

You can specify a text string or numeric value that you want to find.

B Look In

You can limit the search to a certain field.

C Match

You can look for exact matches of the whole field or partial matches.

D Search

You can search above or below the currently selected record.

E Match Case

You can choose whether the search is case-sensitive.

F Found text

The found text is highlighted in the datasheet.

G Replace With

The Replace tab has a Replace With text field, in which you can enter the replacement string.

H Replace

You can click **Replace** to replace one instance of what you are searching for and move to the next instance.

I Replace All

You can click **Replace All** to do a global replace. Be cautious about doing so; it might replace more than you intended.

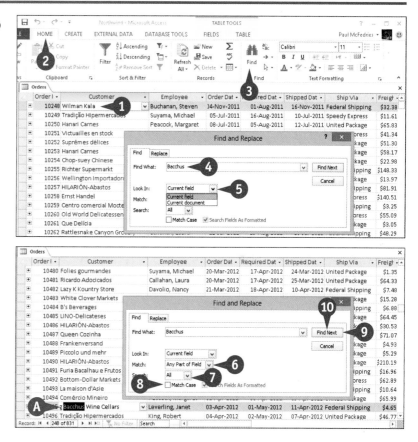

Find Data

If you are working with a table that has only a few records, it is usually easy to locate the record you want fairly quickly. However, if your table contains hundreds or even thousands of records, finding the data you need can be extremely time-consuming. To save time and effort, you can use the Find feature to quickly locate a text string or numeric value within a datasheet.

You can search in one particular field, or you can expand the search to include all the fields in the datasheet. You can also tell Access to match part or all of the field value.

Find Data

1 If you plan to limit the search to only one field, click in that field's column — in any row.

2 Click the **Home** tab.

3 Click **Find** ( ).

4 Type the text to find.

5 Click the **Look In** and click either **Current field** or **Current document**.

6 Click the **Match** and click what you want to match.

Note: The choices are Any Part of Field, Start of Field, and Whole Field.

7 Click the **Search** and click **Up** or **Down** if you want to limit the search to one direction.

8 You can click **Match Case** (changes to) to make the search case-sensitive.

9 Click **Find Next**.

A The Datasheet view jumps to the first instance and highlights it.

10 Continue clicking **Find Next** until the instance that you want is found.

Replace Data

If you find that you need to replace one bit of text with another in a datasheet, this is not difficult or time-consuming if you have only a few instances to replace. However, if you have dozens or even hundreds of instances to replace, doing so by hand can take an extremely long time. To save time, you can take the Find operation one step further by replacing the found value with other text that you specify. For example, if you want to change "Grocery" to "Market," a replace operation can easily make the change throughout a table.

Replace Data

1 To limit the replacement to only one field, click in that field's column — in any row.

2 Click the **Home** tab.

3 Click the Replace button (ᵃᵇ/ₐᶜ).

4 Type the text to find.

5 Type the text that you want to substitute for the found text.

6 Click the **Look In** ☑ and click either **Current field** or **Current document**.

7 Click the **Match** ☑ and click what you want to match.

Note: The choices are Any Part of Field, Start of Field, and Whole Field.

8 Click the **Search** ☑ and click **Up** or **Down** if you want to limit the search to one direction.

9 You can click **Match Case** (☐ changes to ☑) to make the search case-sensitive.

10 Click **Find Next**.

Ⓐ Access jumps to the first instance and highlights it.

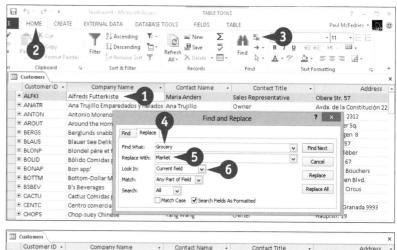

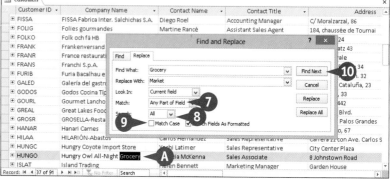

11 Click **Replace**.

B If you do not want to replace that instance, you can click **Find Next** to bypass it.

C The next instance of the text is highlighted.

12 Continue clicking **Replace** or **Find Next** until a message appears that says Access can find no more matches.

13 Click **OK**.

TIPS

How can I replace all instances at once?
Instead of clicking **Replace**, click **Replace All**. Be careful, however, that you do not make any unintentional replacements. For example, if you have a customer named Robert who prefers to be called Bob, you probably would not want to replace all instances of "Robert" with "Bob." His e-mail address might still call him "Robert," and a global replace operation would change the e-mail address and make it incorrect.

What is the Search Fields As Formatted check box, and why is it unavailable?
If a field's Text Format property is set to Rich Text (in the Design view), the field can hold formatting as well as text. For such fields, you can search for strings formatted a certain way. By default, most fields are plain text, so this check box is not available.

Filter to Show Only Blank or Nonblank Entries

Filtering means that instead of displaying all the records, you display only a subset of the records based on some condition that you specify. One of the most common filter operations is to display only those records that are either blank or nonblank for a particular field. For example, if you want to look for records that have no entry in a particular field, you would set up a filter to show the blank entries for that field. Similarly, you may want to find all customers for whom the E-mail Address field is nonblank so that you can send an e-mail announcement.

Filter to Show Only Blank or Nonblank Entries

Apply the Filter

1 Click in the column for the field that you want to search — in a row where that field is blank.

2 Click the **Home** tab.

3 Click the Selection button (▼).

4 Click **Equals Blank** to show only blank entries.

Ⓐ Alternatively, click **Does Not Equal Blank** to show only nonblank entries.

Ⓑ Records that do not match the specification are temporarily hidden.

Remove the Filter

1 Click the Toggle Filter button (▼).

The filter is removed.

Note: To reapply the same filter, click ▼ again.

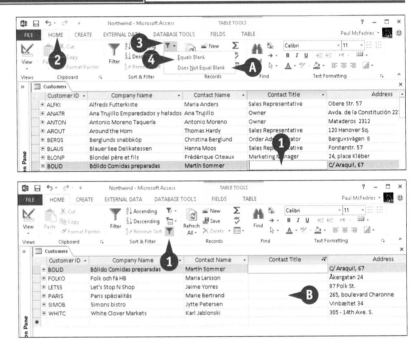

Filter by Selection

You can filter not only for blank versus nonblank entries but also for any specific value in any field. This means that Access looks for those records that have the value in the field and then displays just those matching records. For example, suppose that you want to display all the customer records where the person is an owner of their company. If you have a Contact Title field and such customers have Owner in that field, you could filter the records to show only those that have Owner in the Contact Title field.

Filter by Selection

Apply the Filter

1 Click in a field that contains the value for which you want to filter.

Note: For example, to filter for Owner in the Contact Title field, you would click any instance of **Owner**.

2 Click the **Home** tab.

3 Click .

4 Click the option that you want.

Note: The Equals options look only for entries matching the entire field. The Contains options look for the specified entry as any part of the field.

A Only records that match the filter are displayed.

Remove the Filter

1 Click to remove the filter when finished.

Filter for Multiple Values

Filtering by selection works well, but it finds only one value. For example, you cannot set it to find people with job titles of either "Owner" or "CEO."

To filter for multiple values, you can use the Filter button on the Datasheet tab. It opens a floating pane that contains check boxes for each value in a field, and you can select multiple values to use as the filter. For example, if your table has a Contact Title field and you want to see which contacts are owners or CEOs, you would select only the Owner and the CEO check boxes.

Filter for Multiple Values

Apply the Filter

1 Click in the column for the field that you want to filter.

Note: You can click in any row; it need not be a row containing a value that you want to include.

2 Click the **Home** tab.

3 Click **Filter** (▼).

Ⓐ You can also click ▼ to the right of the field.

A Filter pane appears below the selected field.

4 Deselect the check box next to any value that you do not want to include (☑ changes to ☐).

Ⓑ You can click **Select All** (☑ changes to ☐) to quickly deselect every check box.

5 Click **OK**.

Ⓒ The list is filtered to show only the values that you chose.

Remove the Filter

1 Click ▼ to remove the filter when finished.

Using Text Filters

Access provides a special set of filters for working with text values. These filters take into account that text strings often contain more than just the searched-for value.

For example, if different people entered the records, the same company may be listed as "ACME," "The ACME Corporation," or "ACME Corp." You could set up a text filter to look for all records in which the field begins with "ACME." You can also set up text filters to match field items that contain or end with the text you specify.

Using Text Filters

1 Click in the column for the field that you want to filter.

Note: You can click in any row; it need not be a row containing a value that you want to include.

2 Click the **Home** tab.

3 Click **Filter** ( ).

A You can also click to the right of the field.

A Filter pane appears below the selected field.

4 Click **Text Filters**.

5 Click the text filter that you want to apply.

Note: For example, to find all records that contain a certain text string, you can choose **Contains**.

The Custom Filter dialog box opens.

6 Type the text for the filter.

7 Click **OK**.

Access applies the filter.

B You can remove the filter by clicking , the same as with any other filter.

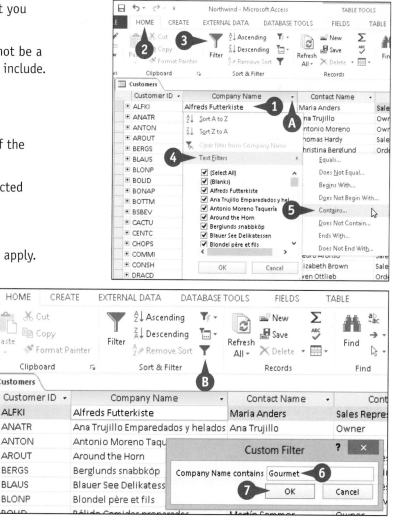

Filter by Form

Filtering by form enables you to filter by multiple fields and specify criteria for as many fields as you like. When you filter by form, you can combine the criteria by using AND, OR, or a combination of the two.

With an AND filter, you choose two or more values, and Access filters the table to include only those records that contain all the chosen values. With an OR filter, you choose two or more values, and the table is filtered to include only those records that contain at least one of the chosen values.

Filter by Form

Using AND

1 Click the **Home** tab.

2 Click the Advanced Filter Options button (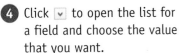).

3 Click **Filter By Form**.

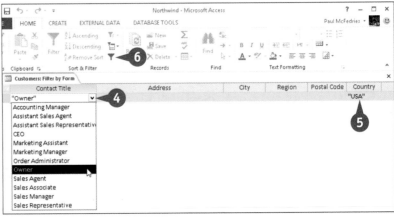

A Filter by Form sheet opens.

Note: If you previously performed a filter operation, the existing filter specification may appear. Delete any unwanted criteria.

4 Click ⌄ to open the list for a field and choose the value that you want.

5 Repeat step **4** for other fields as needed.

6 Click ▼.

Access filters the data.

Using OR

1 Click the **Home** tab.

2 Click 🔽.

3 Click **Filter By Form**.

A Filter by Form sheet opens.

4 Click 🔽 to open the list for a field and choose the value that you want.

5 Click the **Or** tab.

A blank Filter by Form page opens.

6 Repeat step 4 to select another criterion.

Note: Each page represents a separate criterion. Records are included that match the criteria on any page.

7 Click ▼.

The filter is applied.

TIPS

Why is there already criteria in the form?
If you previously performed a filter operation, the last filter that you ran appears in the form — for your convenience. Delete it from the form if you do not want it.

Is there an easier way to set up OR conditions for the same field?
Yes. You can use the Filter by Form page to manually type in a specification for a field. For example, if you want records where the Company field is either "ACME Corporation" or "Colvin Enterprises," you could click in the Company box and type **"ACME Corporation" OR "Colvin Enterprises"**. Make sure that you include the quotation marks and the word OR. You can string together many OR statements for a single field. The Or tab is needed only if the Or condition involves multiple fields.

Save a Filter As a Query

$\int$ ome Filter by Form operations that consist of multiple fields and combinations of AND and OR filters can take quite a bit of time and effort to set up. If you have created such a filter and you think that you might use it again in the future, you can save it as a query so that you can rerun it later without having to set it up again. When you save a filter, a new query is created as a new object in the database. It works just like the queries you learn to create and modify in upcoming chapters.

Save a Filter As a Query

Save the Filter

1 Create a filter and then display it in a Filter by Form sheet.

Note: See the section "Filter by Form" for help if needed. Do not apply the filter yet.

2 Click the **Home** tab.

3 Click 🛅.

4 Click **Save As Query**.

The Save As Query dialog box opens.

5 Type a name for the query.

6 Click **OK**.

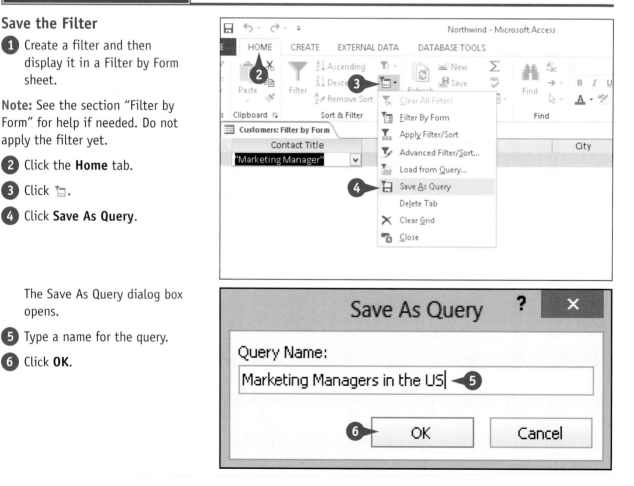

You are returned to the Filter by Form sheet.

7 Right-click the **Filter by Form** tab.

8 Click **Close**.

The Filter by Form sheet closes.

Run the Saved Filter

1 In the All Access Objects list, double-click the query (filter) that you saved.

The results open in a new datasheet.

TIP

What is the difference between a filter and a query?

Filters are fine for quick-and-dirty table operations, but they are not very powerful. To really get at the data, you need to use queries, which are much more sophisticated tools. For example, unlike filters, queries are not simply a different view of the table data. A *query* is a separate database object that actually *extracts* records from a table and places them in a datasheet that you can manipulate.

The other major difference between a query and a filter is that you can save queries and then rerun them any time you like. Filters, on the other hand, are ephemeral: When you close the table, any filters that you have defined vanish into thin air.

See Chapters 7 and 8 to learn how to create and work with queries.

CHAPTER 7

Creating Simple Queries

Queries enable you to save specifications for sort/filter operations as reusable objects. They are the backbone of any data retrieval system and enable users to quickly pull the needed information from large tables. In this chapter, you will learn how to create simple, effective queries that sort and filter the data from one or more tables.

Understanding Queries

If you have a large amount of data in a table, you will not usually want or need to work directly with the raw data. Instead, it is better to work with data that has been sorted and filtered in some way, two operations that you can quickly combine by creating a query. Although the name implies that queries are a sort of question, it is more useful to think of them as *requests*. In the simplest case, a *query* is a request to see a particular subset of your data in a particular order.

A Tables

A query can pull fields from more than one table, provided that they have a relationship between them.

B Field lists

Each table's complete field list appears in a separate window.

C View button

To run the query, click **View**.

D QBE grid

This grid, called the *Query By Example (QBE) grid*, contains the fields chosen to be in the query —one field per column.

E Add a field

To add a field to the QBE grid, double-click it in the field list or drag it to the grid.

F Select a field

To select a column in the grid, click the thin bar above the field.

A Field

The Field row shows the field name.

B Table

The Table row shows what table the field came from.

C Sort

The Sort row indicates the field(s) by which the results should be sorted.

D Show

A field can be omitted from the results by deselecting the **Show** check box.

E Criteria

The Criteria rows hold any filters that you want to apply.

F Or

Additional criteria can be entered in one or more Or rows.

Create a Query with the Simple Query Wizard

T he most basic type of query is one that simply pulls certain fields from two or more related tables and displays the fields in a datasheet. For example, if you have a Products table and a Suppliers table, a basic query could show the ProductName field from the Products table and the CompanyName field from the Suppliers table.

To create these kinds of queries, you can use the Simple Query Wizard, which takes you step-by-step through the process of building the query. Note, however, that you cannot use this wizard to set up any sorting or filtering.

Create a Query with the Simple Query Wizard

1 Click the **Create** tab.

2 Click **Query Wizard**.

The New Query dialog box opens.

3 Click **Simple Query Wizard**.

4 Click **OK**.

The Simple Query Wizard opens.

5 Click the **Tables/Queries** ☑ and click the table (or other query) from which you want to select fields.

6 Click a field.

7 Click ☐ to move the field to the Selected Fields list.

8 Repeat steps **6** and **7** to pull more fields from the same table or query.

9 If needed, repeat steps **5** to **8** to pull fields from another table or query.

10 Click **Next**.

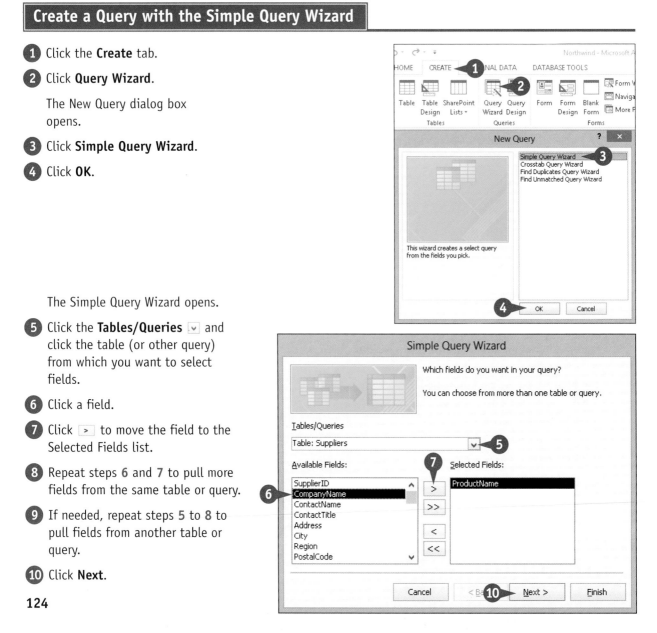

If you selected at least one numeric field, a prompt appears for a detail or summary query.

 Leave **Detail** selected for a query that includes all records.

 Alternatively, you can click **Summary** to summarize the data rather than show every record ($\bigcirc$ changes to $\bigodot$).

Note: This screen does not appear if you did not select any numeric fields in step 6. You will learn about summary queries in Chapter 8, "Creating Complex Queries."

⑫ Click **Next**.

The title page of the wizard appears.

⑬ Type a name for the query, replacing the default name.

⑭ Click **Finish**.

The query results appear in a datasheet.

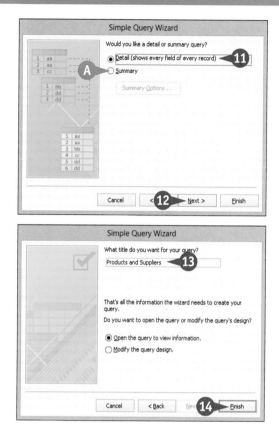

TIPS

Can I use fields from any combination of tables?

No. The tables that you use in a query must be directly related — that is, related with a connecting line between them, not related via some other table that they both connect to individually. If they are related only via another table, you must also include at least one field from the connector table to help Access find the relationship.

What are the other queries in the New Query dialog box used for?

They are for several types of special-purpose queries that are difficult to set up manually:

• A Crosstab query summarizes and groups data in a two-dimensional grid.

• A Find Duplicates query locates records that have the same value in a specified field or fields.

• A Find Unmatched query locates records in one table that have no corresponding entry in a related table. For example, you could find customers who have no orders.

Start a New Query in the Query Design View

The Simple Query Wizard makes it easy to build a basic query, but it does not enable you to add sorting or filtering to your query. Sorting and filtering are essential if you want to create powerful and useful queries, but to include them in a query, you must work in the Query Design view. As with the Table Design view, the Query Design view gives you full access to all the query tools and features.

In this section, you learn how to start a new query in the Query Design view and how to add tables and fields to your query.

Start a New Query in the Query Design View

1 Click the **Create** tab.

2 Click **Query Design**.

A new Query Design window opens, and the Show Table dialog box appears.

3 Click a table that you want to include in the query.

Ⓐ You can also click the **Queries** tab to choose a query to use as a table — to base one query on another.

4 Click **Add**.

5 Repeat steps **3** and **4** to add more tables.

6 Click **Close**.

Ⓑ The selected tables (or queries) appear as field lists in the top part of the window.

7 Drag a field into the first empty column in the query grid.

If you need to add another table, you can drag it into the top part of the query window from the Objects list.

Ⓒ You can also click **Show Table** on the Design tab to reopen the Show Table dialog box to add another table or query.

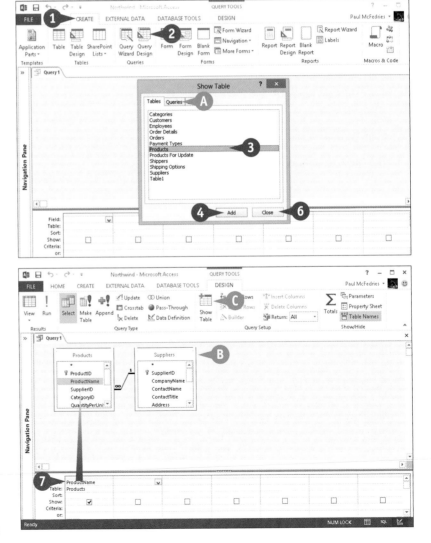

8 Drag more fields into the grid as needed.

Note: The fields can come from different tables as long as the tables are related.

9 Click **View** to check the query results in the Datasheet view.

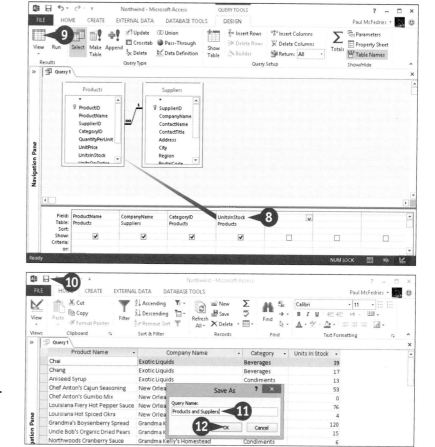

The results appear in a datasheet.

10 Click 💾.

The Save As dialog box opens.

11 Type a name for the query, replacing the placeholder name.

12 Click **OK**.

The query is saved.

TIPS

What is the Run button used for?
Some types of queries perform permanent actions on the data in the table. In such queries, there is a difference between previewing the results in the Datasheet view and actually running the query. That is why there are two buttons: View and Run. For the type of query that you create in this section, though, the two buttons do the same thing.

What if the query results are not what I want?
Rather than save your work, as shown in steps 10 to 12, click the **View** button on the Home tab to return to the Query Design view. Make any changes as needed and then click **View** to preview your work in the datasheet again.

Insert, Arrange, and Remove Query Fields

The order that the fields appear in the datasheet when you run the query is determined by the order that they appear in the query grid. When you double-click a field to add it to a query, Access places the field in the query grid to the right of the existing columns. If you want to insert the field in a different position, you must use a different technique.

You can also rearrange fields after placing them in the grid and remove any fields that you added by mistake.

Insert, Arrange, and Remove Query Fields

Insert a Field in a Specific Position

1 Move ⇧ to the top of the column that the new column should appear to the left of (⇧ changes to ↓) and then click to select the column.

2 Click the **Design** tab.

3 Click **Insert Columns** (ᵘ↑ᵘ).

Ⓐ A new blank column appears.

4 Click the new column's ⌄ and click the field that you want to appear in the column.

Note: As a shortcut, instead of inserting the column, you can drag the new field on top of an existing one; Access creates a new column to the left of the existing column.

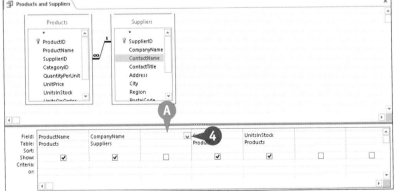

Remove a Field

1. Click the top of a field's column to select it.

2. Click the **Design** tab.

3. Click **Delete Columns** (✕).

   Alternatively, you can press Delete.

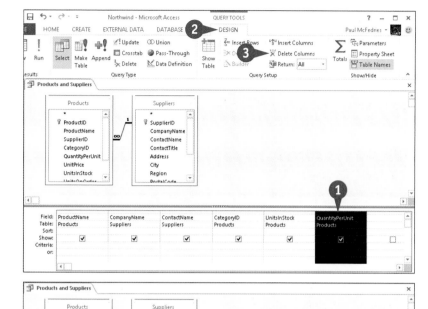

Ⓑ The field is removed from the grid.

Move a Field

1. Click the top of a field's column to select it.

2. Drag the bar above the field left or right to move it (𝕀 changes to 𝕀).

Ⓒ A black line shows where the field is being dragged.

   When you release the mouse button, the field moves to the new location.

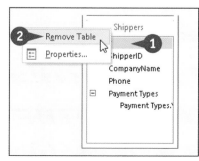

How do I remove a table's field list from the Query Design view?

To remove a table's field list:

1. Right-click the title of the field list.

2. Click **Remove Table**.

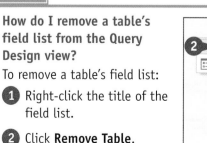

What happens if I remove a table that has fields in use in the query grid?

Those fields are deleted from the grid. Adding the table back again does not automatically restore them in the grid; you must manually add the fields.

Set Field Sorting

You can set a query to sort the results by a certain field, either in ascending or descending order. An *ascending sort* means that a text field is sorted from A to Z, a numeric field is sorted from 0 to 9, and a date field is sorted from earliest to latest. For the opposite sort order, choose a descending sort.

You can specify sorting for more than one field. Access prioritizes the fields from left to right in the grid. The leftmost field that has a sort order set will take precedence; other sorts will operate only in the event of a tie.

Set Field Sorting

1. For the field that you want to use for sorting, click the **Sort** ⌄.

2. Click **Ascending** for an A to Z sort.

Ⓐ You can also click **Descending** for a Z to A sort.

Ⓑ To turn off field sorting, click **(not sorted)**.

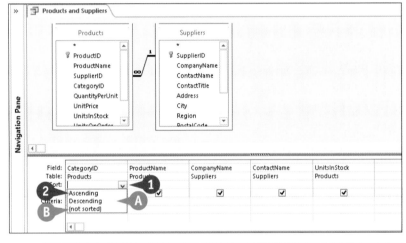

3. Repeat steps **1** and **2** for other fields if needed.

4. Click **View** to check your work.

The results appear sorted by the chosen field(s).

Ⓒ You can return to the Query Design view by clicking **View** again.

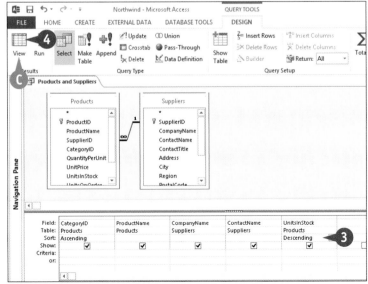

Add an Alias to a Query Field

When you display a query in the Datasheet view, Access displays the field names at the top of each column. However, field names do not have to appear in the query results as their actual names. For example, perhaps you want the Product Name field to appear simply as "Product," or you want the Quantity field to appear as "Qty."

To change the wording of the column heading in the query results, you can create a text alternative called the field's *alias*. Note, however, that you cannot create an alias for a field that already has a defined caption.

Add an Alias to a Query Field

1 Position the insertion point at the beginning of the **Field** box for the field that you want to work with.

2 Type the alias, followed by a colon (**:**).

3 Repeat steps **1** and **2** for other fields if needed.

4 Click **View** to preview the change in a datasheet.

Ⓐ The datasheet column(s) appear with the alias(es).

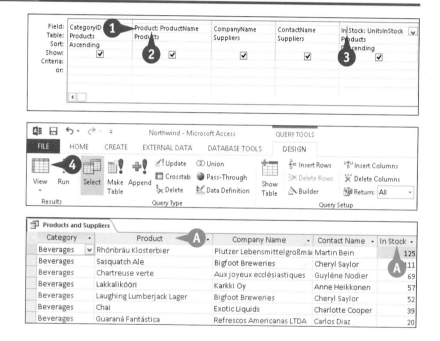

131

Understanding Criteria

The heart of any query is its *criteria*, a set of expressions that determines the records that appear in the results. Criteria is composed of *expressions* that combine operators, functions, and field names with literal values. Access applies the result of the expression to the field in which it was entered in the query design grid, and only those records that match the result are included in the results.

For example, you may include only customers in a certain range of zip codes or only people who have placed orders in the last 12 months.

Numeric Criteria

You can specify a fixed numeric value as a criterion for a number field. Type the number directly into the **Criteria** row in the grid. You do not need quotation marks or any special formatting. Access interprets dates as numbers, too. When using a date, enter hash symbols around it: **#08/23/2013#**. If you forget the hash marks, Access usually adds them for you.

Field:	Quantity	OrderDate
Table:	Order Details	Orders
Sort:		
Show:	✔	✔
Criteria:	100	#8/23/2013#
or:		

Text Criteria

You can specify a text string as a criterion. It can contain multiple words, including punctuation and spacing, but you must enclose it in quotation marks. For example, to set a CompanyName field's criterion to ACME, type **"ACME"** in the **Criteria** row. If you forget the quotation marks, Access usually adds them for you.

Field:	CompanyName	Country
Table:	Customers	Customers
Sort:		
Show:	✔	✔
Criteria:	"ACME"	"USA"
or:		

Criteria Ranges

It is often useful to specify a range of values for a criterion instead of one specific value. You can accomplish this with comparison operators and special keywords, as shown in the following table:

Field:	Quantity	UnitPrice
Table:	Order Details	Order Details
Sort:		
Show:	✔	✔
Criteria:	>=100	<20
or:		

Use	Description	Example
<	Less than	<30
<=	Less than or equal to	<=#1/1/14#
>	Greater than	>100
>=	Greater than or equal to	>=50
<>	Not equal to	<>"Denver"
Like	Matches a pattern of characters	Like "Denver"
And	Matches two or more conditions	>5 And <10
Or	Matches any condition	"CO" Or "CA"
Between ... And	Matches values in a range	Between #1/1/14# And #1/15/14#
In	Selects from a list of values	In ("NM", "NY", "NJ")
Is Null	Includes the record only if the field is empty	Is Null
Is Not Null	Includes the record only if the field is not empty	Is Not Null
*	Wildcard, substituting for any characters	462*
?	Wildcard, substituting for a single character	462??

Filter a Query for a Specific Value

The simplest criterion is one in which you specify a single value for a field. Only records containing that value in that field are included in the query results.

For example, if you have a Products table in your query and that table has a UnitsInStock field, you can display all the out-of-stock products by filtering the query to show those records where the UnitsInStock field value is 0. Similarly, if you just want to see the beverages in the Products table, you could filter the query to show those records where the Category field is "Beverages."

Filter a Query for a Specific Value

Filter a Query for a Numeric Value

1 For the field that you want to filter, type the numeric filter value in the **Criteria** box.

Note: If the value is a date, enclose it in hash marks: **#10/27/2013#**.

Note: If you enter criteria for more than one field, only records that match both criteria are included in the results. Multiple criteria queries are covered later in this chapter.

Filter a Query for a Text String

1 For the field that you want to filter, type the text string filter value, enclosed in quotation marks, in the **Criteria** box.

Note: If you forget the quotation marks, Access usually adds them for you.

Note: If you are not sure of the entire text string, use a wildcard, as in the table in the preceding section. For example, "ACME*" finds ACME, ACME Corp., and Acme Corporation.

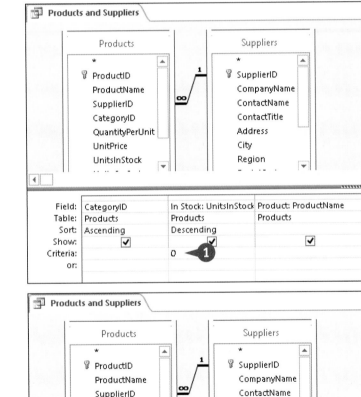

134

Specify a Range of Values

Y ou can specify a range of values in your criteria by using comparison operators. For example, if your query includes a Products table with a UnitsInStock field, you might want to see which products are low in stock by looking for records where the UnitsInStock field is less than 10. Similarly, in a query that includes an Orders table with an OrderDate field, you might want to see just those orders placed between January 1, 2013 and January 31, 2013.

Comparison operators work with all kinds of criteria (text, dates, numbers, and so on). A table of available operators appears in the section "Understanding Criteria."

Specify a Range of Values

Using a Greater-Than or Less-Than Range

1 For the field that you want to filter, type the comparison operator that you want to use in the **Criteria** box: >, <, >=, or =.

2 Type the value to which you want to compare it.

Note: The value can be a number, date, or text string. Remember to enclose text strings in quotation marks.

Using a Between Range

1 In the **Criteria** row, type **Between** and add a space.

2 Type the lower value in the range and add a space.

3 Type **And** and add a space.

4 Type the higher value in the range.

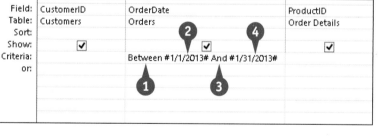

Specify a List of Values

You can create a list of values to use for a criterion to apply to a specified field. Access will include in the query results only those records in which the field value matches any one of the values in the list. For example, if you have an Order Details table with a Discount field, you might want to see those orders where the discount was 15%, 20%, or 25%.

There are two ways to create a list of values. You can separate each value with the word *Or,* or you can use the *In* keyword and then place the values in parentheses as a group.

Specify a List of Values

Create a List by Using Or

1 For the field that you want to filter, type the first value in the **Criteria** box and then add a space.

Note: Enclose the value in quotation marks if it is a text string.

2 Type the word **Or** and add a space.

3 Type the next value and add a space.

4 Repeat steps **2** and **3** to include as many items for the list as needed.

Field:	OrderID	CustomerID	Discount
Table:	Orders	Orders	Order Details
Sort:			
Show:	✔	✔	✔
Criteria:			0.15 Or 0.2 Or 0.25
or:			

Field:	OrderID	CustomerID	Discount
Table:	Orders	Orders	Order Details
Sort:			
Show:	✔	✔	✔
Criteria:			In (0.15,0.2,0.25)
or:			

Create a List by Using In

1 For the field that you want to filter, type **In (** in the **Criteria** box.

2 Type the list of values, separated by commas.

Note: If the values are text strings, enclose each one in separate quotation marks. Make sure that the commas are outside the quotation marks.

3 Type **)**.

Hide a Field in the Query Results

You can hide a field without removing it from the query grid. This is useful when you need to include a field in a query in order to use it for sorting or as part of your criteria but you do not want that field to show up in the results.

For example, suppose that you are creating a query called *Orders in Washington*. You would need the State field to be included so that you can show only Washington orders, but it would be redundant to have "WA" appear in a column for every record.

Hide a Field in the Query Results

1 Click the **Show** check box for the field that you want to hide (☑ changes to ☐).

2 Click **View** to check your work.

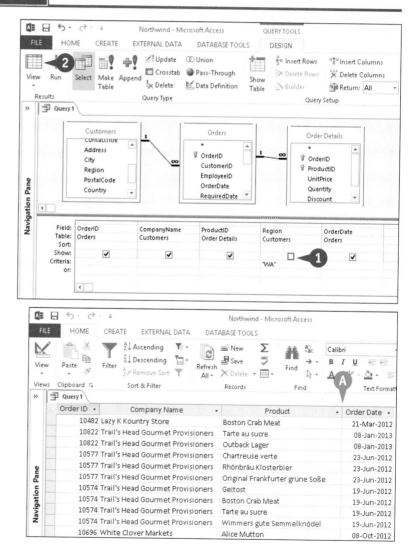

The datasheet opens, showing the query results. Only the records that match the criteria appear.

Ⓐ The field providing the criteria does not appear.

Create Compound Criteria

In many situations, using a single criterion does not show you the data that you want to work with. For example, in a Products table, you might want to see those records in which the UnitsInStock field is low (say, less than 10) *and* the UnitsOnOrder field is 0. For queries like these, you need to set up *compound criteria,* where you enter either multiple expressions for the same field or multiple expressions for different fields.

You use *And* criteria when you want to select records that satisfy two or more different expressions. You use *Or* criteria when you want to display records that satisfy one expression or another.

Create Compound Criteria

Combine Exclusive Criteria (Using And)

1 Create a criterion for a field.

Note: See the preceding sections for help if needed.

2 In the same **Criteria** row, create a criterion for another field.

Combine Nonexclusive Criteria (Using Or)

1 Create a criterion for a field.

2 On the first empty **Or** row, create a criterion for another field.

Note: You can also create a criterion for the same field in step **2**, but if working with the same field, it would be easier to use the word Or in the **Criteria** line, as you learned earlier in this chapter.

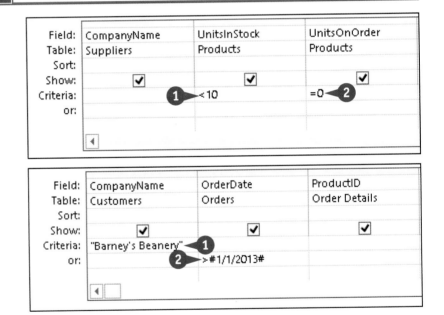

Limit the Records Returned

By default, a query's results contain all the records that match the criteria that you specified. However, there are situations in which you do not want or need to see all the records. For example, in a query that includes an Order Details table with a Quantity field, you might only want to see the biggest orders.

Access enables you to do this by limiting the number of records that a query returns. You can limit it either by a number or by a percentage. For example, you could show only the top 25 records, or you could show the top 5%.

Limit the Records Returned

1 For the field on which you want to impose a limit, click the **Sort** ⬇ and then click **Ascending** or **Descending**.

Note: Access applies the limit to the first field on which the query is sorted, if any. If there is no sorting specified, Access applies the limit to the leftmost field.

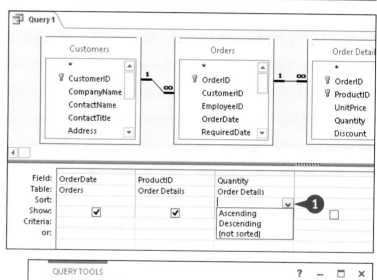

2 Click the **Design** tab.

3 Click the **Return** ⬇ and click the limit that you want.

CHAPTER 8

Creating Complex Queries

Queries can do much more than just sort and filter data from a table. They can summarize and calculate data, append data from one table to another, identify duplicate data, prompt the user for parameters at runtime, and much more. In this chapter, you learn how to take advantage of the powerful tools for special-purpose queries in Access 2013.

Understanding Summary Queries

Asummary query includes a column that performs a mathematical operation — such as summing or averaging — on the values of a particular field. A summary query derives either a single value for the entire query or several values for the records that have been grouped within the results. This means that you can use a summary query to distill a large quantity of data down to useful information. You can use summary queries whenever you do not care about the individual records but want to understand the big picture.

A No individual records

Individual records do not appear in the results of a summary query. Each row in the query datasheet represents a summary of a group of records. It is possible but not typical for a group to consist of a single record.

B Group By

A summary query typically contains only a few fields. It needs only the field(s) by which you want to group the data and the field(s) by which you want to calculate. There is typically one field by which the data is grouped. In this example, each row represents a different month.

Orders Quantities By Month

OrderDate By Month ▾	Sum Of Quantity ▾	Avg Of UnitPrice ▾
June 2012	1635	$25.59
July 2012	2054	$27.15
August 2012	1861	$26.14
September 2012	2343	$26.66
October 2012	2679	$26.81
November 2012	1856	$25.40
December 2012	2682	$30.94

C Sum

The Quantity field has been set up to use the Sum function to sum the Quantity values for the month as a whole. Access automatically generated the column title Sum Of Quantity.

D Average

The UnitPrice field has been set up to use the Average function to average the unit price values for the month as a whole. Access automatically generated the column title Avg Of UnitPrice.

Aggregate Functions

Summary queries summarize data using *aggregate functions* built in to Access. These are math operations that calculate statistics about the data. Some of the aggregate functions require the data to be numeric, such as Sum; others, such as Count, work on any data type.

The following are the available aggregate functions:

Function	Purpose
Sum	Totals numeric values.
Avg	Totals numeric values and divides by the number of records in the group.
Min	Finds the lowest value (smallest number, first text alphabetically, earliest date).
Max	Finds the highest value (largest number, last text alphabetically, latest date).

Function	Purpose
Count	Finds the number of records in the group.
StDev	Calculates the standard deviation. This is used to see how close the values are to the average.
Var	Calculates the variance. This is another way of measuring how close the values are to the average.
First	Finds the first record's entry in the group.
Last	Finds the last record's entry in the group.
Expression	Allows a custom formula to be entered.
Where	Refers the query to the Criteria row. This enables you to include fields in the query purely for criteria purposes without grouping or calculating by that field.

Simple Query Wizard Summaries

Ⓐ Summary Options

When you choose a summary query with the Simple Query Wizard, a Summary Options button becomes available in the wizard.

Ⓑ Select the calculations

You can click check boxes for each calculation that you want (☐ changes to ☑). Each check box that you click translates into a column in the query results, so choose carefully to avoid information overload.

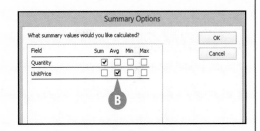

Ⓒ Query Design view summaries

In the Query Design view, you can display a Total row in the grid. For each field included, the Total row must be set either to Group By or to one of the functions shown in the previous table.

Create a Summary Query with the Simple Query Wizard

The easiest way to create a summary query is to use the Simple Query Wizard, as you learn in Chapter 7, "Creating Simple Queries." You follow the same procedure for adding fields from one or more tables or queries. After you have done that, the Simple Query Wizard gives you the opportunity to specify that you want to create a summary query. From there, you set up the calculations that you want to use and decide if you want your results grouped on a field's values.

Create a Summary Query with the Simple Query Wizard

1 Click the **Create** tab.

2 Click **Query Wizard**.

The New Query dialog box opens.

3 Click **Simple Query Wizard**.

4 Click **OK**.

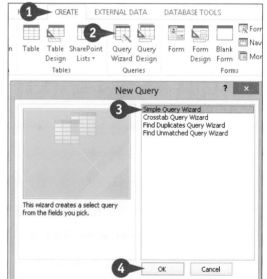

The Simple Query Wizard opens.

5 Click here and choose the table (or other query) from which you want to select fields.

6 Click a field.

7 Click 🔽 to move the field to the Selected Fields list.

8 Repeat steps **6** and **7** to pull more fields from the same table.

9 If needed, repeat steps **5** to **8** to pull fields from another table.

10 Click **Next**.

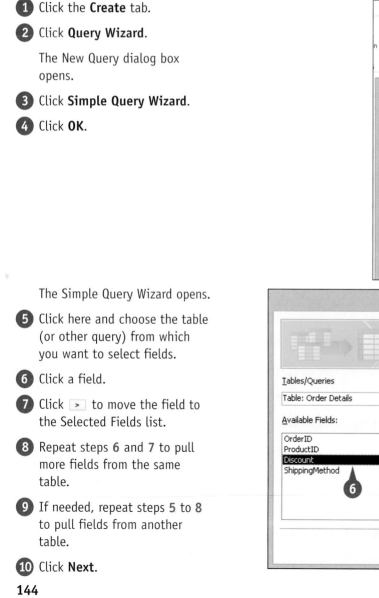

The detail or summary page of the wizard appears.

11 Click **Summary** (○ changes to ⦿).

12 Click **Summary Options**.

Simple Query Wizard

Would you like a detail or summary query?

○ Detail (shows every field of every record)

⦿ Summary

Summary Options ...

Cancel   < Back   Next >   Finish

The Summary Options dialog box opens.

13 Click the check box for each calculation that you want to perform (☐ changes to ☑).

14 If you want a record count, click **Count records in _table name_** (☐ changes to ☑).

Note: _Table name_ will be replaced by the name of the table or query from which that field is being taken. It is Order Details in this example.

15 Click **OK**.

Summary Options

What summary values would you like calculated?

Field	Sum	Avg	Min	Max
Quantity	☑	☐	☐	☐
UnitPrice	☐	☑	☐	☐

OK

Cancel

☐ Count records in Order Details

TIPS

Which fields should I use?

A summary query is clearest and most concise when it uses very few fields. Include one field by which to group and then only the fields by which you want calculations to appear for those groups. If you use more fields than that, the datasheet becomes so complex that it defeats the purpose of a summary query — to summarize a large collection of data in a concise format.

Can I choose fields from different tables?

Yes. The same rules apply as with a detail query. Fields can come from different tables as long as those tables are related. Consult the Relationships window (click the **Database Tools** tab and then click **Relationships**) if you are not sure about the relationships.

Create a Summary Query with the Simple Query Wizard (continued)

When you create a summary query that includes a field that uses the Date/Time data type, the Simple Query Wizard enables you to group the results according to the values in that field. You do this by selecting a grouping interval for the field's date values, and that interval can be by day, month, quarter, or year.

This option alone makes the wizard very valuable. It is easy to set up such intervals in the wizard, but it is very complicated and difficult to set them up manually in the Query Design view.

Create a Summary Query with the Simple Query Wizard (continued)

You are returned to the Simple Query Wizard.

16 Click **Next**.

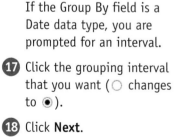

If the Group By field is a Date data type, you are prompted for an interval.

17 Click the grouping interval that you want (○ changes to ⊙).

18 Click **Next**.

The title page of the wizard appears.

19 Type a name for the query, replacing the default name.

20 Click **Finish**.

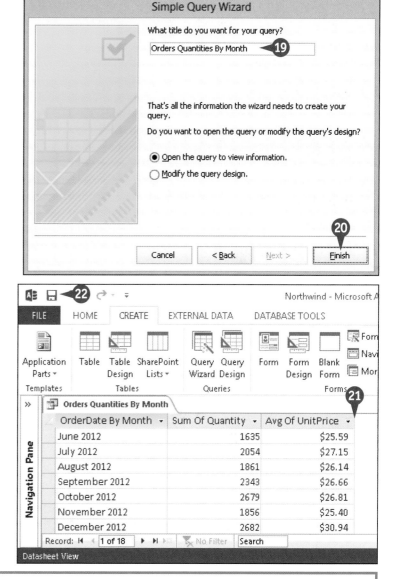

Simple Query Wizard

What title do you want for your query?

Orders Quantities By Month ◄ **19**

That's all the information the wizard needs to create your query.

Do you want to open the query or modify the query's design?

◉ Open the query to view information.

○ Modify the query design.

20

| Cancel | < Back | Next > | Finish |

The query results appear in a datasheet.

21 Widen the columns if needed to display the column headings.

Note: To automatically size a column to its content, double-click between the column headings. To manually size it, drag the right border of a column heading.

22 Click .

Access saves the summary query.

Northwind - Microsoft A

FILE   HOME   CREATE   EXTERNAL DATA   DATABASE TOOLS

Application Parts ▾ | Table | Table Design | SharePoint Lists ▾ | Query Wizard | Query Design | Form | Form Design | Blank Form | Form | Nav | Mor

Templates | Tables | Queries | Forms

22

21

Orders Quantities By Month

OrderDate By Month ▾	Sum Of Quantity ▾	Avg Of UnitPrice ▾
June 2012	1635	$25.59
July 2012	2054	$27.15
August 2012	1861	$26.14
September 2012	2343	$26.66
October 2012	2679	$26.81
November 2012	1856	$25.40
December 2012	2682	$30.94

Record: I◄ ◄ 1 of 18 ► ►I ► No Filter Search

Datasheet View

TIPS

Can I make changes to a summary query after creating it with the wizard?

Yes. You can edit it in the Query Design view. In most respects, a summary query is just like any other query. However, it has a Total row in the grid that detail queries do not have. You will learn more about summary queries in the Query Design view in the next section.

When I view the query in the Query Design view, why is there a weird extra field that starts with "Year"?

When you specify grouping by a date range, the Simple Query Wizard adds a formula that represents the interval. Its syntax can be quite complex; that is why it is best to create such fields with the wizard. Widen its column in the grid to see the entire formula at once.

Create a Summary Query in the Query Design View

I f you want more control over the creation of a summary query, you can create it in the Query Design view by specifying the fields manually. For example, the Simple Query Wizard gives you a choice of only four summary values: Sum, Average, Maximum, and Minimum. If you want to use summary values such as Count or Standard Deviation, you need to use the Design view.

Also, if you know exactly what you want and if the syntax that you need is not complicated, it can be faster to use this method than the wizard.

Create a Summary Query in the Query Design View

1 Click the **Create** tab.

2 Click **Query Design**.

A new Query Design window opens, and the Show Table dialog box appears.

3 Double-click the tables that you want to include in the query.

Ⓐ You can also click a table and then click **Add**.

Ⓑ You can also click the **Queries** tab and add an existing query, just as you would a table.

4 Click **Close**.

The selected tables (or queries) appear as field lists in the top part of the window.

5 Drag the fields that you want on to the grid.

6 Click the **Design** tab.

7 Click **Totals**.

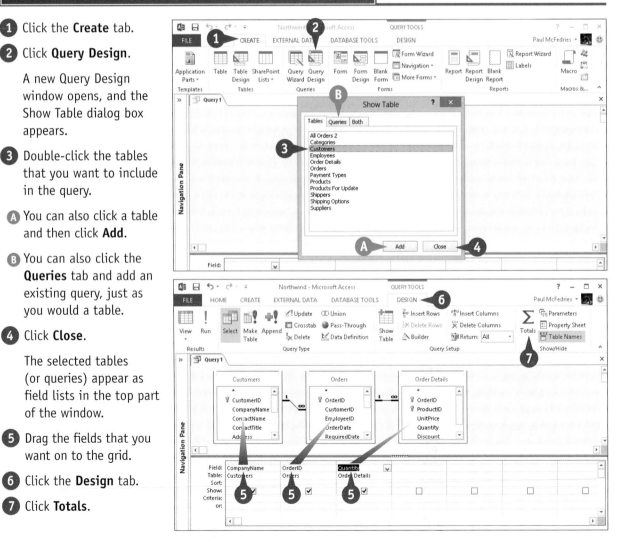

The Total row appears on the grid.

8 For each field, click the **Total** ☑ and click the calculation to perform.

C Leave one field set to **Group By**; these groups will form the rows of the results.

9 Click **View**.

The query results appear in a datasheet.

10 Click 🖫.

The Save As dialog box opens.

11 Type a name for the query, replacing the default name.

12 Click **OK**.

The query is saved.

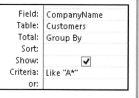

TIPS

How can I rename the column headings?

Use an alias, as you learn to do in Chapter 7. In the

| Sum of Quantity: Quantity |
| Order Details |
| Sum |
| |
| ✔ |

Query Design view, type an alias and a colon in front of the field name in the **Field** row.

Can I sort and use filter criteria in a summary query?

Yes. A summary query is just like a detail query in most respects. You

Field:	CompanyName
Table:	Customers
Total:	Group By
Sort:	
Show:	✔
Criteria:	Like "A*"
or:	

can even include a field in the query that does not appear in the query results just for filtering.

Understanding Calculated Fields

You often need to perform some kind of analysis on the query results. To do that, you need to introduce calculations into your query by creating what is called a *calculated field*. This is a column where the "field" is a calculation and the field values are the results of the calculation for each record. The calculation can be any combination of operator, field, and literal values.

For example, if you have a table of orders with a UnitPrice field and a Quantity field, you could create a calculated field named *Total* that multiples these two values.

Assign a Column Name

Use the same technique for naming the new column that you did with aliasing in Chapter 7, but do it in a blank column. Type the new name at the beginning of the **Field** box and then follow it with a colon.

Field:	Total:	✔
Table:		
Sort:		
Show:	☐	
Criteria:		
or:		

Write the Expression

After the colon, write the expression — that is, the math formula — by using standard math operators, with field names enclosed in square brackets. For example, to multiply the UnitPrice by the Quantity, type the following: **[UnitPrice]*[Quantity]**.

Field:	Total: [UnitPrice]*[Quantity]	
Table:		
Sort:		
Show:	✔	
Criteria:		
or:		

Here are the math operators that Access recognizes:

Addition	+
Subtraction	−
Multiplication	*
Division	/
Exponentiation	^

Create a Calculated Field

Calculated fields enable you to create powerful queries that use the full power of Access's expression-building features. For example, suppose that you have a Products table with a UnitPrice field and you want to display the unit price for each product plus a 5% increase. You can do that by creating a calculated field based on the following expression: **[UnitPrice] * 1.05**.

Similarly, suppose that you have a table of employees with FirstName and LastName fields and you want to see the names combined. You can do that by creating a calculated field that uses the following expression: **[FirstName] & " " & [LastName]**.

Create a Calculated Field

Create a Calculated Field

1. In the **Field** row for a blank column, type a title for the new column, followed by a colon (:).

2. Type the formula to calculate.

Note: Remember to enclose field names in square brackets.

Set a Number Format for the Calculated Field

1. Right-click the calculated field.

2. Click **Properties**.

   The Property Sheet opens.

3. Click the **Format** ☑ and click the number format that you want.

4. Click ✕.

   The Property Sheet closes.

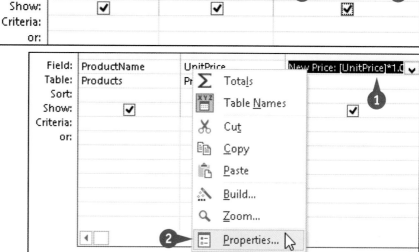

Understanding Action Queries

All the queries that you have worked with to date have been select queries. A *select query* is one in which Access uses the query criteria to select the matching rows from one or more tables. However, Access has several other query types that are designed to perform actions on the data, such as changing values, adding records, deleting records, and writing records to a new table. These are the so-called *action queries*. Unlike a select query, an action query makes permanent changes to the table.

Types of Action Queries

In the Query Design view, the Query Type group has buttons for the various types of queries. Here are the action queries that are the most useful:

- **Make Table:** This creates a new table; it is a way of copying records from an existing table to a new one.

- **Append:** This adds records to the end of an existing table. This is a way of copying records from an existing table to another existing table.

- **Update:** This changes values across the entire table based on criteria that you specify. For example, you can increase prices by a certain percentage.

- **Delete:** This deletes records from the table based on criteria that you specify.

Be Careful!

Because an action query makes permanent changes to a table, you should back up the table before running one on it. One way is to copy the table by selecting it in the Objects list, pressing `Ctrl` + `C`, and then pasting it by pressing `Ctrl` + `V`. In the Paste Table As dialog box, specify a name for the copy, click **Structure and Data** (○ changes to ◉), and click **OK**.

Paste Table As

Table Name:

Copy Of Products

Paste Options
- ○ Structure Only
- ◉ Structure and Data
- ○ Append Data to Existing Table

OK

Cancel

To avoid accidentally rerunning an action query later, either delete it from the Objects list when you are finished with it or hide it there by right-clicking it and clicking **Hide in This Group**.

To unhide hidden objects, right-click the bar at the top of the navigation pane and click **Navigation Options**. In the Navigation Options dialog box, click **Show Hidden Objects** and then click **OK**.

Run a Make Table Query

A Make Table query creates a new table. You can use this query to archive old records, for example, or to split a table into two separate tables based on the status of a certain field.

For example, at the end of the fiscal year, you might want some of your tables to be "frozen" while you tie things up for year-end. (This applies particularly to tables that track invoices.) Instead of letting the new work pile up until the table can be released, you can run a Make Table query to create a new table from the existing one.

Run a Make Table Query

1 Create a select query as you would any other query in the Query Design view.

Note: Make sure that you include all the fields that the new table should contain. Also, make sure that your criteria captures the needed records.

2 To check your work before running the query, click **View**.

3 Click **View** again to return to the Query Design view.

4 Click the **Design** tab.

5 Click **Make Table**.

The Make Table dialog box opens.

6 Type a name for the new table.

7 Click **OK**.

8 Click **Run**.

Access creates the new table.

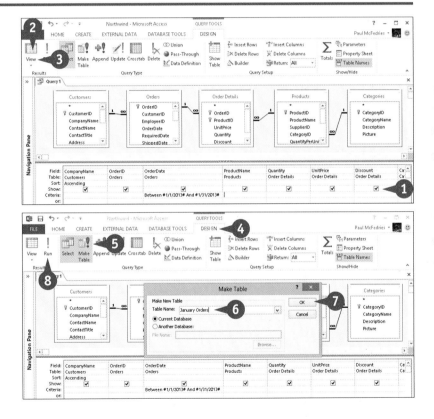

Run a Delete Query

If you need to delete one or two records from a table, just select each record and choose the Home tab's **Delete** command. But what if you have a large number of records to delete? For example, you might want to clean out an Orders table by deleting any old orders that were placed before a certain date. Or you might want to delete records for products that have been discontinued. For these and similar examples, you can set up a Delete query that uses criteria to identify which records to delete. When you run the query, Access deletes the matching records.

Run a Delete Query

1 Create a select query as you would any other query in the Query Design view.

A Include criteria that identifies the records to be deleted.

Note: This query acts on entire records, regardless of the fields that you include. Therefore, you need to include only those fields required to set up the criteria.

2 To check your work before running the query, click **View**.

3 Click **View** again to return to the Query Design view.

4 Click the **Design** tab.

5 Click **Delete**.

B The rows in the grid change. The Sort and Show rows disappear, and a Delete row appears.

6 Click **Run**.

A warning dialog box opens.

7 Click **Yes**.

Access deletes the records that match your criteria.

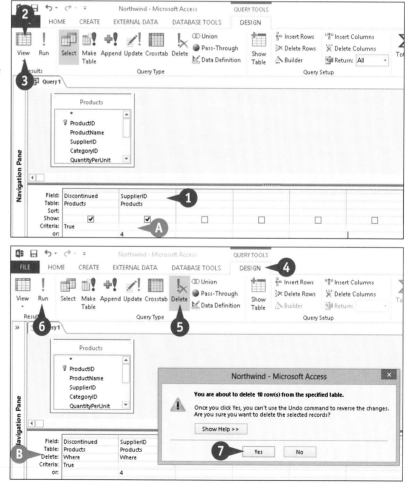

Run an Append Query

Instead of creating a new table using a Make Table query, you might prefer to add records from one table to an existing table. You can accomplish this using an Append query, which takes the records that match some criteria from one table and copies them to another table. Appending records does not remove them from the original source.

Note that for an Append query to work, the corresponding fields in the receiving table must use the same data type as the fields that you specify in your query.

Run an Append Query

1 Create a select query.

A Add the fields that you want to include in the appended records.

B Include criteria that identifies the records to be appended to another table.

2 To check your work before running the query, click **View**.

3 Click **View** again to return to the Query Design view.

4 Click the **Design** tab.

5 Click **Append**.

The Append dialog box opens.

6 Click the **Table Name** and click the table to which you want the records appended.

7 Click **OK**.

8 Click **Run**.

A warning dialog box opens.

9 Click **Yes**.

The records are appended.

Note: The records are not appended where it would violate data integrity rules, such as duplicate records not being allowed for a certain field.

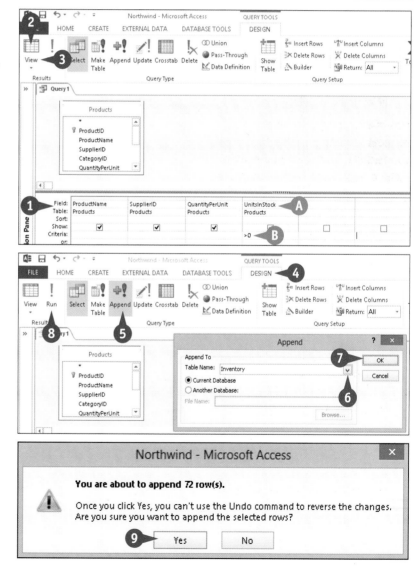

Run an Update Query

What if you want to replace the contents of a field with a new value, but only for records that meet certain criteria? You can do this by creating an Update query. Unlike a select query, which displays only a subset of the table, an Update query actually makes changes to the table data. You select a field, specify the new field value, set up some criteria (optionally), and then run the query. Access runs through the table and changes the field entries to the new value. If you enter criteria, only records that match the criteria are updated.

Run an Update Query

1. Click the **Design** tab.

2. Click **Update**.

Ⓐ An Update To row appears in the grid.

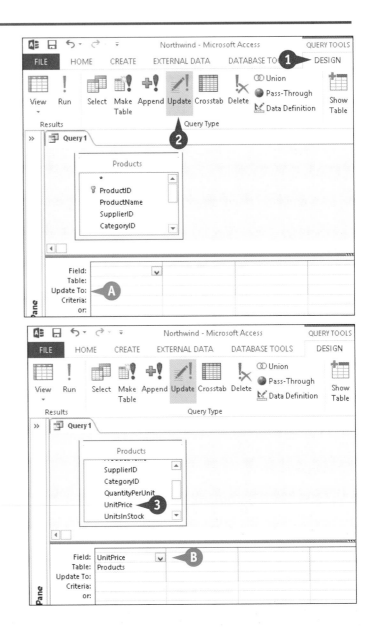

3. Double-click the field that you want to update.

Ⓑ The field is placed in the grid.

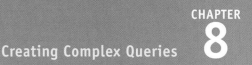

4 In the **Update To** row, type the formula to use for the update.

Note: A 5% increase in the unit price is shown here.

5 Click **Run**.

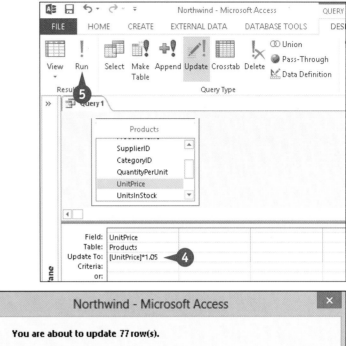

A warning dialog box opens.

6 Click **Yes**.

The query runs and updates the values.

What is the correct syntax for an Update To formula?
Enclose field names in square brackets and use standard math operators:

- + (addition)
- – (subtraction)
- * (multiplication)
- / (division)
- ^ (exponentiation)

Do not use any currency symbols and express numbers as plain digits.

What are some examples of formulas?
Some examples include the following:

- To increase Price by $2: **[Price]+2**
- To decrease Price by 5%: **[Price]*0.95**
- To decrease Price by one-third: **[Price]*0.67**
- To multiply Price by itself: **[Price]*[Price]** or **[Price]^2**

Prompt the User for a Parameter

After you have a query running properly, you usually do not have to worry about the query design any longer. However, in certain situations, the query itself undergoes regular change. For example, if your query filters customer orders using a State field, you might find yourself constantly changing the State criterion.

Instead of constantly editing the query, you can configure the query to prompt the user for a value to use as a variable. In the customer orders example, you could create a parameter that asks for the state each time the query is run.

Prompt the User for a Parameter

Create the Prompt

1 Create the query as you normally would in the Query Design view.

2 In the **Criteria** row, type the prompt message in square brackets.

Test the Parameter

1 Click **Run**.

Note: Because this is a select query, there is no difference between Run and View. You can use either one.

The prompt for the parameter appears.

2 Type the variable in the text box.

3 Click **OK**.

The datasheet opens with just the records that match the variable.

A If you want to rerun the prompt from the Datasheet view without returning to the Design view, click the **Home** tab and then click **Refresh All**.

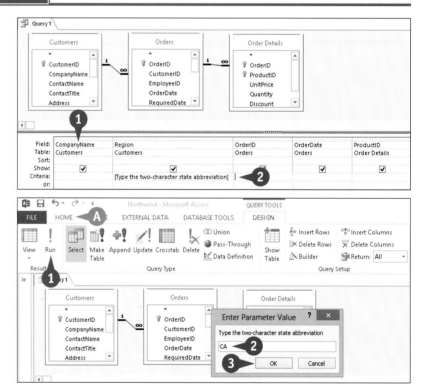

158

Understanding Parameter Syntax

One of the difficulties in creating a parameter prompt is making it easy for users to enter the values that they want without generating an error or unwanted results. To help with this, you can modify the basic prompt and combine it with other criteria to permit a variety of responses.

Here are some examples that use the simple prompt [Which State?] as their basis:

Entry in Criteria	Permissible Responses
[Which State?]	Entire state abbreviation.
Like [Which State?]	Entire state abbreviation. OR Any portion of field contents with a wildcard. For example, use **C*** to see CA, CO, and CT or ***A** to see CA, IA, PA, and WA.
Like [Which State?] or Is Null	Entire state abbreviation. OR Any portion of field contents with a wildcard. OR Press `Enter` or click **OK** without entering anything to display all records.
Like [Which State?] & "*"	Entire state abbreviation. OR Any portion of field contents with a wildcard, where the wildcard applies to the value in any position. For example, ***A** displays all values with A anywhere in their name. OR Press `Enter` or click **OK** without entering anything to display all records.

CHAPTER 9

Creating Forms

Forms provide an easy-to-use interface for data entry and editing. Forms are especially helpful for databases that will have less-experienced users assisting you because on-screen forms can mimic familiar paper forms. In this chapter, you learn how to create forms, group and arrange fields on them, and define their tab order.

Understanding Forms

The datasheet is a reasonable tool if you are only entering one or two records, but if you are entering a dozen records or even a hundred, you need to leave the datasheet behind and use the Access data-entry tool of choice: the form. A *form* is a collection of controls — usually labels and text boxes, but also lists, check boxes, and option buttons — each of which represents either a field or the name of a field. Forms make data entry easier and more efficient.

A One record at a time

The default form shows the fields as fill-in boxes for one record at a time. This makes it easier for users to enter a new record without becoming confused by the multiple rows and columns of a datasheet.

B Object display

In the Datasheet view, imported objects such as graphics appear as text names, but on a form, depending on the data type, Access might be able to display them as they actually appear. For example, pictures of employees can be displayed with each employee record.

C Form header

A form can have a running header that appears the same no matter which record is displayed. You can put anything that you want in this header. In this example, hyperlinks to other forms appear, making it easy for the user to navigate between forms.

D Search

To search for a particular record, the user can type a word or phrase in the Search box and then press Enter. The records are filtered so that only records that contain the word or phrase appear when the user scrolls through them with the record navigation controls. The user can click **No Filter** to remove the filter.

E Record navigation

To move between records, users can use the Record navigation buttons. These are the same as in a datasheet, but they are more useful here because you cannot see other records without them.

F Tabbed or pop-up forms

A form can appear on a tab, as shown here, or as a pop-up window, as shown on the preceding page. This is controlled by the pop-up setting in the form's properties.

G Multitabbed forms

A form can consist of multiple tabbed pages, with different form controls on each tab.

Order Details

Order #51

Status: Closed

Create Invoice · Ship Order · Complete Order · Delete Order · Close

| Customer | Company Z | Salesperson | Anne Hellung-Larsen |
| E-mail Address | | Order Date | 4/5/2006 |

Order Details | Shipping Information | Payment Information

Product	Qty ▾	Unit Price ▾	Discount ▾	Total Price ▾	Status ▾
Northwind Traders Olive Oil	25	$21.35	0.00%	$533.75	Invoiced
Northwind Traders Clam Chowder	30	$9.65	0.00%	$289.50	Invoiced
Northwind Traders Crab Meat	30	$18.40	0.00%	$552.00	Invoiced
Total	85			$1,375.25	

Record: I◄ ◄ 21 of 48 ► ►I ►⊡ No Filter Search

H Datasheet-style forms

There are several design styles for forms besides the standard one shown on the preceding page. For example, a form can resemble a datasheet and can show multiple records at once.

I Subforms

A *subform* shows the records from a different table or query that are related to the main record shown. In this example, the orders for a particular customer are being pulled from the Orders table depending on which customer is chosen in the main form.

J Navigation buttons

This subform does not have navigation buttons at the bottom. That is because having two sets of buttons (one for the main form and one for the subform) would be confusing. Navigation buttons are turned off with the Navigation Buttons property for the subform.

Create and Save a Form

The easiest way to create a form is to use a predefined form layout. Access has several of these layouts, but the basic, split, and multiple-items forms are the ones that you will use most often.

A *basic* form layout shows just the data from one record at a time. A *split* form displays a datasheet on top and a form below, and when you click a record in the datasheet, the record data appears in the form. A *multiple-items* form is a tabular layout that shows the field names at the top and the records in rows.

Create and Save a Form

Create a Basic Form

1 In the Objects list, click the table or query for which you want to create a form.

2 Click the **Create** tab.

3 Click **Form**.

The form appears.

Note: You might also see a subform showing a related table, if any usable relationships exist.

Create a Split Form

1 In the Objects pane, click the table or query for which you want to create a form.

2 Click the **Create** tab.

3 Click **More Forms**.

4 Click **Split Form**.

Ⓐ The form appears in the upper part of the screen.

Ⓑ The datasheet for the table or query appears in the lower part of the screen.

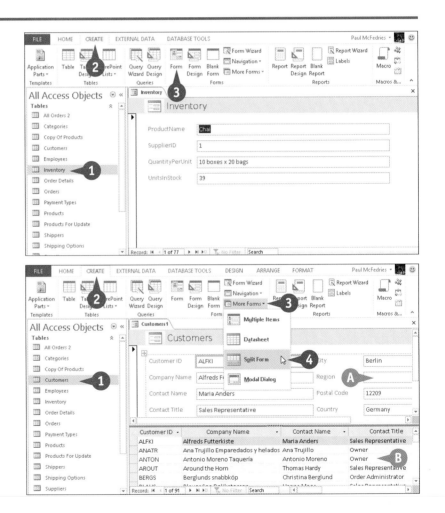

Create a Multiple-Items Form

1. In the Objects pane, click the table or query for which you want to create a form.

2. Click the **Create** tab.

3. Click **More Forms**.

4. Click **Multiple Items**.

   A form appears with multiple records visible at the same time.

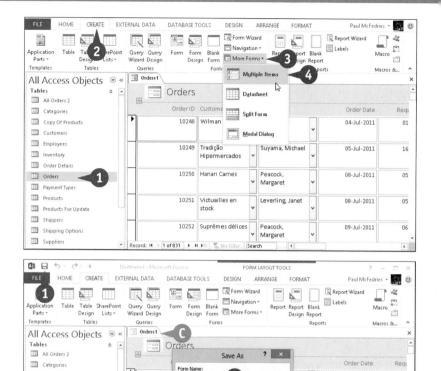

Save a Form

1. Click 💾.

   The Save As dialog box opens.

2. Type a name for the form.

3. Click **OK**.

   The form is saved.

Ⓒ You can right-click the form tab and then click **Close** on the shortcut menu to close the form.

What other form types can I create?

Click the **Home** tab, click the **More Forms** button, and then click one of the following:

- **Datasheet:** This looks just like a regular datasheet, but it is actually a form. This is useful when you want to show a datasheet on a subform, for example.

- **Modal Dialog:** This looks just like a dialog box, but it is actually a form. This is useful for creating navigational menu systems.

What if I do not want a subform on a form created with the Form button?

If you do not require the subform, you can delete it from the form. First click any border of the subform to select it. You will know that it is selected when you see a thick border around the subform. Click the **Home** tab and then click **Delete** (alternatively, press Delete).

Create a Form with the Form Wizard

The basic, split, and multiple-items forms are fine for very simple form needs, but it is likely that in most cases the resulting form will not suit your needs exactly. For a bit more control over your forms, you need to use the Form Wizard, which takes you step-by-step through the entire form-creation process.

The Form Wizard enables you to create a form based on more than one table or query, not necessarily using all the available fields from them. With the Form Wizard, you gain some flexibility without having to do all the form design work yourself.

Create a Form with the Form Wizard

1 Click the **Create** tab.

2 Click **Form Wizard**.

The Form Wizard appears.

3 Click the **Tables/Queries** and click the table or query from which you want to select fields.

4 Click a field.

5 Click > to move the field to the Selected Fields list.

Note: Add fields in the order in which you want them to appear on the form.

A If you make a mistake, you can remove a field by clicking < .

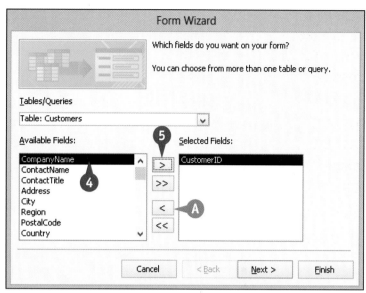

6 Repeat steps **4** and **5** to add more fields from the chosen table or query.

7 Repeat steps **3** to **6** for other tables or queries if needed.

Note: If you choose fields from more than one table or query, they must be related.

8 Click **Next**.

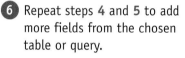

TIPS

Can I use fields from more than two tables or queries?

Yes. But you are not prompted for subform information. Instead, all the fields appear on a single form. It is possible to create subforms within subforms using the Form Design view but not using the wizard.

Is it okay to not use all the fields from the table or tables?

Yes. But keep in mind that users filling out that form will have no way of entering values in the fields that do not appear on the form. With an AutoNumber field, that is not a problem because the user cannot enter data into that field anyway, but any other field will be blank if it is not included on the form.

Create a Form with the Form Wizard (continued)

The Form Wizard is useful not only for selecting the exact fields to include but also for choosing a format and appearance for the form. You can also change the fields and format later in the Form Design view, but it is often easier to specify upfront what you want via the wizard.

In particular, you can use the Form Wizard to determine the form layout to use when you choose fields from two related tables. For example, if your form includes fields from the Customers and Order Details tables, you can choose one table for the main form and the other for the subform.

Create a Form with the Form Wizard (continued)

If you chose fields from two different tables or queries, you are asked which one should be the subform.

 Click the option that best represents the layout that you want.

 If you would rather have a linked form than a subform, click **Linked forms** (○ changes to ◉).

Note: A *linked form* means that Access creates a second form instead of a subform. The main form includes a button that, when clicked, displays the second form.

⓫ Click **Next**.

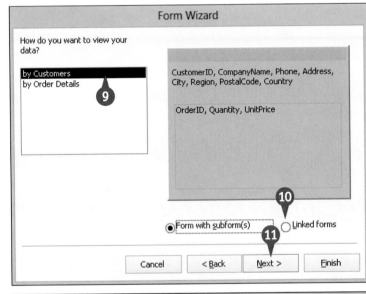

The layout page of the wizard appears.

⓬ Click the layout that you want for the form (○ changes to ◉).

Note: If you are creating a form with a subform, this screen asks you to choose the layout for the subform rather than for the main form. For a form/subform layout, the main form is always columnar when constructed by the wizard.

⓭ Click **Next**.

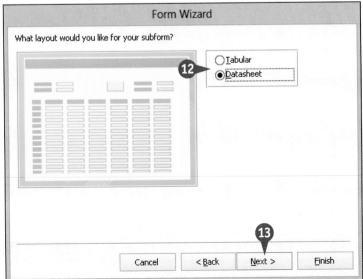

The title page appears.

14 Type a name for the form, replacing the default name.

15 If you created a subform, type a name for the subform, replacing the default name.

16 Click **Finish**.

> **Form Wizard**
>
> What titles do you want for your forms?
>
> Form: Customers **14**
>
> Subform: Order Details Subform **15**
>
> That's all the information the wizard needs to create your form.
>
> Do you want to open the form or modify the form's design?
>
> ● Open the form to view or enter information.
> ○ Modify the form's design.
>
> **16**
>
> Cancel   < Back   Next >   Finish

The form appears in the Form view.

If some of the labels appear truncated, you can fix this problem in the Form Design view.

Note: See the section "Arrange Fields on a Form" for more on fixing truncated fields.

> **Customers**
>
> Customers
>
> Customer ID   ALFKI
> Company Name   Alfreds Futterkiste
> Phone   030-0074321
> Address   Obere Str. 57
> City   Berlin
> Region
> Postal Code   12209
> Country   Germany
>
> Order Details
>
> | Order ID | Quantity | Unit Price |
> |---|---|---|
> | 10643 | 15 | $45.60 |
> | 10643 | 21 | $18.00 |
> | 10643 | 2 | $12.00 |
> | 10692 | 20 | $43.90 |
> | 10702 | 6 | $10.00 |
>
> Record: 1 of 12   No Filter   Search
>
> Record: 1 of 91   No Filter   Search

TIPS

Do I need to save the form before I close it?

No. When you specify a name in step 14 and optionally in step 15, you are supplying the object names to be used. Access automatically saves the form and subform, if applicable, with those names.

I made a mistake; how do I delete the form that I just created?

Delete the form as you would any other object:

1 Locate the form in the Objects list.

2 Right-click the form name.

3 Click **Delete**.

4 In the warning dialog box that appears, click **Yes**.

Create a Form in the Layout View

The Form Wizard offers the easiest path to creating a form, but it does not give you much flexibility in terms of the form layout. The Form Design view, which you learn about in the "Create a Form in the Design View" section, gives you complete flexibility but is more complex to learn and use. In between these extremes is the Form Layout view, which lets you create a form by dragging and dropping fields on to a blank page. It is not as powerful as the Design view, but it is much easier to use.

Create a Form in the Layout View

Create the Form

1 Click the **Create** tab.

2 Click **Blank Form**.

A blank form appears, along with a Field List pane.

3 Click **Show all tables**.

A A list of all the tables appears; each table's field list is collapsed.

4 Click ⊞ next to a table.

A list of the fields in the table appears (⊞ changes to ⊟).

5 Drag a field from the Field List on to the form.

You can also double-click a field to add it to the form.

6 Repeat step **5** to add more fields.

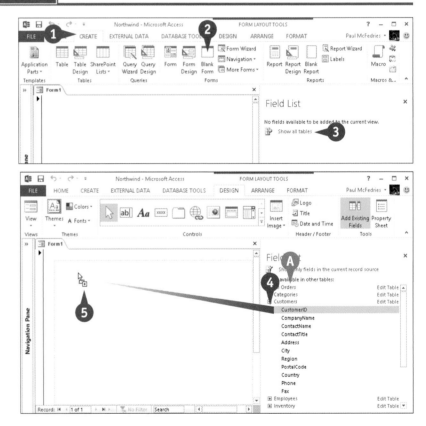

Adjust the Spacing between Labels and Fields

B This is the field label.

C This is the field.

1 Click any label to select it.

2 Position ▷ between the field and its label (▷ changes to ↔).

3 Click and drag to the left or right to change the spacing.

The change affects all the fields.

Adjust Label Alignment

1 Click any label to select it.

2 Position ▷ above the top label so that a black arrow appears and then click.

Access selects the entire column.

3 Click the **Format** tab.

4 Click the Align Right button (≡).

Access aligns the labels on the right.

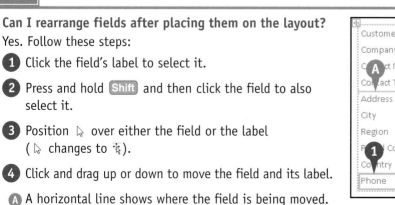

TIP

Can I rearrange fields after placing them on the layout?
Yes. Follow these steps:

1 Click the field's label to select it.

2 Press and hold **Shift** and then click the field to also select it.

3 Position ▷ over either the field or the label (▷ changes to ✣).

4 Click and drag up or down to move the field and its label.

A A horizontal line shows where the field is being moved.

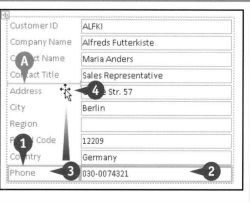

Create a Form in the Design View

Although the Layout view is a step up from the Form Wizard in terms of control, the resulting form still might not satisfy your needs. For maximum form flexibility, you need to use the Form Design view, which gives you total control over the form, including the positioning of the controls, the formatting of the text, and the colors.

This section shows you how to create a basic form layout using the Design view. The rest of the sections in this chapter and in Chapter 10, "Editing Forms," show you how to customize your form using the Design view tools.

Create a Form in the Design View

1 Click the **Create** tab.

2 Click **Form Design**.

A new form appears in the Form Design view.

A The Field List appears.

B If the Field List does not appear, click the **Design** tab and then click **Add Existing Fields**.

3 In the Field List, click ⊞ next to the table from which you want to select fields.

⊞ changes to ⊟, and the list of fields appears.

4 Click and drag a field on to the design grid.

Both the field and its associated label appear.

C This is the field label.

D This is the field.

5 Drag and drop more fields on to the form.

Note: You can drag more than one field at a time by selecting multiple fields in the Field List before dragging. Hold down Ctrl and then click the fields that you want.

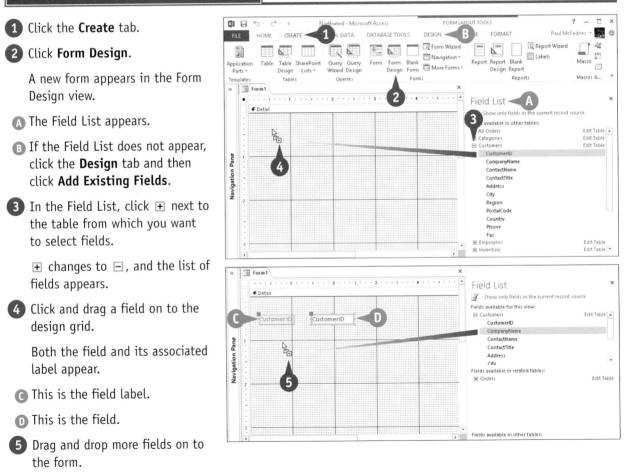

Delete a Field from the Design View

If you no longer need a form object, you can either remove an entire field, including its label, or remove only the label. When you remove the label, this enables the field to remain on the form but without a label. This can be useful, for example, when you want a single label, such as Name, followed by two different fields, such as FirstName and LastName. It can also be useful when fields on the form are obvious and do not need labels to name them, such as Notes or Memo.

Delete a Field from the Design View

Delete a Field and Its Label

1 Click the field — not its label — to select it.

A A selection box appears around the field.

2 Press Delete.

Both the field and its label are deleted.

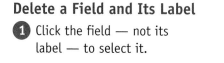

Delete Just the Field Label

1 Click the field label — not the actual field — to select it.

B A selection box appears around the label.

2 Press Delete.

The label is deleted, but the field remains.

Note: You cannot delete the field but leave its label. You can, however, place freestanding labels on a form. See Chapter 10 for more information.

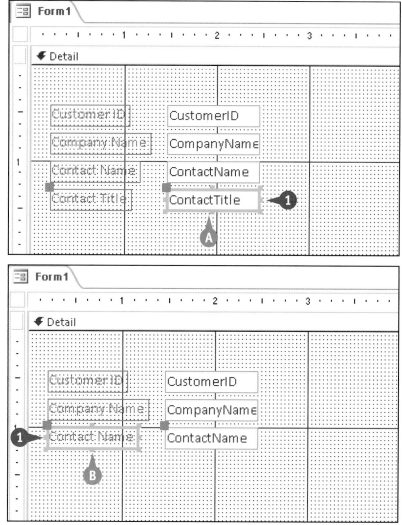

Arrange Fields on a Form

Onne advantage of working in the Form Design view, as opposed to the Layout view, is the flexibility it offers in arranging fields. You can freely drag a field around on the grid or make a field align or conform in size with other fields.

An invisible rectangular frame surrounds each label and field. When you select an item, Access displays a selection box on this frame, which includes selection handles at the frame's corners and midpoints. You can use this frame to resize any label or field to change its shape or dimensions, as well as to move the label or field.

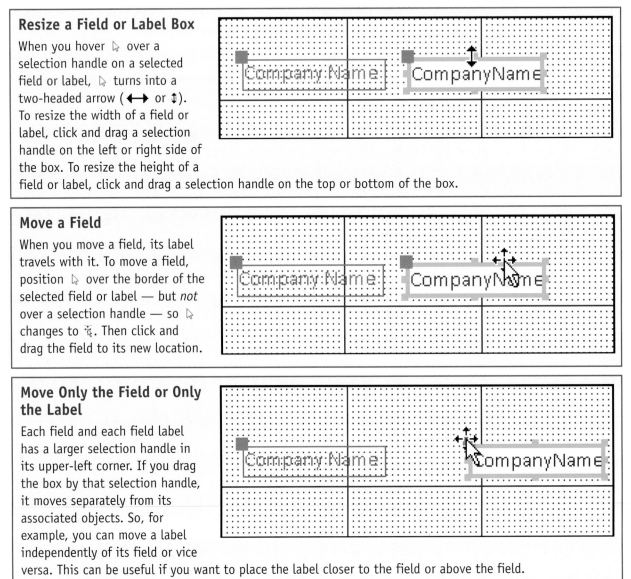

Resize a Field or Label Box

When you hover ℞ over a selection handle on a selected field or label, ℞ turns into a two-headed arrow (↔ or ↕). To resize the width of a field or label, click and drag a selection handle on the left or right side of the box. To resize the height of a field or label, click and drag a selection handle on the top or bottom of the box.

Move a Field

When you move a field, its label travels with it. To move a field, position ℞ over the border of the selected field or label — but *not* over a selection handle — so ℞ changes to ℞. Then click and drag the field to its new location.

Move Only the Field or Only the Label

Each field and each field label has a larger selection handle in its upper-left corner. If you drag the box by that selection handle, it moves separately from its associated objects. So, for example, you can move a label independently of its field or vice versa. This can be useful if you want to place the label closer to the field or above the field.

Align Fields and Labels

It is often useful to right-align or left-align a series of fields or field labels. You can select several fields and then click one of the alignment buttons to make the fields align neatly with one another. Click the **Arrange** tab, click **Align** ( ), and then choose an alignment from the menu that appears.

Note that Access aligns the selected controls with a single *base control*, which is the control that is the farthest positioned in whatever direction you are aligning the controls. For example, if you want to align the controls on their right edges, the base control is the one that is farthest to the right.

Make Field Sizes Consistent

Sometimes, a form looks best when all the fields are the same size. Access enables you to select multiple items and then automatically size them horizontally to either the widest item in the selection or the narrowest. You can also size the selected items vertically to the tallest or shortest item in the selection.

Select the fields and/or labels that you want to size consistently, click the **Arrange** tab, click the **Size/Space** button ( ), and then click a sizing command.

Align Fields in a Grid

Access gives you an easy way to arrange your form controls: the control layout. This simple layout acts as a kind of table, and your controls are slotted neatly into the layout's rows and columns. In a *stacked* layout, the controls are arranged vertically in two columns, with field names in the left column and fields in the right column. In a *tabular* layout, the controls are arranged horizontally in two rows, with field labels in the top row and fields in the bottom row.

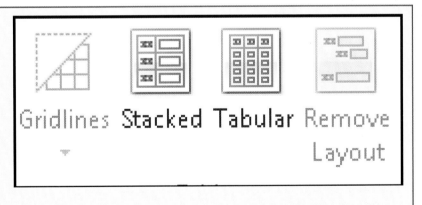

Select the items that you want to align, click the **Arrange** tab, and then click either **Stacked** ( ) or **Tabular** ( ).

175

Group Fields Together

When working with fields, it can be easier to work with multiple fields together than to select and move each one individually. You can do this by creating a *group*, which is a collection of fields you can format, size, and move together, similarly to the way you format, size, and move a single control.

Access treats a group as a single item with its own frame. To select an entire group, you just need to select one item from the group.

Group Fields Together

1 Drag a marquee around a group of fields to select them.

Note: To create a marquee, click and drag an imaginary box from a spot above and to the left of the fields to a spot below and to the right of the fields. You can also press and hold Shift and then click each field that you want to select.

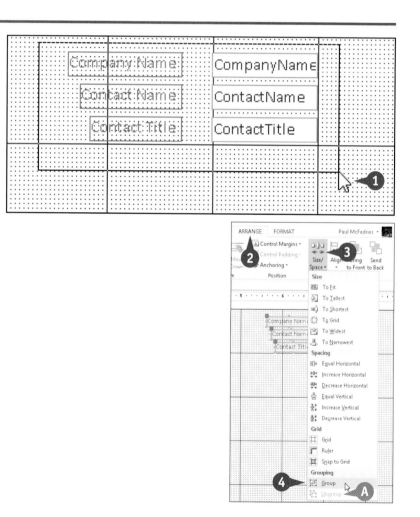

2 Click the **Arrange** tab.

3 Click **Size/Space** (🔳).

4 Click **Group**.

The fields are grouped together.

Ⓐ To ungroup the fields, click any item in the group to select it, click the **Arrange** tab, click 🔳, and then click **Ungroup**.

Note: Grouping works only with fields that are not part of a layout grid (stacked or tabular). If the Group command is unavailable, select the fields, click the **Arrange** tab, and then click **Remove Layout** to remove them from the grid.

Define the Tab Order on a Form

You can navigate a form by pressing the Tab key. As you press Tab, the order in which Access selects the controls is called the *tab order*. Access sets the tab order according to the order that you added the controls to the form. You will often find that this order does not correspond to the "natural" order of the controls, so pressing Tab causes the selection to jump haphazardly around the form. To fix this, Access lets you control the tab order yourself.

Define the Tab Order on a Form

1 Click the **Design** tab.

2 Click **Tab Order** ().

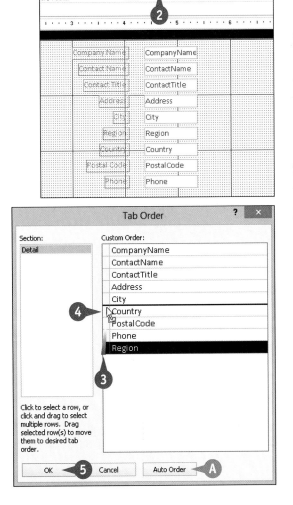

The Tab Order dialog box opens.

3 Click to the left of a field name to select it.

4 Drag the selected field name up or down in the list.

Ⓐ Alternatively, you can click **Auto Order** to set the tab order based on the positions on the form.

Note: Auto Order orders fields from top to bottom. If two fields have the same vertical position, it orders them from left to right.

5 Click **OK**.

The dialog box closes, and Access puts the new tab order into effect.

177

CHAPTER 10

Editing Forms

The basic forms that you create in Chapter 9 can be improved by applying formatting and by using special sections, such as headers and footers. In this chapter, you will learn how to use formatting and design features to make forms easier to use and more attractive.

Display the Header and Footer

The Detail section of a form should be a data-only area. If you want to display a form title or the current date or some other information not related to the data, you can take advantage of the form's header and footer.

The *form header* appears above the Detail area, so it is a good choice for the form title, a company logo, or any other items that you want displayed separately from the form data. The *form footer* appears below the Detail area. It is a good place to add nondata items such as the current date or instructions on how to fill in the form.

Display the Header and Footer

1 In the Design view, right-click one of the section bars (such as **Detail**).

2 Click **Form Header/Footer**.

Note: The command is a toggle; click it again to turn the header/footer display off.

A You can also click **Page Header/Footer**, which creates separate Page Header and Page Footer sections, both of which appear only when you print the form.

B The form header appears at the top of the form, with its own title bar.

C The form footer appears at the bottom.

Resize Sections of a Form

eader and footer sections start out with a relatively small height, but you can enlarge them as much as is needed to hold the content that you want to place there. You can also resize the main section of the form — the Detail section — to accommodate the fields there.

It is also sometimes helpful to temporarily enlarge a section so that you have more room to work and then tighten the spacing up again when its content is finalized.

Resize Sections of a Form

1 In the Design view, position ⊾ at the bottom edge of a section of the form (⊾ changes to ↨).

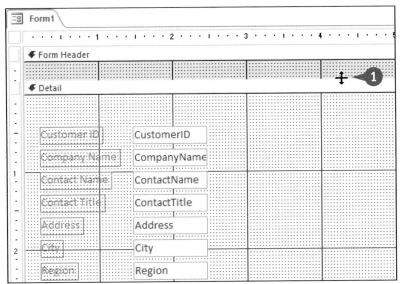

2 Click and drag up or down to change the height of that section of the form.

A A horizontal bar denotes the new position of the bottom edge of the section.

B The form footer does not have a divider below it. To enlarge the form footer, drag its bottom border down.

Note: If you want only the header but not the footer, or vice versa, resize the unwanted section so that it takes up no space at all.

Note: If you do not want the header and footer at all, turn them off, as described in the section "Display the Header and Footer."

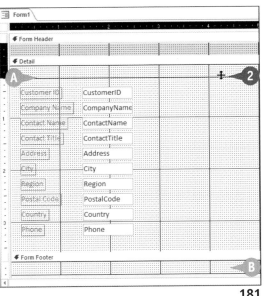

Select Sections of a Form

After turning on headers and footers, you will have a multisection form that consists of at least three sections: Form Header, Detail, and Form Footer. You can select and work with each of these sections individually. For example, you could add a label to just the Form Header section. (See "Add a Label," later in this chapter.) Similarly, you could add a background image to just the Detail section. (See "Add a Background Image," later in this chapter.)

To make sure that formatting applies to the correct sections, you must learn how to select a section and how to select an entire form.

Select Sections of a Form

Select an Individual Section

1. In the Design view, click the title bar of the section that you want to select.

Ⓐ The title bar turns black, indicating that the section beneath it is active.

Select an Entire Form

1. In the Design view, click the square in the upper-left corner of the form.

Ⓑ A small black square appears within the square, indicating that the form is selected.

Note: Any individual section title bars that were previously selected become unselected.

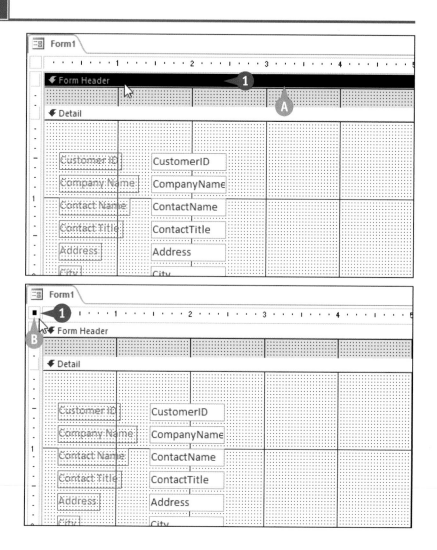

Add a Form Title

A form title appears in the form header and provides a name for the form. Adding a title to your form is usually a good idea so that users have some idea what the form is used for. If the form header does not already appear when you insert a form title, Access turns on the form header.

You can manually create a form title by adding a label text box to the form header area, but Access makes it easy by providing a button on the Design tab specifically for this purpose.

Add a Form Title

1 In the Design or Layout view, click the **Design** tab.

2 Click **Title**.

Ⓐ If the form header was not already visible, it now appears, containing a box with dummy text, such as "Form1."

3 Type the text for the title.

Note: Because the dummy text was already selected, typing new text replaces it.

4 Click outside the box when finished.

The title is added to the form.

Apply a Theme

A *theme* is a preset collection of formatting that you can apply to your form. Themes are used consistently across all Office 2013 applications to apply formatting, allowing you to standardize color and font choices for everything you create, regardless of which application you create it in.

Generally speaking, themes define three formatting elements for the object to which they are applied: fonts, colors, and object effects. However, in Access, only colors and fonts are affected.

Apply a Theme

1 In the Design or Layout view, click the **Design** tab.

2 Click **Themes**.

A gallery of themes appears.

3 Click the theme that you want.

Ⓐ You can point to a theme without clicking it to see a preview of it on the form.

The theme is applied to the form.

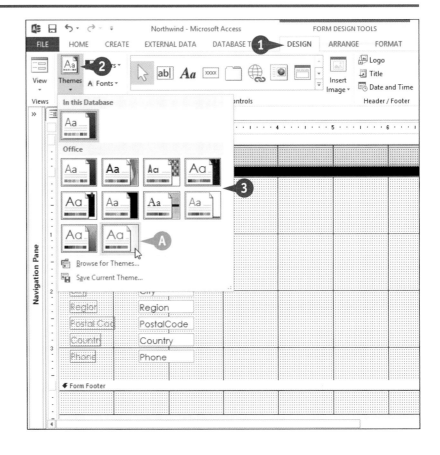

Browse for a Theme to Apply

The list of themes that appears when you click the Themes button is compiled from two specific locations on your hard disk. The built-in themes are taken from C:\Program Files\Microsoft Office\ Document Themes 15, and any custom themes that you have created are taken from C:\Users\ *username*\AppData\Roaming\Microsoft\Templates\Document Themes (where *username* is the name you use to log into Windows). If you want to apply a theme that is stored in some other location, such as on a network or on a CD, you must browse for it.

Browse for a Theme to Apply

1. In the Design or Layout view, click the **Design** tab.

2. Click **Themes**.

3. Click **Browse for Themes**.

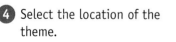

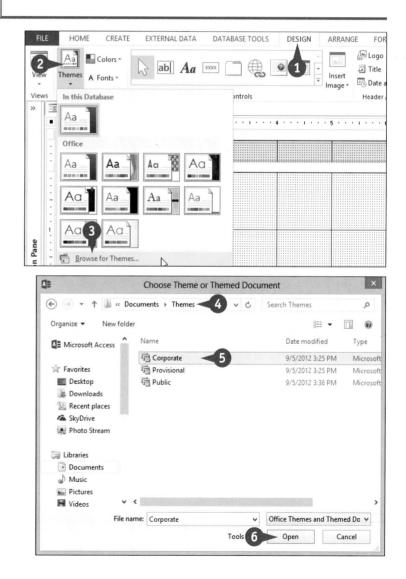

The Choose Theme or Themed Document dialog box opens.

4. Select the location of the theme.

5. Click the theme or other file from which you want to apply font and color settings.

6. Click **Open**.

The theme is applied.

Apply a Font Theme or Color Theme

Applying a theme changes both the fonts and the colors used. If you want to change only the fonts or the colors, you should apply a font theme or a color theme instead. Each has its own separate gallery that you can access from the Design tab.

Like regular themes, font and color themes are consistent across all Office applications and can be shared among them to create consistency among all the business documents, spreadsheets, databases, and presentations that you create.

Apply a Font Theme or Color Theme

Apply a Font Theme

1 In the Design or Layout view, click the **Design** tab.

2 Click **Fonts**.

A gallery of font themes appears.

3 Click the font theme that you want.

The new fonts are applied to the form.

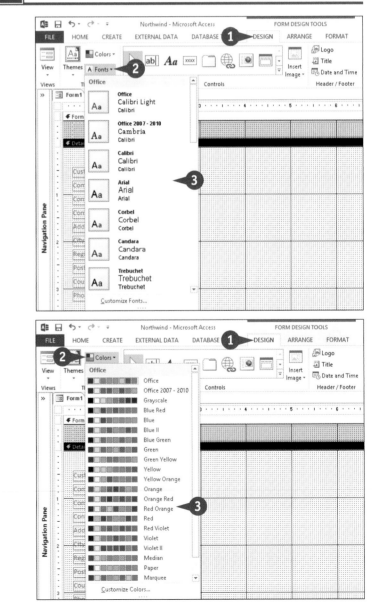

Apply a Color Theme

1 In the Design or Layout view, click the **Design** tab.

2 Click **Colors**.

A gallery of color themes appears.

3 Click the color theme that you want.

The new colors are applied to the form.

Create a Custom Font Theme

You can add visual appeal to your form by selecting a different font theme. Each font theme has two defined fonts: a *heading font* for text that appears in the Form Header (or Page Header) section, and a *body font* for text that appears in the Detail (or the Form Footer or Page Footer) section. Access offers more than 20 font themes, but if none of the predefined themes is suitable, you can create a custom font scheme.

Any custom font themes that you create are also accessible by other Office applications, such as Word and PowerPoint.

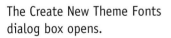

Create a Custom Font Theme

1 In the Design or Layout view, click the **Design** tab.

2 Click **Fonts**.

3 Click **Customize Fonts**.

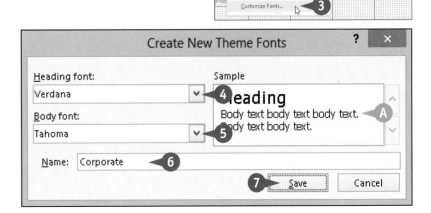

The Create New Theme Fonts dialog box opens.

4 Click the **Heading font** ⌄ and click a heading typeface.

5 Click the **Body font** ⌄ and click a body typeface.

Ⓐ The Sample preview box shows what the heading and body fonts look like.

6 Type a name for the new font theme.

7 Click **Save**.

The new font theme will be available in the Fonts gallery the next time you use it.

Create a Custom Color Theme

Acolor theme defines colors for 12 placeholders that Office applications use when formatting a document; however, not all these colors are used in Access forms. For example, the Hyperlink color placeholder defines the color of underlined hyperlinks in tables and forms. In addition, whenever you use a color picker — such as on the Font Color button's drop-down menu — the colors from the current theme are available for selection.

You can create your own custom color themes if none of the existing ones meet your needs. Just as with font themes, you can share color themes among all your Office applications.

Create a Custom Color Theme

1 In the Design or Layout view, click the **Design** tab.

2 Click **Colors**.

3 Click **Customize Colors**.

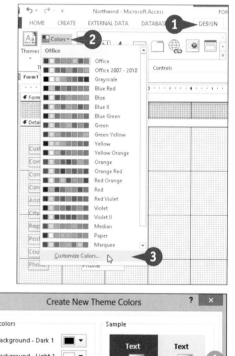

The Create New Theme Colors dialog box opens.

4 Click the color button for one of the placeholders.

A palette of color choices opens.

5 Click the color that you want.

6 Repeat steps **4** and **5** for each placeholder that you want to change.

A The Sample preview box shows what the colors look like.

7 Type a name for the new color theme.

8 Click **Save**.

The new color theme will be available in the Colors gallery the next time you use it.

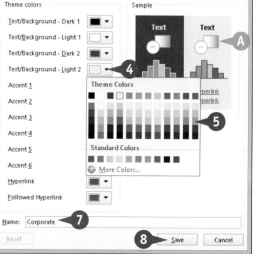

188

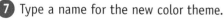

Create a Custom Theme

You can create a theme that combines your preferred fonts and colors so that you do not have to go through the two-step process of applying a certain color theme and a certain font theme each time you want to format a form or other object.

First, you define the form's colors and fonts the way you want them. You can do this by applying any of the preset color and font themes or by creating your own custom color and font themes, as you learn earlier in this chapter. Then, you use the following steps to save them as a new theme.

Create a Custom Theme

1 In the Design or Layout view, apply the colors and fonts that you want to be used in the theme.

2 Click the **Design** tab.

3 Click **Themes**.

4 Click **Save Current Theme**.

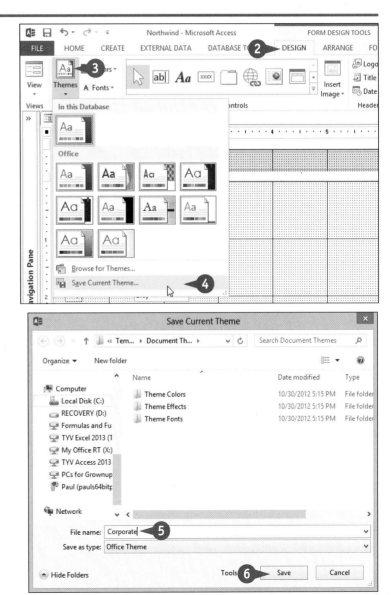

The Save Current Theme dialog box opens.

5 Type a name for the theme.

6 Click **Save**.

The new theme will appear in the Themes list the next time you use it.

Adjust Internal Margins and Padding

Your forms will be more attractive and easier to use if the controls have some extra space within and around them. You can ensure this by adjusting the margins and the padding. The *margin* is the amount of space inside a field's box between the edge and the text. You can adjust the margins for individual fields, but forms look better if all the fields have the same margins.

In a stacked or tabular layout, *padding* refers to the amount of space outside the box. When you adjust the padding, you change the amount of space between fields and between a field and its label.

Adjust Internal Margins and Padding

Change the Margins

1 In the Design view, select the field(s) for which you want to change the margins.

Note: To select fields, drag an imaginary box around them while holding down the left mouse button. When you release the mouse button, everything inside the area that you dragged across will be selected.

2 Click the **Arrange** tab.

3 Click **Control Margins**.

4 Click the margin setting that you want.

Access applies the margin setting to the selected fields.

Change the Padding

1 In the Design view, select the field(s) for which you want to change the padding.

2 Click the **Arrange** tab.

3 Click **Control Padding**.

4 Click the padding setting that you want.

The new padding setting is applied to the selected fields.

Note: You can also change margins and padding in the Layout view.

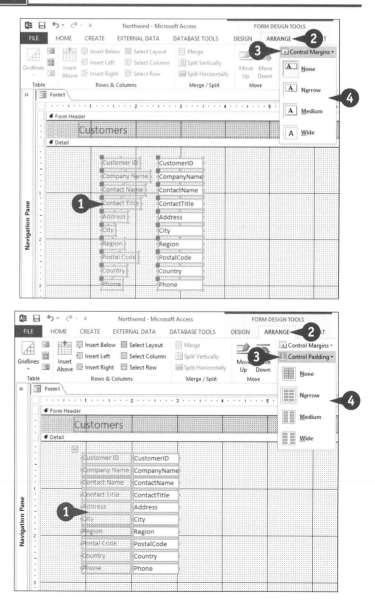

190

Add a Label

A *label* is a text area that is not connected to a field or function. A label displays *static text,* which means the text that cannot be edited or copied by the user of the form. Labels are most often used to display the name of a field, but they have many other uses, as well. For example, they can be used as the form subtitle; this should go in the Form Header section, below the title. You can also use labels to add explanatory text to the form: instructions for filling out the form, data restrictions, and so on.

Add a Label

1 In the Design view, click the **Design** tab.

2 Click the Label button (*Aa*).

↳ changes to **A**.

3 Drag a box where you want the label to be and then release the mouse button.

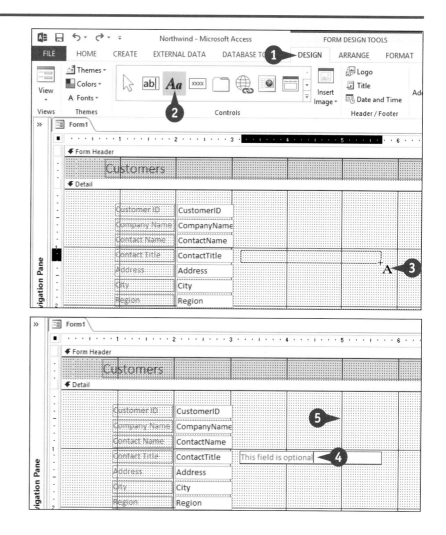

A label box appears, containing a flashing insertion point.

4 Type the label text.

5 Click outside the label when finished.

Format Label Text

You can apply some of the same types of formatting to a label as you would to text in Word or most other word-processing programs. For example, you can change the typeface, specify a font size, and applying formatting such as bold, italic, and underline.

The main difference is that in Access, text formatting is available only when the outer frame of the label is selected; you cannot select different formatting for certain characters within a single label box.

Format Label Text

1 In the Design view, click the frame of the label that you want to format.

Note: You can select multiple labels at once by holding down **Shift** as you click each one.

Note: You can format labels you create yourself and labels that are associated with fields.

2 Click the **Format** tab.

3 Click the Font ☑ and click a font.

Note: You can also use the Font list on the Home tab.

4 Click the Font Size ☑ and click a size.

5 Click one or more of these buttons to apply formatting:

Ⓐ Bold (**B**)

Ⓑ Italic (*I*)

Ⓒ Underline (U)

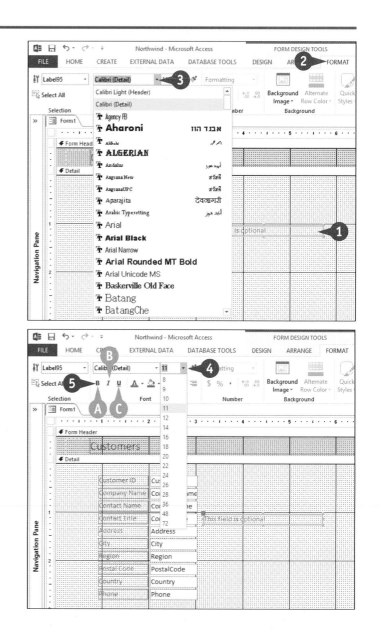

6 Click an alignment button:

D Left (≡)

E Center (≡)

F Right (≡)

7 Click the Font Color ⌄ and click a color.

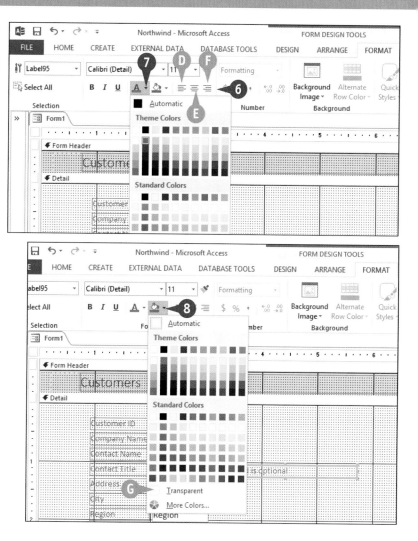

8 To place a colored background in the label box, click the Background Color ⌄ and click a color.

G You can click **Transparent** to remove the colored background.

TIPS

Can I format the text in a field?

Yes. Just select a field instead of a label and then apply the formatting as you learn in this section. It works exactly the same way.

What is the paintbrush button on the Format tab?

This is the Format Painter button ( ). It copies formatting from one place to another. To use it:

1 Select a label or field that has the formatting you want to copy.

2 Click .

3 Click the label or field to which you want to apply the formatting.

If you want to click more than one field or label in step **3**, double-click instead of single-clicking in step **2**. Click the button again to turn it off when finished.

Change the Background Color

You can set a background color for each section individually. For example, this would allow the form header to be in a contrasting color to the detail section. Alternatively, you can set all the sections in the same color for a uniform appearance.

When choosing a background color, make sure that it does not clash with the color of the field label text. For example, the default label text color is black, so any dark background will cause a problem. Either use a light color for the background or change the color of the label text.

Change the Background Color

1 In the Design view, click the title bar of the section for which you want to change the background color.

2 Click the **Format** tab.

3 Click the Background Color ☑ to display the available colors.

4 Click **More Colors**.

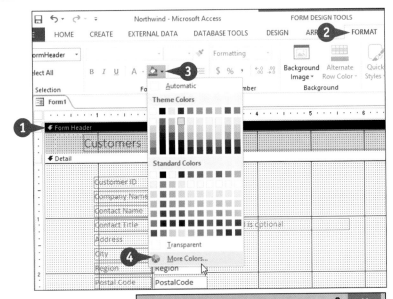

The Colors dialog box opens.

5 Select the color that you want:

Ⓐ You can use the **Standard** tab to choose from basic colors.

Ⓑ You can use the **Custom** tab to define a color numerically.

6 Click **OK**.

The color is applied to the background.

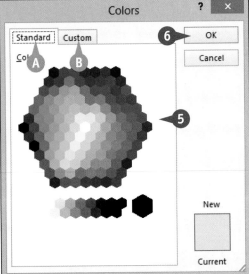

Add a Background Image

A background image can add interest to a form. As the name implies, it sits behind the fields, providing a backdrop. For the best results, choose an abstract image rather than a photo of a person or building.

By default, the fields have a solid, filled background, so they will contrast nicely with a background image and stand out for easy viewing. If you prefer the fields to blend into the background image, set the fill for each field to **Transparent**, as you learn to do in the section "Format Label Text." Labels are already set to a transparent fill by default.

Add a Background Image

1. Click the **Format** tab.

2. Click **Background Image**.

3. Click **Browse**.

The Insert Picture dialog box opens.

4. Navigate to the folder containing the image that you want to use.

5. Click the image.

6. Click **OK**.

The image appears behind all sections of the form.

Note: To remove the background image from the form, on the Design tab, click **Property Sheet**. Choose **Form** from the drop-down menu on the Property Sheet. Click the **Format** tab and then delete the filename from the **Picture** property.

Add a Hyperlink

A hyperlink on a form is like a label, except that it is a live link to the destination it represents. That destination can be a web page, a file on your PC or network, an e-mail address, or another object in the database, such as a table, form, or report.

The hyperlinks you learn to create in this section exist only on the form; they are not stored in database fields. If you want to store hyperlinks in a table, you can use a Hyperlink field type. See "Change a Field's Data Type" in Chapter 2 to learn how to change a field type to Hyperlink.

Add a Hyperlink

1 In the Design view, click the bar of the section in which you want to place the hyperlink.

2 Click the **Design** tab.

3 In the **Controls** group, click the Hyperlink button ( ).

Note: The Controls group's gallery contains many different content types that you can insert in a form. You may want to explore some of the others on your own.

The Insert Hyperlink dialog box opens.

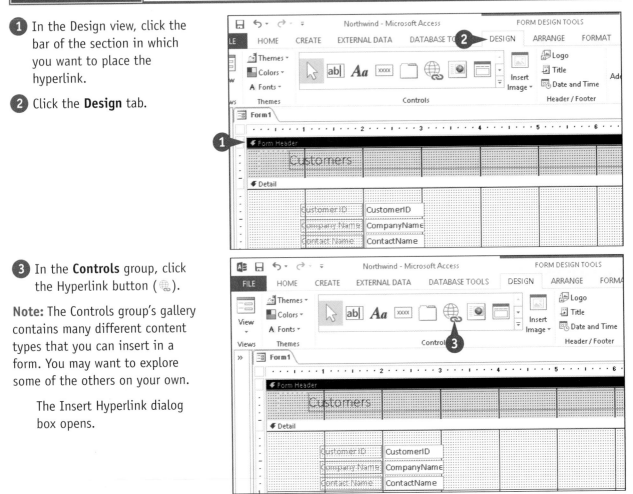

④ Type the URL.

Ⓐ You can also click **Browsed Pages** to choose a recently used URL.

⑤ Type the text that should appear on the form.

⑥ Click **ScreenTip**.

The Set Hyperlink ScreenTip dialog box opens.

Note: A *screen tip* is text that pops up when the user points at the hyperlink with the mouse pointer.

⑦ Type the screen tip text that you want to use.

⑧ Click **OK**.

Access returns you to the Insert Hyperlink dialog box.

⑨ Click **OK**.

Access adds the hyperlink to the form.

⑩ Click the hyperlink's frame and then drag it to the location that you want.

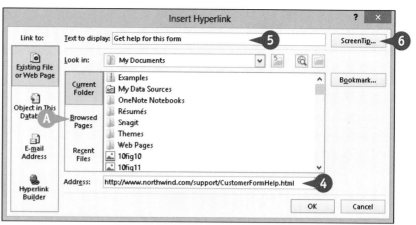

TIPS

Can I hyperlink to other locations besides the Internet?
Yes. A hyperlink can link to any file in any location, including your own hard drive or network; it does not have to be on the Internet. By default, in the Insert Hyperlink dialog box, the current folder contents are displayed. You can browse your hard drive or network locations using this interface to choose any accessible file. You can also link to a database object by clicking **Object in This Database** and then clicking the object, such as a table, form, or report.

What does the E-mail Address type of hyperlink do?
It inserts a hyperlink that, when clicked, opens a new message window in your default e-mail program. To set up an e-mail address hyperlink, click the **E-mail Address** button in the Insert Hyperlink dialog box and then fill in the fields provided.

Add a Tabbed Section

When there are too many fields or labels to fit on a form at a usable size, you can use a tab control to create multiple tabs, or pages, on the form. Like the tabs on the Ribbon in Access, the tabs on the form can be clicked to switch to their associated set of fields and other controls.

A tab control is also useful when you need the form to show multiple sets of the same (or similar) data. For example, you might want the form to be capable of showing separate data for various company divisions.

Add a Tabbed Section

Add a Tab

1 Click the **Design** tab.

2 Click the Tab Control button ().

3 Drag to create a rectangle representing the tab area and then release the mouse button.

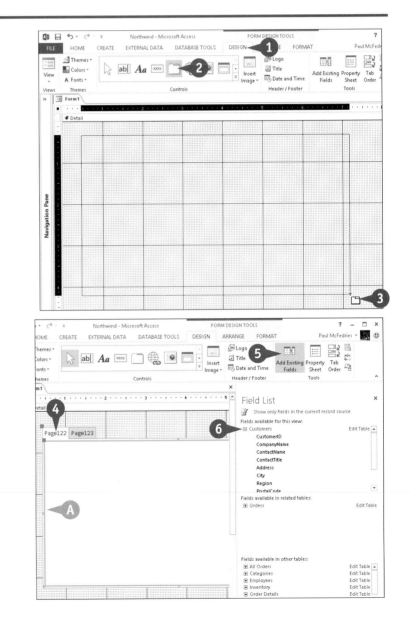

A tab control appears on the form with two tabs.

4 Click a tab.

Ⓐ A frame appears, representing that tab's page.

5 Click **Add Existing Fields**.

The Field List pane appears.

6 Click ⊞ next to a table name (⊞ changes to ⊟).

The list expands to show that table's fields.

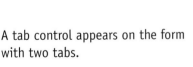

7 Drag and drop fields from the Field List on to the frame.

Note: You can also add nonfield items, such as labels and hyperlinks.

8 Click the other tab to add fields to it.

Add Another Tab

1 Click the outer frame of the tab control.

2 Click the **Design** tab.

3 Click the Controls ☰ and then click the Insert Page button (🗅).

Access adds another tab to the tab control.

Rename a Tab

1 Click the tab that you want to rename.

2 Click **Design**.

3 Click **Property Sheet**.

The Property Sheet pane appears.

4 Click **Format**.

5 Type the tab text in the **Caption** box.

The tab is renamed.

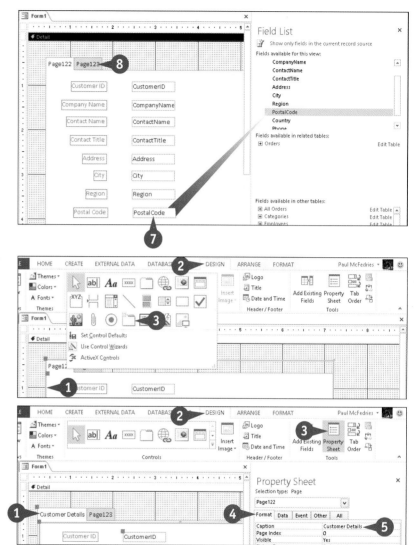

How do I delete a tab?

Right-click the tab that you want to remove and click **Delete Page** on the shortcut menu. Alternatively, click the tab that you want to remove and then press Delete.

Can I hide a tab without deleting it?

Yes, you can hide a tab by setting its **Visible** property to **No**. Click the tab to select it, click the **Design** tab, and then click **Property Sheet** to open the Property Sheet task pane. Click the **Format** tab, click the **Visible** ⌄, and then click **No**.

Insert a Logo or an Image

You can add visual appeal to a form by adding a logo to the form header. This will most often be a company logo, but you might also want to use different logos for different projects, teams, or departments. Just as the Title feature inserts a label in the form header, the Logo feature inserts a graphic in the form header.

If you want to insert a graphic anywhere else, you can use the Image feature. Images are like logos, except that you can choose where to put them and you can define the size of the frame.

Insert a Logo or an Image

Insert a Logo

1 Click the **Design** tab.

2 Click **Logo**.

The Insert Picture dialog box opens.

3 Select a location.

4 Click the picture to be inserted.

5 Click **OK**.

The picture is inserted in the Form Header section.

Depending on the resolution of the image file, it may cause the Form Header section to expand. The form header may also change its background color.

Resize a Logo

1 If needed, expand the Form Header section to make room for the image to be enlarged.

2 Click the logo.

3 Drag a corner selection handle (⌖ changes to ⬉).

Note: If you do not maintain the proportions, extra blank space may appear on either the sides or the top and bottom, but the picture will not be distorted.

The logo is resized.

Insert an Image

1. Click the **Design** tab.

2. Click **Insert Image**.

3. Click **Browse**.

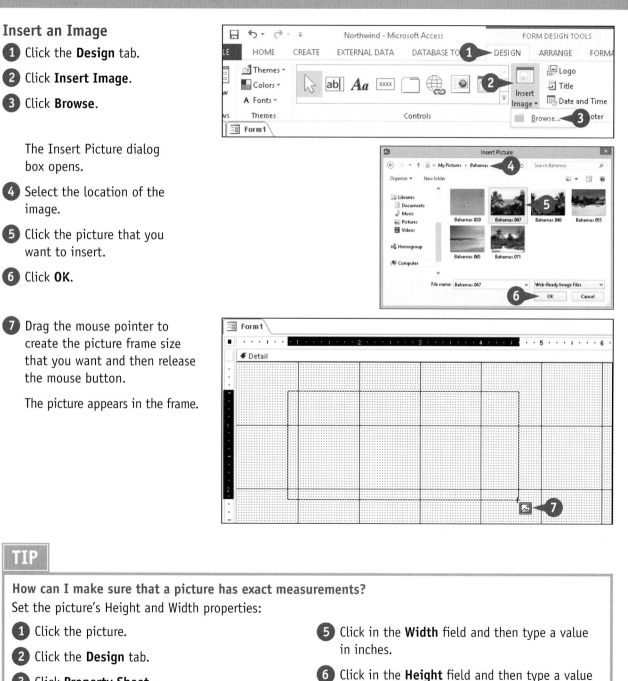

The Insert Picture dialog box opens.

4. Select the location of the image.

5. Click the picture that you want to insert.

6. Click **OK**.

7. Drag the mouse pointer to create the picture frame size that you want and then release the mouse button.

The picture appears in the frame.

How can I make sure that a picture has exact measurements?

Set the picture's Height and Width properties:

1. Click the picture.

2. Click the **Design** tab.

3. Click **Property Sheet**.

4. On the Property Sheet, click the **Format** tab.

5. Click in the **Width** field and then type a value in inches.

6. Click in the **Height** field and then type a value in inches.

Set Conditional Formatting

You can make form data easier to analyze by applying a conditional format to a field. A *conditional format* is formatting that Access applies only when a field meets the condition you specify. For example, you could set up a Balance field to display its value in red if the balance is negative, or you could color the Order Total field green for customers whose order amount exceeds a certain value.

When you set up your conditional format, you can specify the font, border, and background pattern, which helps to ensure that when a field meets your criteria, it stands out from the other fields in the form.

Set Conditional Formatting

1 In the Design view, click the field that you want to format.

Note: Make sure that you select the field, not its label.

2 Click the **Format** tab.

3 Click **Conditional Formatting**.

The Conditional Formatting Rules Manager dialog box opens.

4 Click **New Rule**.

The New Formatting Rule dialog box opens.

5 Click a rule type.

6 Click  and choose a condition.

7 Click  and choose a comparison operator.

8 Click here and type the value or text string.

9 In the **Preview** area, define the formatting for records where the condition is met:

Ⓐ Bold (**B**)

Ⓑ Italic (*I*)

Ⓒ Underline (U)

Ⓓ Background Color ( )

Ⓔ Font Color ( )

Ⓕ Enable/Disable ( ) toggles the display of the formatting.

10 Click **OK**.

Ⓖ The new rule appears in the Conditional Formatting Rules Manager dialog box.

11 To add another rule, you can repeat steps **4** to **10**.

12 Click **OK**.

The conditions are applied to the selected field.

Note: You can switch to the Form view and then scroll through a few records to check the conditional formatting.

Why would I want to use the Enable/Disable button?
You can toggle off the conditional formatting with the Enable/Disable button for either default formatting or for any of your conditions in order to preserve your conditional settings without using them all the time. For example, perhaps you only want to use conditional formatting when a form is viewed on-screen, so you would turn it off before printing the form.

How do I delete one of the multiple conditions that I have set up?
To remove a rule, click the **Format** tab and then click **Conditional Formatting** to open the Conditional Formatting Rules Manager dialog box. Click the rule that you want to delete, click **Delete Rule**, and then click **OK**.

CHAPTER 11

Creating Reports

A *report* is a database object that organizes and formats your table or query data to make it presentable and meaningful to other people. With reports, you can organize data into groups; display subtotals and grand totals for appropriate fields; and add lines, graphics, and fonts to put your data in its best light. Best of all, as you see in this chapter, various Access tools and wizards make it easy to create basic reports.

Understanding Report Views

You have seen in previous chapters that each type of Access object offers multiple views, such as the Datasheet and Design views for a table, and the Form, Layout, and Design views for a form. Reports come with the most views of just about any other object — four in all. Each view has a specific function for which it is best suited, so it pays to understand what each view offers you and when it is best to use it.

Layout View

The Layout view enables you to configure the overall formatting and layout of the report but not to change individual elements, such as text boxes. You can add grouping and sorting levels, totals, and other information as well as apply themes.

Design View

The Design view is where you can fine-tune the fields and labels to be included on the report. Only in this view can you add nonfield controls, such as labels. A report in the Design view often bears little resemblance to the finished layout. For example, compare the Design and Layout views shown here; the Layout view shows approximately how the fields will appear in the actual printout. However, the Design view shows items according to section and does not always place everything where it will actually be. As you are learning to use the Design view, it is often best to begin the report by using the Report Wizard or another automated method to help you set up the fields.

Report View

The Report view shows the report approximately as it will be printed, but it does not simulate the edges of the paper on-screen, so you cannot see the actual margins that will be used. Even if the report is too wide to fit on the paper, it still appears on-screen as one whole page. You cannot edit the report in the Report view.

Print Preview

Print Preview shows the report exactly as it will be printed. It shows page margins by simulating the edges of the paper on-screen. If the report is too wide to fit on the paper, it is truncated where the page break would truncate it. You cannot edit the report in Print Preview.

Create a Simple Report

By far, the easiest way to create a report is to use the Report command. It lets you create no-frills reports with just a few clicks of the mouse. The Report command — which you can use only on existing tables or queries — is fast and requires no input from you. This is the way to go if, rather than print a form or datasheet, you prefer to generate a report. After you create a report, you can save it for later reuse or simply re-create it the next time you need it.

Create a Simple Report

1. Click the table or query in the Objects list.

2. Click the **Create** tab.

3. Click **Report**.

Ⓐ The report appears in the Layout view.

4. To save the report, click the Save button ().

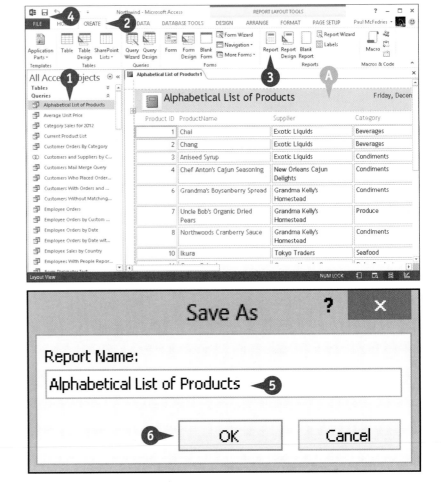

The Save As dialog box opens.

5. Type a name for the report.

6. Click **OK**.

The report is saved.

Apply a Theme to a Report

A *theme* is a preset collection of formatting that you can apply to your report. Throughout Office 2013, themes define three formatting elements for the object to which they are applied: fonts, colors, and object effects. However, in Access reports, only colors and fonts are affected. Office 2013 provides you with ten themes that you can use to quickly apply consistent formatting to a report so that it matches other reports or company specifications.

Themes work the same way for reports as for forms; for more details, see Chapter 10, "Editing Forms."

Apply a Theme to a Report

1 In the Layout view or Design view, click the **Design** tab.

2 Click **Themes**.

Access displays a gallery of themes.

A You can point to a theme to see a preview of it on the report.

3 Click the theme that you want.

The theme is applied.

Note: See Chapter 10 for information on creating your own custom themes. Chapter 10 also explains how you can apply color themes or font themes separately.

Preview and Print a Report

After creating a report, you will probably want to print it — for example, if you need multiple copies for distribution to others. Access enables you to set a number of print options before printing the report, including choosing the printer, a page range, and the number of copies.

You can also check the report first in Print Preview to make sure that it looks the way you want it. If you are confident that the report is laid out properly, you can also print it directly from any other view.

Preview and Print a Report

Open a Report in Print Preview

1 In the All Access Objects list, right-click the report.

2 Click **Print Preview**.

The report appears in Print Preview.

Switch an Open Report to Print Preview

1 Click the **Home** tab.

2 Click the **View** ▼.

3 Click **Print Preview**.

The report appears in Print Preview.

Print a Report from Print Preview

1 Click **Print**.

The Print dialog box opens.

2 Change any print settings, if necessary:

Ⓐ Click the **Name** ☑ to choose a different printer.

Ⓑ Click here to set a page range (○ changes to ◉).

Ⓒ Click here to specify a number of copies to print.

3 Click **OK**.

The report is printed.

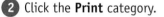

Print a Report from Other Views

1 Click **File**.

The File options appear.

2 Click the **Print** category.

3 Click **Print**.

The Print dialog box opens.

4 Perform steps **2** and **3** in the subsection "Print a Report from Print Preview."

The report is printed.

How can I see more of the report at once?
The Zoom group on the Print Preview tab contains buttons for One Page, Two Pages, and More Pages. If you click **More Pages**, you can choose a four-, eight-, or twelve-page display.

How can I export the report?
The Data group on the Print Preview tab contains buttons for exporting to Microsoft Word (in rich text format), to a text file, to an Excel file, and to several other formats.

Create a Report with the Report Wizard

The simple report is fine for very basic reporting, but it is likely that in most cases the resulting report will not suit your needs exactly. For more control over your reports, you need to use the Report Wizard, which takes you step-by-step through the entire report-creation process.

You can use the Report Wizard to create a report without having to manually design it while still having some control over its layout and formatting. After creating a report this way, you can then edit it in the Design view to fine-tune its appearance.

Create a Report with the Report Wizard

1. Click the **Create** tab.

2. Click **Report Wizard**.

   The Report Wizard opens.

3. Click the **Tables/Queries** [v] and click the table or query on which to base the report.

4. Click a field.

5. Click [>] to move the field to the Selected Fields list.

6. Repeat steps **4** and **5** for all the fields that you want to include.

   Ⓐ If necessary, you can click [<] to remove a field.

7. Click **Next**.

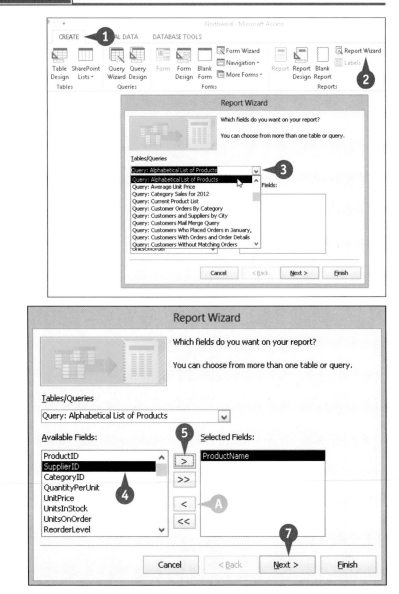

The grouping page of the wizard appears.

⑧ Click a field by which you want to group the records.

⑨ Click ⟩ to group by the chosen field.

Ⓑ The sample changes to show grouping by that field.

⑩ Click **Next**.

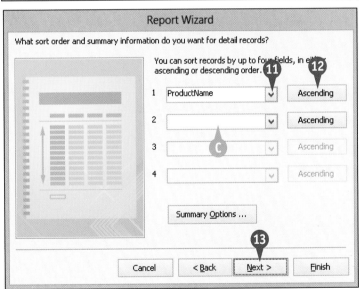

The sort order page appears.

⑪ In the first drop-down list, click ⋁ to choose a field by which you want to sort.

⑫ Click here to switch between an Ascending and a Descending sort.

Ⓒ You can define additional sort levels, if needed.

⑬ Click **Next**.

TIPS

How can I group by something other than unique values?

Click **Grouping Options** after step **9** to access the Grouping Intervals dialog box. From there, you can define a grouping interval. For text, you can group by the first letters of the entry. For numeric values, you can group by numbers (such as 10s or 100s).

Can I have fields from more than one table or query in the same report?

Yes. Repeat steps **3** to **6** to select another table or query before clicking **Next** in step **7**. As long as the tables or queries are related in some way, Access will pull data from them, just as it does when you create a query.

The Report Wizard is useful not only for selecting the exact fields that you want in your report, but also for making it easy to apply a grouping option to the records. The Report Wizard also allows you to choose the report layout, orientation, and formatting. You can change the fields, grouping, layout, and other options later in the Report Design view, but it is often easier to specify upfront what you want via the wizard. Finally, the Report Wizard also enables you to preview your report.

Create a Report with the Report Wizard (continued)

The layout page appears.

14 Click the layout that you want to use (○ changes to ◉).

15 Click the page orientation that you want (○ changes to ◉).

16 Click **Next**.

The title page appears.

17 Click here and type a name for the report, replacing the generic name that appears.

18 Click to choose how the report should be viewed after it is created (○ changes to ◉).

19 Click **Finish**.

If you clicked the Preview the Report option in step 18, the report appears in Print Preview.

If you clicked the Modify the Report's Design option in step 18, the report appears in the Design view.

TIPS

How can I change the name of a report after creating it with the Report Wizard?
First, close the report. Then, from the Objects list, right-click the report and choose **Rename** from the shortcut menu. Type a new name and then press Enter.

How can I make the report extend to multiple pages horizontally if the fields do not fit on a single page width?
Before step **16**, deselect **Adjust the field width so all fields fit on a page** (☑ changes to ☐). The report will then expand horizontally to fill as many pages as needed for all the fields to be at their original sizes.

Create a Report in the Layout View

The Report Wizard offers the easiest path to creating a report, but it does not give you much flexibility in terms of the report layout. The Report Design view gives you complete flexibility but is more complex to learn and use. In between these extremes is the Report Layout view, which enables you to create a report by dragging and dropping fields on to a blank page.

Because you can easily switch between views, you can create the initial layout in the Layout view and then fine-tune it in the Design view.

Create a Report in the Layout View

1 Click the **Create** tab.

2 Click **Blank Report**.

A blank report window appears in the Layout view.

3 In the Field List, if a list of tables does not already appear, click **Show all tables**.

4 Click ⊞ next to a table's name.

A list of the fields in the table appears (⊞ changes to ⊟).

5 Drag a field on to the report.

Ⓐ The field name appears at the top, and records from the table appear beneath it.

6 Repeat step **5** to add other fields to the report as needed.

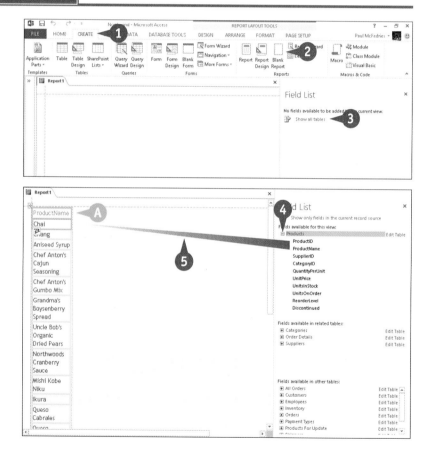

Set the Page Size and Orientation

The default page size for a report is Letter size, which is 8.5 × 11 inches. If you will be printing your report on paper that uses a different size, Access offers 17 different page sizes, including Legal (8.5 × 14 inches) and US B (11 × 17 inches).

You can also switch the report layout between portrait and landscape. Portrait prints across the shorter dimension of the paper, so it is best for reports that have only a few fields. Landscape prints across the long dimension, so use it if your report has many fields.

Set the Page Size and Orientation

Set the Page Size

1 In the Design or Layout view, click the **Page Setup** tab.

2 Click **Size**.

3 Click a paper size.

Access adjusts the report to suit the new page size.

Set the Page Orientation

1 In the Design or Layout view, click the **Page Setup** tab.

2 Click **Portrait** or **Landscape**.

Access adjusts the report to accommodate the new orientation.

Change the Report Layout Type

Access gives you an easy way to arrange your report fields: the control layout. This simple layout acts as a kind of table, and your fields are slotted neatly into the layout's rows and columns. In a *stacked* layout, the controls are arranged vertically in two columns, with field names in the left column and fields in the right column. In a *tabular* layout, the controls are arranged horizontally in two rows, with field labels in the top row and fields in the bottom row.

Ⓐ The default type of report created in the Layout view is tabular.

Ⓑ A tabular layout places each field name across the top row, with the individual records beneath.

C You can click here to change to a stacked layout.

D A stacked layout places each record in its own area, one on top of the other, with all its fields in one place.

E When switching between stacked and tabular layouts, make sure that you click the Select All icon (⊞) to select the entire data grid before making the change. If you select only certain fields, only those fields will be changed. That enables you to create layouts in which some fields are arranged in a tabular layout and others are stacked.

Set Page Margins

You can get more space on the printed page to display your report data by using smaller page margins. The *margins* are the blank areas that surround the printed data. For example, if you find that Access is printing extra pages because your data is a bit too wide or a bit too long to fit on a single page, you can reduce either the left and right margins or the top and bottom margins.

If you or another person will be writing notes on the printouts, consider using wider margins to allow more room for the notes.

Set Page Margins

Use a Page Margin Default

1 In the Design or Layout view, click the **Page Setup** tab.

2 Click **Margins**.

3 Click a margin setting.

The margin setting is applied.

A By default, margins appear on-screen in Print Preview. If you do not want this to happen, deselect **Show Margins** (☑ changes to ☐).

Set Custom Page Margins

1 Click the **Page Setup** tab.

2 Click **Page Setup**.

The Page Setup dialog box opens.

3 Click in a text field and type a margin setting for that side of the page.

4 Repeat step **3** as needed for the other sides.

5 Click **OK**.

The margin setting is applied.

Set Control Margins and Padding

Your reports will be more attractive and easier to read if the controls have some extra space within and around them. You can ensure this by adjusting the margins and the padding. The margin controls for individual items are for the text within the text boxes or label frames.

You can also set an amount of padding for one or more controls. *Padding* is like margins, but it refers to the space between fields — that is, the extra white space on the outside of a text box or another control.

Set Control Margins and Padding

Set Control Margins

 In the Design or Layout view, select the controls.

Note: Hold down **Shift** and then click multiple controls; you can also drag a lasso around them.

② Click the **Arrange** tab.

③ Click **Control Margins**.

④ Click the setting that you want.

Access applies the control margin setting to the selected controls.

Set the Control Padding

① In the Design or Layout view, select the controls.

Note: Hold down **Ctrl** and then click multiple controls; you can also drag a lasso around them.

② Click the **Arrange** tab.

③ Click **Control Padding**.

④ Click the setting that you want.

Access applies the control padding setting to the selected controls.

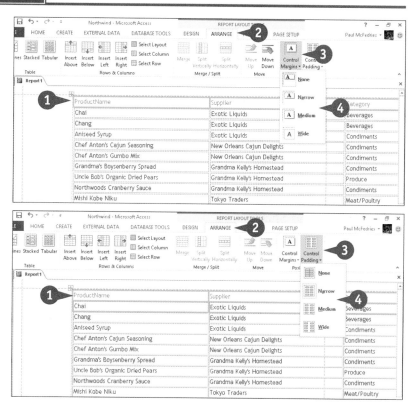

Format Report Text

When you apply a theme to a report, the font formatting is applied automatically. You can modify this, applying some of the same types of formatting to report text as you would text in Word. For example, you can change the typeface, specify a font size and color, and apply formatting such as bold, italic, and underline. As with forms, font formatting on reports applies to entire boxes only, not to individual characters. Therefore, if you want characters formatted differently from others, they must be in separate controls or labels.

Format Report Text

Set the Font

① In the Design or Layout view, click the label or field that you want to format.

To select more than one label or field, hold down Ctrl as you click them.

② Click the **Format** tab.

③ Click the Font ☑ and click the font that you want.

Access applies the font.

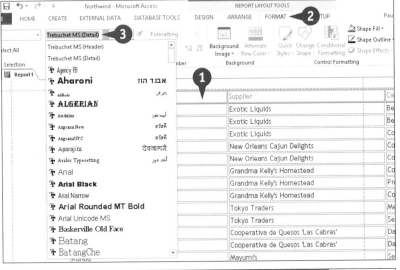

Set the Font Size

① Click the label or field that you want to format.

To select more than one label or field, hold down Ctrl as you click them.

② Click the **Format** tab.

③ Click the Font Size ☑ and click the font size.

Note: If you choose a larger size, the text may appear truncated. Enlarge a field's box if needed, moving other boxes to make room.

Access changes the font to the new size.

Set the Font Attributes

1 Click the label or field that you want to format.

To select more than one label or field, hold down Ctrl as you click them.

2 Click the **Format** tab.

3 Click the buttons for the attributes that you want:

Ⓐ Bold (**B**)

Ⓑ Italic (*I*)

Ⓒ Underline (U)

Access applies the font attributes.

Set the Font Color

1 Click the label or field that you want to format.

2 Click the **Format** tab.

3 Click the Font Color ⯆.

The Font Color palette appears.

4 Click the color that you want.

Access applies the color.

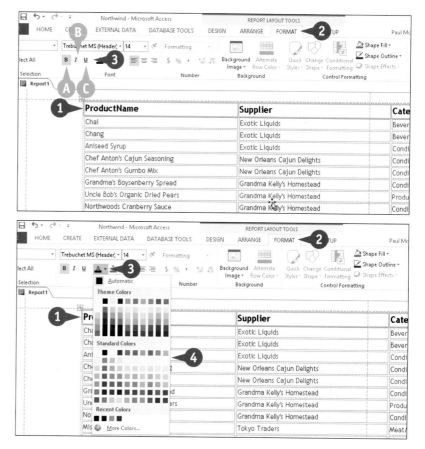

TIPS

What are the different color sections in the Font Color palette?

- **Theme Colors** refers to the color themes that you can apply throughout Office applications in Office 2013. These colors shift when you apply a different theme.
- **Standard Colors** are fixed colors that do not change with the color theme.
- **Recent Colors** are colors that you have already applied in this database. Using one of these colors ensures consistency across objects.

What does the Background Color button do?

The Background Color button (⯆) applies a background fill to controls. For example, you may want to use a colored background for certain labels. Keep in mind that if you use a dark fill color, you should set the text color to white (or a light color).

Size and Align Report Fields

As you design your report, you may need to adjust the sizing and alignment of the fields and their labels. When you change the width of a field, its label also changes automatically, and the fields to its right shift to make room or to reduce the space.

When you create a report in the Layout view, the fields are usually properly aligned with one another, but if you create or modify the report in the Design view, some of the fields may not be quite aligned with one another. You can easily align multiple fields by selecting them and then choosing an alignment type.

Size and Align Report Fields

Size a Field

1 In the Design or Layout view, click the label or field.

2 Position � over the right edge of the control (� changes to ◄─►) and then drag to the right or left.

The field is resized, and any fields to its right are moved.

Align Fields with One Another

1 In the Design view, select the fields.

Note: Hold down **Shift** as you click each field.

2 Click the **Arrange** tab.

3 Click **Align**.

4 Click the alignment that you want.

The selected fields align with one another.

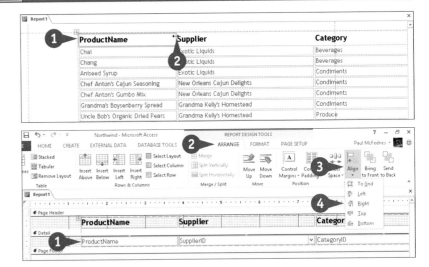

Insert a Page-Numbering Code

Because reports are designed to be printed, they should include page-numbering codes. Reports generated with the Report Wizard or other quick methods contain a page-numbering function in the Page Footer section. In reports that you generate from blanks, you must insert your own page-numbering codes. Page numbering can be placed in either the report header or footer. The *report header* appears above the Detail area, whereas the *report footer* appears below the Detail area.

Note: The following steps are for reports that do not already contain page numbering.

Insert a Page-Numbering Code

1 In the Design view, click the **Design** tab.

2 Click **Page Numbers**.

The Page Numbers dialog box opens.

3 Click a page number format (○ changes to ◉).

Note: Page N displays "Page" along with the number, like this: "Page 2." **Page N of M** displays "Page" along with the current page number, "of," and the total page count, like this: "Page 2 of 4."

4 Choose a position for the page numbers (○ changes to ◉).

5 Click the **Alignment** ▾ and click an alignment for the page numbers.

Ⓐ You can deselect **Show Number on First Page** (☑ changes to ☐) to omit the page number from the first page.

6 Click **OK**.

The page numbering code is inserted in either the header or the footer, depending on your selection.

CHAPTER 12

Grouping and Sorting Data

The reports you learn about in Chapter 11 provide a complete listing of the records in the data set. In this chapter, you learn how to create reports that group and sort data, distilling down a large amount of information into a manageable, meaningful report.

Understanding Grouping and Summarizing

When you have a lot of data, it can be difficult to discern its overall meaning. As you learn in the previous chapter, the Report Wizard gives you options for grouping the records based on the values in one or more fields, as well as summarizing the report records. If you need to fine-tune the grouping and summarizing options set up through the wizard or if you are building your report from scratch, you can specify the report's sorting and grouping from the Design view. Access provides several ways of grouping and summarizing data to make it easier to understand.

Ⓐ Grouping

You can group a report by a field, such as by category. In this example, each category has its own section of the report.

Ⓑ Aggregate functions

You can summarize each group with one or more aggregate functions, such as Sum (shown here), Average, or Count.

Product Inventory By Category

Category	Product	Supplier	Units In Stock
Beverages Ⓐ			
	Chai	Exotic Liquids	39
	Chang	Exotic Liquids	17
	Chartreuse verte	Aux joyeux ecclésiastiques	69
	Côte de Blaye	Aux joyeux ecclésiastiques	17
	Guaraná Fantástica	Refrescos Americanas LTDA	20
	Ipoh Coffee	Leka Trading	17
	Lakkalikööri	Karkki Oy	57
	Laughing Lumberjack Lager	Bigfoot Breweries	52
	Outback Lager	Pavlova, Ltd.	15
	Rhönbräu Klosterbier	Plutzer Lebensmittelgroßmärkte AG	125
	Sasquatch Ale	Bigfoot Breweries	111
	Steeleye Stout	Bigfoot Breweries	20
		TOTAL	559
Condiments			
	Aniseed Syrup	Exotic Liquids	
	Chef Anton's Cajun Seasoning	New Orleans Cajun Delights	
	Chef Anton's Gumbo Mix	New Orleans Cajun Delights	0 Ⓑ
	Genen Shouyu	Mayumi's	39
	Grandma's Boysenberry Spread	Grandma Kelly's Homestead	120
	Gula Malacca	Leka Trading	27
	Louisiana Fiery Hot Pepper Sauce	New Orleans Cajun Delights	76

Ⓒ Reports based on summary queries

As you learn in Chapter 8, "Creating Complex Queries," you can create summary queries that distill table data into aggregate functions. You can then create reports based on one of those queries.

Order Summaries By Customer

Customer	Total Units Ordered	Total Value of Orders
Alfreds Futterkiste	174	$4,273.00 Ⓒ
Ana Trujillo Emparedados y he	63	$1,402.95
Antonio Moreno Taquería	359	$7,023.98
Around the Horn	650	$13,390.65
Berglunds snabbköp	1001	$24,927.58
Blauer See Delikatessen	140	$3,239.80
Blondel père et fils	666	$18,534.08
Bólido Comidas preparadas	190	$4,232.85
Bon app'	980	$21,963.25
Bottom-Dollar Markets	956	$20,801.60
B's Beverages	293	$6,089.90
Cactus Comidas para llevar	115	$1,814.80
Centro comercial Moctezum	11	$100.80
Chop-suey Chinese	465	$12,348.88
Comércio Mineiro	133	$3,810.75
Consolidated Holdings	87	$1,719.10
Drachenblut Delikatessen	160	$3,763.21

⒟ Sorting

If you want your report data sorted without worrying whether the data in the report's table or query was sorted, you can specify a sort field from within the Report Design view.

⒠ Sorting levels

Access supports multiple sorting levels, which means that you can sort your report based on two or more fields. For example, if you sort your Product Inventory report based on the Category field, you can also add a second sort level that sorts within each category by the Product Name field.

⒡ Sorting text

For a text field, you can sort the values from A to Z (an ascending sort) or Z to A (descending).

⒢ Sorting dates

For a date field, you can sort the values from oldest to newest (ascending) or newest to oldest (descending).

⒣ Sorting numbers

For a numeric field, you can sort the values from 0 to 9 (ascending) or 9 to 0 (descending).

Product Inventory By Category

Product Invent ⒟ ⒠ By Category

Category	Product Name	Supplier	Units In Stock
Beverages	Chai	Exotic Liquids	39
Beverages	Chang	Exotic Liquids	17
Beverages	Chartreuse verte	Aux joyeux ecclésiastiques	69
Beverages	Côte de Blaye	Aux joyeux ecclésiastiques	17
Beverages	Guaraná Fantástica	Refrescos Americanas LTDA	20
Beverages	Ipoh Coffee	Leka Trading	17
Beverages	Lakkalikööri	Karkki Oy	57
Beverages	Laughing Lumberjack Lager	Bigfoot Breweries	52
Beverages	Outback Lager	Pavlova, Ltd.	15
Beverages	Rhönbräu Klosterbier	Plutzer Lebensmittelgroßmärkte AG	125
Beverages	Sasquatch Ale	Bigfoot Breweries	111
Beverages	Steeleye Stout	Bigfoot Breweries	20
Condiments	Aniseed Syrup	Exotic Liquids	13
Condiments	Chef Anton's Cajun Seasoning	New Orleans Cajun Delights	53
Condiments	Chef Anton's Gumbo Mix	New Orleans Cajun Delights	0
Condiments	Genen Shouyu	Mayumi's	39

Customer Orders for 2012

Cust ⒡ er Orders for 2012 ⒢ ⒣

Customer	Employee	Order Date	Product	Quantity
Alfreds Futterkiste	Nancy Davolio	15-Jan-2012	Original Frankfurter grüne So	2
Alfreds Futterkiste	Nancy Davolio	15-Jan-2012	Raclette Courdavault	15
Alfreds Futterkiste	Nancy Davolio	16-Mar-2012	Rössle Sauerkraut	2
Alfreds Futterkiste	Nancy Davolio	16-Mar-2012	Grandma's Boysenberry Spre	16
Alfreds Futterkiste	Janet Leverling	09-Apr-2012	Flotemysost	20
Alfreds Futterkiste	Janet Leverling	09-Apr-2012	Escargots de Bourgogne	40
Alfreds Futterkiste	Michael Suyama	25-Aug-2012	Spegesild	2
Alfreds Futterkiste	Michael Suyama	25-Aug-2012	Rössle Sauerkraut	15
Alfreds Futterkiste	Michael Suyama	25-Aug-2012	Chartreuse verte	21
Alfreds Futterkiste	Margaret Peacc	03-Oct-2012	Vegie-spread	20
Alfreds Futterkiste	Margaret Peacc	13-Oct-2012	Aniseed Syrup	6
Alfreds Futterkiste	Margaret Peacc	13-Oct-2012	Lakkalikööri	15
Ana Trujillo Emparedac	Margaret Peacc	04-Mar-2012	Queso Cabrales	2
Ana Trujillo Emparedac	Margaret Peacc	04-Mar-2012	Teatime Chocolate Biscuits	7
Ana Trujillo Emparedac	Margaret Peacc	04-Mar-2012	Konbu	10
Ana Trujillo Emparedac	Margaret Peacc	04-Mar-2012	Mozzarella di Giovanni	10

Group Report Results

I f you use the Report Wizard to create a report, as detailed in Chapter 11, you have the opportunity to specify grouping in the wizard.

You can also set up grouping in the Layout or Design view afterward or change the grouping. If you arrange the grouping in the Layout view, the grouping field is moved automatically into the newly created group header. If you arrange it in the Design view, you must manually cut and paste the field.

Group Report Results

Group from the Layout View

1 In the Layout view, click the **Design** tab.

2 Click **Group & Sort** ([≡]).

The Group, Sort, and Total pane appears.

3 Click **Add a group**.

A shortcut menu appears, showing the available fields by which you can group your data.

4 Click the field by which you want to group.

A A Group On line appears.

B An additional set of buttons appears for creating another level of grouping, if needed.

Group from the Design View

1 In the Design view, perform the steps in the subsection "Group from the Layout View" to create a grouping.

2 On the design grid, click the field on which you have grouped and then press `Ctrl` + `X` to cut it to the Clipboard.

3 Click the header for the field on which you have grouped.

4 Press `Ctrl`+ `V` to paste the field into that header section.

Access will now display the field in the report's grouping header.

TIPS

Can I have multiple levels of groupings?

Yes. After you create a grouping, a fresh set of Add a Group and Add a Sort buttons appears below it. Click **Add a group** to create a group subordinate to your original one.

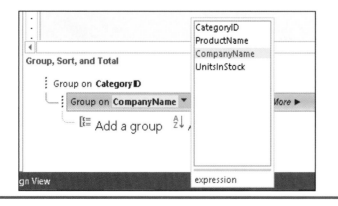

How can I set grouping options?

Click **More** on the group's bar. Additional drop-down lists appear for setting options. For example, you can choose grouping intervals, choose to have only a group header or footer, and choose whether to keep a group together on one page.

Group a Numeric Field by Intervals

By default, Access groups a field based on the entire value of each unique item in the grouping field. That is exactly what you want if you are using a text field, but it does not work well if you are using a numeric field. For example, if your report contains order data, it does not make sense to group the report based on the Quantity field because you will just end up with a huge number of groups. Instead, you can group a numeric field using intervals, such as 1-10, 11-20, and so on.

Group a Numeric Field by Intervals

1 Click the **Design** tab.

2 Click **Group & Sort** ([≡]).

The Group, Sort, and Total pane appears.

3 Click **More**.

4 Click this ▼.

Access displays the interval options for the grouping.

5 Click the interval that you want to use (○ changes to ●).

Ⓐ If you prefer to use some other interval, click **Custom** (○ changes to ●) and then type the interval value.

Access will now display the report grouped on the numeric field, using the interval that you selected.

Group a Date Field

As with a numeric field, grouping a report based on a date field usually presents problems because your report ends up grouped by the individual dates in the grouping field. This might be what you want, but in most cases it creates too many groups for the report to be useful. A better way to go is to group the date field based on some larger interval, such as by week, month, quarter, or year. This will usually give you a more meaningful and more readable report.

Group a Date Field

1 Click the **Design** tab.

2 Click **Group & Sort** (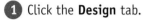).

The Group, Sort, and Total pane appears.

3 Click **More**.

4 Click this ▼.

Access displays the date interval options for the grouping.

5 Click the interval that you want to use (○ changes to ◉).

Ⓐ If you prefer to use some other interval, click **Custom** (○ changes to ◉), type the interval value, and then select an interval unit.

Access will now display the report grouped on the date field, using the interval that you selected.

Group Records Using an Expression

Although you will most often use a field to group a report, you can also define your own grouping *expression,* which is a collection of operators, operands, field names, and functions that returns some value for each record. You can then group the report based on the values returned by the expression.

For example, suppose that you have a product inventory report that includes UnitPrice and UnitsInStock fields. Multiplying these values together gives you an "inventory value" number. If you want to group the records based on inventory value, here is the expression to use: **=[UnitPrice] * [UnitsInStock]**.

Group Records Using an Expression

1 Click the **Design** tab.

2 Click **Group & Sort** ( ).

The Group, Sort, and Total pane appears.

3 Click **Add a group**.

Access adds a grouping.

4 Click this .

5 Click **expression**.

The Expression Builder dialog box appears.

6 Type your expression.

7 Click **OK**.

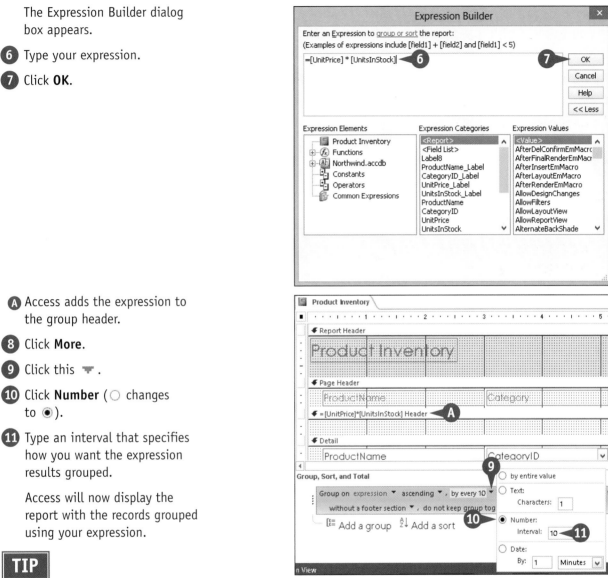

A Access adds the expression to the group header.

8 Click **More**.

9 Click this ▼ .

10 Click **Number** (○ changes to ◉).

11 Type an interval that specifies how you want the expression results grouped.

Access will now display the report with the records grouped using your expression.

TIP

Can I also use an expression for sorting?

Yes. For example, in the product inventory report, you could use the expression **=[UnitPrice] * [UnitsInStock]** to sort the report based on the inventory value. Similarly, suppose that you have an invoices report that includes the fields Quantity, Price, and Discount. If you want to sort the report based on the total value of each invoice, you would use the following expression:

=[Quantity] * [Price] * (1 - [Discount])

To sort your report based on an expression, open the Group, Sort, and Total pane, click **Add a sort**, click **expression**, and then follow steps 6 to 11 in this section.

Sort Report Results

You can sort the results in a report, with or without grouping. If you have grouped your report, you can sort your report by sorting on the groups themselves. You can also sort the entries within each group. For example, if you have grouped a report based on product categories, you can sort within each category based on product supplier names.

If you have not grouped your report, you define the sorting separately. In this case, you can define your sort based on any field in the report.

Sort Report Results

Sort the Groups

Note: Begin these steps in the Design view, with a group already defined.

1 Click ▯≣.

The Group, Sort, and Total pane appears.

2 Click ▼ to choose a sort order for the group.

3 To sort within the group based on another field, click **Add a sort** and then select the field.

Access will now display the report with the groups sorted.

Group, Sort, and Total

Group on **CategoryID** ▼ from smallest to largest ▼ **2** ▶

▯≣ Add a group ⅍↓ Add a sort **3**

Sort with No Grouping

1 Click ▯≣.

The Group, Sort, and Total pane appears.

2 Click **Add a sort**.

A list of available fields appears on which you can sort your data.

3 Click the field on which you want to sort.

A sort bar appears.

Group, Sort, and Total

▯≣ Add a group ⅍↓ Add a sort

2

CategoryID
ProductName **3**
CompanyName
UnitsInStock

Group, Sort, and Total

Sort by **ProductName** ▼ *More* ▶

▯≣ Add a group

n View

expression

236

Count Records

You can use a Count function in a report to list the number of records. You can add record counts whether you have grouped or sorted the report.

Access gives you several count options. For example, you can display just the total number of records within the report, which is called the *grand total*. If your report is grouped, you can also display *subtotals,* which are the total number of records within each group. You can display these subtotals in the group header, group footer, or both. You can also display each subtotal as a percentage of the grand total.

Count Records

Note: Begin these steps in the Design view, with a group or sort specification already defined.

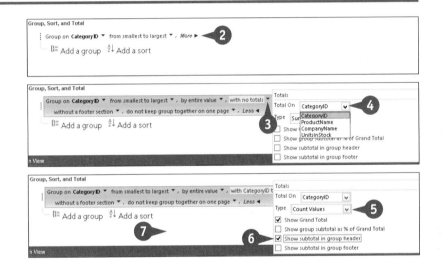

1 Click .

The Group, Sort, and Total pane appears.

2 Click **More**.

The available options expand. The options may be different than shown here depending on the field type.

3 Click this ▼ to open a menu of options.

4 Click the **Total On** ⌄ and click the field on which you want to total.

5 Click the **Type** ⌄ and click **Count Values** if it does not already appear.

6 Click the check boxes to indicate where and how the count should appear (☐ changes to ☑).

7 Click away from the menu to close it.

Access will now include in the report the record counts that you selected.

237

Add an Aggregate Function

Counting is only one of many math operations that you can perform on records in a report. You can also add other functions, including sum, average, minimum, maximum, and standard deviation. These are all referred to as *aggregate functions* because they summarize (aggregate) data.

For example, if you have a report that shows product inventory, you might want to know the total number of products that you have in stock. You can do that by adding a Sum function based on the field that holds the units in stock for each product.

Add an Aggregate Function

Note: Begin these steps in the Design view, with a group or sort specification already defined.

1 Click [≡.

The Group, Sort, and Total pane appears.

2 Click **More** if the extended options do not already appear.

3 Click this ▼ to open a menu of total options.

④ Click the **Total On** ☑ and click the field on which you want to total.

⑤ Click the **Type** ☑ and click the function that you want.

⑥ Click the check boxes to indicate where and how the function should appear.

⑦ Click away from the menu to close it.

Ⓐ The function appears in the report design.

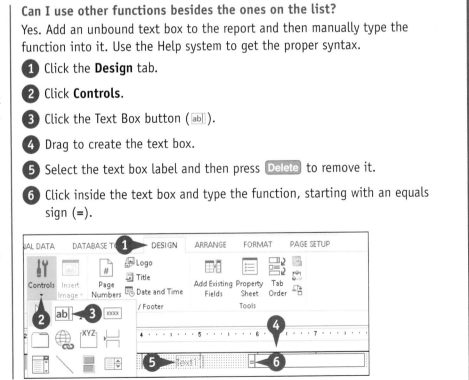

TIPS

How can I move a function between sections?

A function is in an unbound text box. You can move unbound text boxes between sections with a cut-and-paste operation but not with a drag-and-drop operation. Select the text box containing the function and press Ctrl + X. Click the bar for the section into which you want to insert the function and press Ctrl + V.

Can I use other functions besides the ones on the list?

Yes. Add an unbound text box to the report and then manually type the function into it. Use the Help system to get the proper syntax.

① Click the **Design** tab.

② Click **Controls**.

③ Click the Text Box button (ab|).

④ Drag to create the text box.

⑤ Select the text box label and then press Delete to remove it.

⑥ Click inside the text box and type the function, starting with an equals sign (=).

Hide the Group Header and Footer

When you create a report grouping, Access creates two new report sections: a *group header* and a *group footer*. You can use the header to identify the group and the footer to print summary information about the group. For example, at the bottom of each group, you could print the sum of a particular field or the total number of records in the group. (See the section "Count Records," earlier in this chapter.)

However, if you do not use the group header or the group footer, you can hide these features to reduce clutter in the Report Design view.

Hide the Group Header and Footer

1. If the group header section contains controls that you want to save, move them to another section.

2. Click the **Design** tab.

3. Click **Group & Sort** ( ).

   The Group, Sort, and Total pane appears.

4. Click **More**.

5. Click this .

6. Click **without a header section**.

Ⓐ Access removes the group header section.

7. Click this .

8. Click **without a footer section**.

   Access removes the group footer section.

Keep a Group Together on a Page

Access offers an option called *Keep Whole Group Together on One Page.* This option tells Access to print each group on a single page, if possible. If there is not enough room after one group ends to print the next group on the same page, Access starts a new page.

Another option is called *Keep Header and First Record Together on One Page,* and it tells Access to print the group header on the same page as the first group record. This prevents the group header from appearing by itself at the bottom of a page.

Keep a Group Together on a Page

1 Click the **Design** tab.

2 Click **Group & Sort** ( ).

The Group, Sort, and Total pane appears.

3 Click **More**.

4 Click this .

5 Click the option that you prefer to use.

Access will print the report based on the option that you selected.

Change the Grouping or Sorting Priority

If you have added two or more groupings to your report, Access maintains a priority for the grouping levels. The first grouping is given top priority, which means that Access groups the entire report based on that field. The second grouping is given the next priority, which means that Access only groups the records within the main grouping. To get a different look at the report, you can move a grouping level up or down in the priority list.

The same priority idea applies also to sorting, so if your report uses multiple sort levels, you can also move them up or down in the sort priority.

Change the Grouping or Sorting Priority

1 Click the **Design** tab.

2 Click **Group & Sort** ([≡]).

The Group, Sort, and Total pane appears.

3 Click the grouping or sorting level that you want to change.

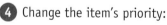

4 Change the item's priority:

Ⓐ Click the Move Up button (⬆) to move the item to a higher priority.

Ⓑ Click the Move Down button (⬇) to move the item to a lower priority.

Access adjusts the grouping or sorting priority.

Remove a Grouping or Sorting

If you have added two or more groupings to your report, you might find that the extra grouping levels actually make your report harder to read because it is now broken down into too many groups within groups. In that case, you can simplify the report by deleting a grouping level.

If you have added one or more sorting levels to your report, you can also remove any sorting level that you no longer require.

Remove a Grouping or Sorting

1 If the group's header or footer section contains controls that you want to save, move them to another section.

2 Click the **Design** tab.

3 Click **Group & Sort** (☷).

The Group, Sort, and Total pane appears.

4 Click the grouping or sorting level that you want to remove.

5 Click ✕.

Access deletes the grouping or sorting level.

CHAPTER 13

Creating Mailing Labels

In addition to standard reports, Access can also create mailing labels. This enables you to print labels without first exporting the data into a word-processing program as well as set up reusable label definitions for recurring mailings.

Create Labels

If you are working on your Christmas card list, a print newsletter, or a direct mail marketing campaign, you eventually have to mail out a number of pieces. You can make this tedious chore quite a bit easier by printing a mailing label for each recipient. If you have all your recipients in an Access table, you can generate the mailing labels directly from it. Labels are a special type of report. They print multiple records per page in a layout designed to correspond to self-stick labels that feed into your printer.

Create Labels

① In the Objects list, click the table or query containing the fields that you want.

② Click the **Create** tab.

③ Click **Labels** (⊟).

The Label Wizard opens.

④ Click the **Filter by manufacturer** ⌄ and click the label manufacturer.

⑤ Click the unit of measure that you want to use (○ changes to ⦿).

⑥ Click the label type (○ changes to ⦿).

Note: Continuous-feed labels are typically used only by dot matrix printers.

⑦ Click the label product number.

Note: If you do not know the product number, choose one that matches the dimensions and number of labels across that you have.

⑧ Click **Next**.

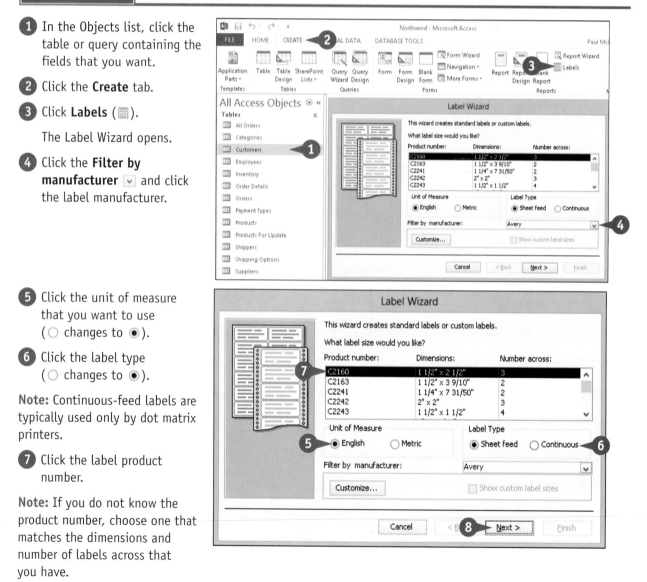

The font and color page of the wizard appears.

9 Click the **Font name** ☑ and click a font for the labels.

10 Click the **Font size** ☑ and click a font size.

11 Click the **Font weight** ☑ and click a font weight.

12 If needed, click **Italic** (☐ changes to ☑).

13 If needed, click **Underline** (☐ changes to ☑).

14 Click the **Text color** ⋯ to open the Color palette.

15 Click a color for the text.

Ⓐ For more choices, you can click **Define Custom Colors**.

16 Click **OK**.

17 Click **Next**.

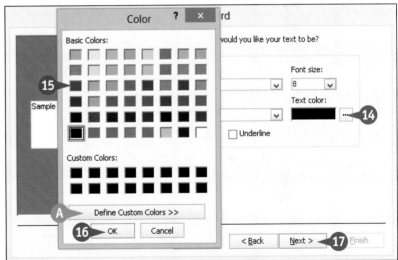

How can I create a custom label definition?

1 In the first screen of the Label Wizard, click **Customize** to open the New Label Size dialog box.

2 Click **New** to open the New Label dialog box.

3 Define the new label according to its size, type, and orientation.

4 Type a name for the new label definition.

5 Click **OK**.

6 Click **Close** in the New Label Size dialog box.

Create Labels (continued)

After choosing the size and formatting for the label, you set up the fields that should appear on it. These come from the table or query that you selected before you started the wizard. In most cases, these will include the fields that hold the recipient names as well as the recipient address data, including the street address, state or province, country, and zip or postal code.

You can also configure your labels to appear sorted on one or more fields.

Create Labels (continued)

The available fields page of the wizard appears.

18 Click a field and click **>** to move it to the Prototype Label list.

A You can click a line to move the insertion point into it.

19 Type any spaces or other punctuation that should separate the fields within a line.

20 Repeat steps **18** and **19** as needed to create the complete label.

21 Click **Next**.

The sort page appears.

22 Click a field by which you want to sort and click **>** to move it to the Sort By list.

23 Repeat step **22** to specify additional sorting if needed.

24 Click **Next**.

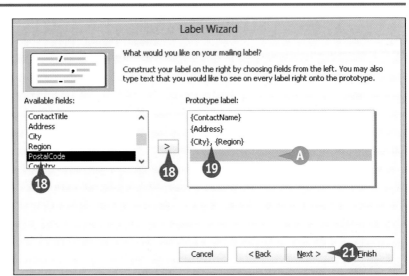

The name page appears.

25 Type a name for the label report.

26 Click **Finish**.

> **Label Wizard**
>
> What name would you like for your report?
>
> Customer Labels **◄ 25**
>
> That's all the information the wizard needs to create your labels!
>
> What do you want to do?
>
> ● See the labels as they will look printed.
>
> ○ Modify the label design.
>
> Cancel   < Back   Next **26** →   Finish

The report appears in Print Preview, ready to print on label paper.

> Customer Labels 1   ✕
>
> Alejandra Camino   Alexander Feuer   Ana Trujillo
> Gran Via, 1   Heerstr. 22   Avda. de la Constitución 2222
> Madrid,   Leipzig,   México D.F.,
> Spain 28001   Germany 04179   Mexico 05021
>
>
> Anabela Domingues   André Fonseca   Ann Devon
> Av. Inês de Castro, 414 Av. Brasil, 442   35 King George
> São Paulo, SP   Campinas, SP   London,
> Brazil 05634-030   Brazil 04876-786   UK WX3 6FW

TIPS

How can I change the font after the report has been generated?

Right-click the report's tab and then choose **Layout View** from the shortcut menu. Click the **Format** tab and then select the text that you want to format. Use the controls in the Font group to format the text.

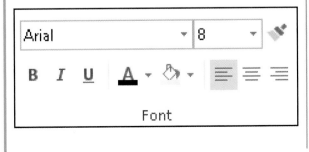

When I look at the labels in the Design view, the fields are enclosed in a =TRIM() **function. Why?**

The =TRIM() function removes extraneous spaces around entries. For example, if the City field's entry has several spaces after it and you do not use =TRIM(), those spaces will appear between the City and Region values on the label.

> ◢ Detail
>
> ContactName
> Address
> =Trim([City] & ", " & [Region])
> =Trim([Country] & " " & [PostalCode])

Add a Field to an Existing Line

As shown in the "Create Labels" section, you can configure a label to include multiple fields on a single line, such as a City field and a Region field. You can also separate such fields using commas and spaces. When you do this, the Label Wizard combines the fields and text into a single text box and encloses everything within a TRIM() function. If you want to add or remove a field within a line of the label, you must understand the syntax used to construct this function.

Syntax of the =TRIM() function

Syntax	Explanation
=Trim([City] & ", " & [Region])	This is an example of a complete =TRIM() function.
=Trim( )	The =TRIM() function trims off any excess blank spaces in the fields.
[City]	Field names appear in square brackets.
&	Fields are concatenated with an ampersand.
", "	Literal text or space is enclosed in quotation marks.

Additions to a =TRIM() function

To add another field within an existing =TRIM() function, you must make sure that the new field is enclosed in square brackets, separated from other fields by an ampersand (**&**) and separated from other fields with any literal text or punctuation marks in quotation marks.

So, to add the PostalCode field to the example shown here, you would change the function's code to **=Trim([City]& ", "&[Region]& " "&[PostalCode])**.

✦ Detail

ContactName
Address
=Trim([City] & ", " & [Region])
=Trim([Country] & " " & [PostalCode])

Add a Field to a Label As a Separate Line

In addition to adding a field to an existing =TRIM() function on a label, you can also add fields as separate text boxes on their own lines. For example, if you forgot to add an Address line, you could insert one in the Design view.

If the field will be by itself in its own text box, you do not have to use the =TRIM() function; you can simply add the field as you would on a form or on an ordinary report.

Add a Field to a Label As a Separate Line

1 In the Design view, drag the existing fields to make room for the new line, if necessary.

Note: To move a field, click on its border and then drag.

2 Click the **Design** tab.

3 Click **Controls**.

4 Click the Text Box button (ab|).

5 Click and drag to create a new text box where you want to place the field.

6 Type the field name in the new text box (if a single field).

Note: You can also type a **=Trim()** function to include multiple fields on the same line; see the section "Add a Field to an Existing Line" for more information.

The field name appears in the box.

Note: To delete a field, select it and then press Delete.

Color the Label Background

There are two ways to color a label background: You can color the overall background of the label, or you can color the individual text boxes in which the text appears.

When choosing a label background, make sure that the color does not clash with the color of the label text. For example, the default label text color is black, so any dark background will cause a problem. Either use a light color for the background or change the color of the label text, as described next in the "Color the Label Text" section.

Color the Label Background

1 In the Design view, click **Detail** to select the entire Detail section.

A You can also click an individual text box to select it.

2 Click the **Format** tab.

3 Click the Background Color and click a background color.

B You can click **Automatic** to revert to the default theme background color.

C You can click **Transparent** to use no background color.

D You can click **More Colors** to create a custom background color.

E Access applies the chosen background color to either the entire label or the individual text box.

F Fields on the label remain white by default; you can set their colors to Transparent if you prefer.

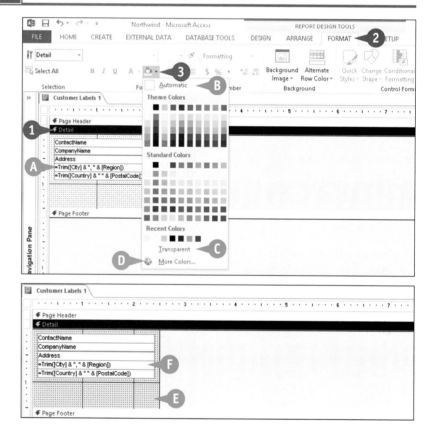

Color the Label Text

You can change the color of a label's text. This is especially useful after changing the label background color so that the text continues to contrast with the background for good visibility. For more, see the preceding section, "Color the Label Background."

Note that Access does not allow you to apply a different color to only part of the text in a text box; you must apply the new color to the entire text box.

Color the Label Text

1 In the Design view, select one or more text boxes containing the text that you want to color.

Note: You can select multiple text boxes by holding down **Shift** as you click each one. You can also drag a lasso around them.

2 Click the **Format** tab.

3 Click the Font Color ⌄ and click a text color.

Ⓐ You can click **Automatic** to revert to the default theme text color.

Ⓑ You can click **More Colors** to create a custom text color.

Ⓒ Access applies the chosen color to the text in the text box(es) that you selected.

Apply Font Formatting to the Label Text

You can change the font formatting for the label text in the same way in the Design view that you can using the Label Wizard — changing the font and size and applying bold, italic, and underline. You can also set the horizontal alignment — left-aligned, centered, or right-aligned — of the label text.

If you have spent some time getting the formatting of a label text box just right, you might want to apply the same formatting to another text box. Rather than start from scratch, you can copy formatting between text boxes with the Format Painter tool.

Apply Font Formatting to the Label Text

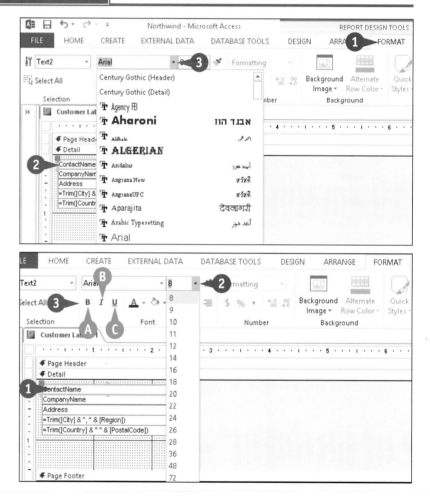

Change the Font

1 In the Design view, click the **Format** tab.

2 Select one or more text boxes for which you want to change the font.

3 Click the Font ⌄ and click the font that you want.

Access applies the font to the text.

Change the Font Size and Attributes

1 Select one or more text boxes that you want to format.

2 Click the Font Size ⌄ and click the size that you want.

Access resizes the text.

3 You can click one or more of these buttons to apply more attributes:

Ⓐ Bold (**B**)

Ⓑ Italic (*I*)

Ⓒ Underline (U)

Access applies the font attributes.

Change the Text Alignment

1 Select one or more text boxes with text you want to align.

2 Click one of the alignment buttons:

D Left (≡)

E Center (≡)

F Right (≡)

Access applies the alignment to the text.

Copy Formatting to Another Text Box

1 Select a text box that is already formatted the way you want.

2 Click the Format Painter button (✿).

3 Click the text box that you want to format.

Access copies the formatting to the second text box.

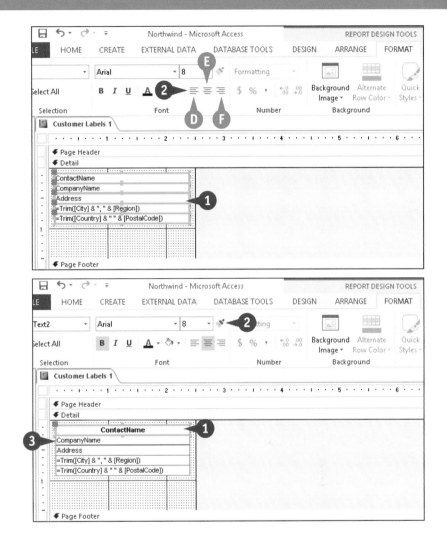

How can I format one field in a text box differently from the others?

You cannot. Font formatting is applied to the entire text box, not to individual characters. If you want a certain field to be formatted differently, place it in its own text box.

After I enlarged the font, the text appeared truncated. How can I fix this?

You may need to resize the text box to adjust for the larger font size. You can do this in one of the following ways: dragging a selection handle; double-clicking a selection handle; or right-clicking the text box, clicking **Size**, and then clicking **To Fit**. Keep in mind, however, that in the Design view, the text in the text boxes is the code to produce the label text, not the label text itself. Switch to the Layout view for a more realistic picture of whether the text on the labels will be truncated.

Export Labels to Word

You may prefer to print labels in Microsoft Word rather than Access because of the increased options that are available in Word for formatting. Also, Word has powerful tools for setting up printed pages, so by transferring your labels to Word you can take advantage of these tools.

You can use the Export Wizard to export the labels — or any other report — to a new Word document.

Export Labels to Word

1 Click the **External Data** tab.

2 In the Export group, click **More**.

3 Click **Word**.

The Export – RTF File Wizard opens.

4 Change the path and filename if needed.

A You can click **Browse** to choose a location.

5 Click here to open the file in Word after the export (☐ changes to ☑).

6 Click **OK**.

7 If you see a message about some data not being displayed, click **OK** to continue.

The final screen of the Export Wizard appears with a confirmation.

⑧ Click **Close**.

The labels open in Word.

Should I be worried about a message that warns that some data may not be displayed?

Not necessarily. In most cases, the results are fine when exported into Word. If needed, you can adjust margins, columns, and other formatting settings in Word after the export. For example, to adjust the margins in Word, click the **Page Layout** tab, click **Margins**, click **Custom Margins**, and then use the **Margins** tab of the Page Setup dialog box to set your new margins.

If I export the labels to Word frequently, do I have to repeat these steps each time?

No, you can save the export steps for easy recall later on. In the final screen of the Export Wizard, click **Save export steps** (☐ changes to ☑). This enables you to rerun the export later from Saved Exports on the External Data tab. See the section "Using Saved Import or Export Specifications" in Chapter 15 for more information.

CHAPTER 14

Performing a Mail Merge

One common use for a database is to store names and addresses of people to whom you send written correspondence. You can combine the capabilities of Access with those of a word-processing program, such as Microsoft Word, to easily produce hundreds or even thousands of personalized copies of a letter with a few simple mouse clicks.

Start a Mail Merge

You can begin a mail merge either from Access or from Word. In this chapter, you will learn how to do it from Access. Either way, you will work primarily in Word because that is where you set up the main document. The Access database serves as a passive supplier of data when the actual merge occurs.

The Mail Merge Wizard gives you the choice of creating a new Word document to serve as the main document or using an existing one. This chapter assumes that you will create a new Word document as part of the mail merge process.

Start a Mail Merge

1 Click the table that you want to use as a data source for the merge.

Note: Make sure that the table contains adequate fields to address a postal mailing. At the minimum, it should include the name, address, city, state, and zip code.

2 Click the **External Data** tab.

3 Click **Word Merge**.

The Microsoft Word Mail Merge Wizard opens.

4 Click **Create a new document and then link the data to it** (○ changes to ⦿).

5 Click **OK**.

Microsoft Word opens a new document and then opens the Mail Merge task pane.

6 Click **Letters** (○ changes to ⦿).

A You can click other document types if you prefer.

7 Click **Next: Starting document**.

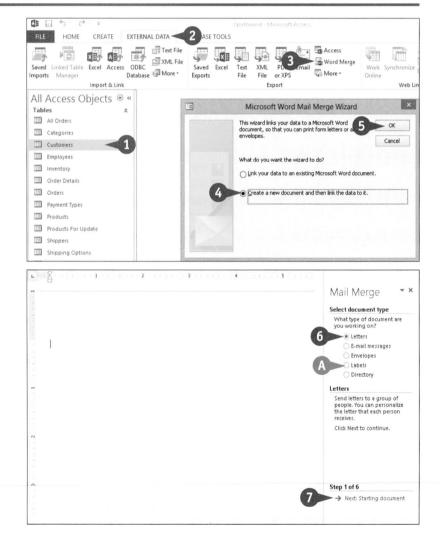

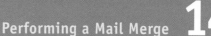
You are prompted to select a starting document.

8 Make sure that **Use the current document** is selected (○ changes to ◉).

9 Click **Next: Select recipients**.

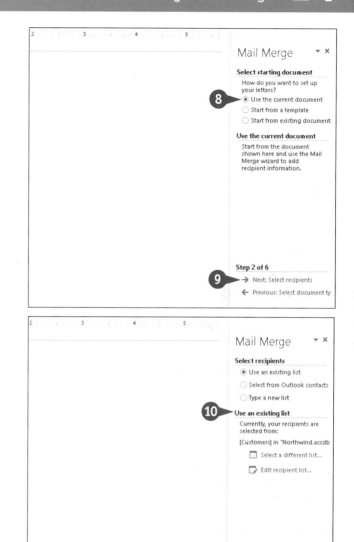

You are prompted to select recipients.

10 Leave the data source settings as they are.

Note: Because you started the merge from Access, the correct Access table is already selected.

11 Click **Next: Write your letter**.

The next set of options appears in the task pane.

Note: The rest of the sections in this chapter take you through the steps required to complete the mail merge.

Do I need to do anything special in Access to prepare the table to be used for mail merge?
If you are going to use the mail merge results for postal mailings, the table should include all the fields you need for that purpose: full name, address, city, state, and zip code. Otherwise, you will not be able to construct complete, usable addresses.

Do I have to use the Mail Merge Wizard?
No. You can use the commands on the Mailings tab in Word to manually set up a mail merge. This chapter does not cover those methods, but you can learn about them by using Help in Word.

Create the Main Document in Word

The main document is the one that contains all the parts of the letter that stay the same for each copy. For example, if you are writing a letter to customers, the main document will contain your return address, the message to the customers, and your signature line.

You can create all the text for the main document at once, or you can insert fields in the letter. Inserting fields is covered later in this chapter.

Create the Main Document in Word

1 Start the mail merge as described in the section "Start a Mail Merge."

2 In Word's Step **4** of **6** of the Mail Merge Wizard, type all the parts of the letter except those that should be personalized.

A Leave blanks where you will put the fields, such as the address and the greeting.

The letter is now ready for you to insert merge fields, which you will learn to do in the following sections.

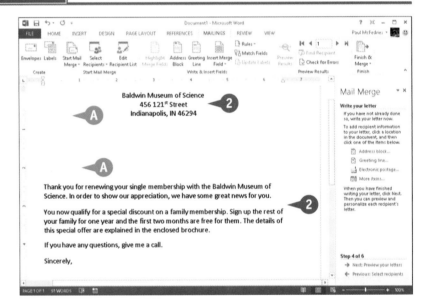

Insert an Address Block

If you have selected a table that contains all the elements needed to construct a mailing address block (name, address, city, state, and zip code), you can use the Address Block field code to automatically insert all the fields needed for the address in a single step. Word is able to determine which fields to use in most cases.

If the Address Block field code does not deliver the results you expect, you can instead insert the individual field codes, as covered later in this chapter.

Insert an Address Block

1 Perform the steps in the previous two sections.

2 In the main document, put the insertion point where the address block should be placed.

3 In the task pane, click **Address block**.

A Alternatively, click the **Mailings** tab and then click **Address Block**.

The Insert Address Block dialog box opens.

B You can choose a different format for the recipient's name.

C You can choose to include or omit the company name.

D You can see how the records from your database will appear in the letter.

Note: If the sample does not look right, see the later section "Match Fields" for help.

4 Click **OK**.

E An <<AddressBlock>> field code appears in the document.

Note: Field names in a main document are surrounded by double arrow brackets.

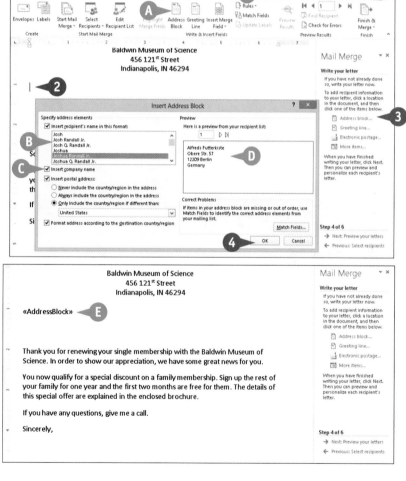

Insert a Greeting Line

A greeting line field code inserts a greeting, such as "Dear," along with one or more fields. If you want to greet the letter recipient with multiple fields, such as Prefix, First Name, and Last Name, using a greeting line field code is more efficient than inserting the individual fields one by one.

If the greeting line field code does not deliver the results you expect, you can instead insert the individual field codes, as covered later in this chapter.

Insert a Greeting Line

1 Perform the steps in the previous sections.

2 In the main document, put the insertion point where the greeting line should be placed.

3 In the task pane, click **Greeting line**.

A Alternatively, click the **Mailings** tab and then click **Greeting Line**.

The Insert Greeting Line dialog box opens.

4 Click this ☑ to choose a prefix type for the greeting.

5 Click this ☑ to choose how the name will appear.

6 Click this ☑ to choose what punctuation will follow the greeting.

7 Click this ☑ to choose a greeting to use if the record lacks the fields needed to construct a regular greeting.

B You can preview the greeting line here.

8 Click **OK**.

C Access adds a <<GreetingLine>> field code.

If Word is not able to correctly match up the fields from the database table to the right spots in the address block when you are inserting a greeting line, you can manually match up the fields yourself.

For example, if your Access table uses a field named *Region* for the state or province, Word might not recognize that field as a match for the State portion of the address block. In that case, you can tell Word that your Region field matches the State field in the address block.

Match Fields

1 Perform the steps in the previous sections.

2 In the Insert Address Block or Insert Greeting Line dialog box, click the **Match Fields** button.

A If neither of those dialog boxes is open, you can click the **Mailings** tab and then click **Match Fields** ( ).

The Match Fields dialog box opens.

3 Click to open the drop-down menu for a field placeholder and then select the corresponding field in the data source.

4 Repeat step **3** for each field that you need to match.

5 Click **OK**.

6 If you have either the Insert Address Block or Insert Greeting Line dialog box open, click **OK** to close it.

The fields are now matched as you have indicated.

Insert Individual Fields

In addition to creating an address block, you may also want to insert other fields from the database table. For example, after the address block, you might want to insert the person's phone number.

You can also insert individual field codes to create your own version of the address block instead of using the <<AddressBlock>> code. For example, you might want to create a custom address block that includes not only the standard address fields, but also the person's e-mail address and phone number.

Insert Individual Fields

1. Perform the steps in the previous sections.

2. Position the insertion point where you want the field code to be placed.

3. Click the **Mailings** tab.

4. Click the top half of the **Insert Merge Field** button.

Ⓐ You can also click **More items** in the task pane.

Ⓑ If you click the **Insert Merge Field** ▼ instead, a menu of available fields opens; you can click one of the fields there instead of using the dialog box.

The Insert Merge Field dialog box opens.

5. Click the field that you want to insert.

6. Click **Insert**.

Ⓒ Access inserts a field code.

7. Repeat steps **5** and **6** to insert other fields if needed.

Note: You may want to type some punctuation between steps **6** and **7** to separate the fields, such as a space between the first and last names.

8. Click **Close**.

Word returns you to the merge document.

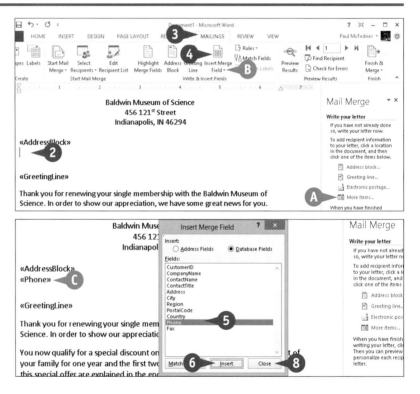

266

Preview the Merge Results

Before you print the mail merge, you might want to preview the merge on-screen to save paper in case there are problems that need correcting.

Word enables you to page through the records one at a time, examining each one to make sure that the addresses are valid and the fields are appropriately set up to display the right information. If you see a record that you do not want to include in the merge, you can exclude it.

Preview the Merge Results

1 Perform the steps in the previous sections.

2 In the Mail Merge task pane, click **Next: Preview your letters**.

«AddressBlock»
«Phone»

«GreetingLine»

Thank you for renewing your single membership with the Baldwin Museum of Science. In order to show our appreciation, we have some great news for you.

You now qualify for a special discount on a family membership. Sign up the rest of your family for one year and the first two months are free for them. The details of this special offer are explained in the enclosed brochure.

If you have any questions, give me a call.

Sincerely,

To add recipient information to your letter, click a location in the document, and then click one of the items below.

 Address block...
 Greeting line...
 Electronic postage...
 More items...

When you have finished writing your letter, click Next. Then you can preview and personalize each recipient's letter.

Step 4 of 6

→ Next: Preview your letters
← Previous: Select recipients

Ⓐ The document changes to show the first copy of the letter as it will appear when printed.

3 Click » to display the next record and then continue until you have checked all the records.

Ⓑ You can click **Exclude this recipient** to exclude a record that you did not intend to include.

Baldwin Museum of Science
456 121ˢᵗ Street
Indianapolis, IN 46294

Alfreds Futterkiste
Obere Str. 57
12209 Berlin
Germany
030-0074321

Dear Sir or Madam,

Mail Merge

Preview your letters

One of the merged letters is previewed here. To preview another letter, click one of the following:

<< Recipient: 1 >>

 Find a recipient...

Make changes

You can also change your recipient list:

 Edit recipient list...

Exclude this recipient

When you have finished

Filter the Recipient List

Besides excluding individual records, you can filter the recipient list more broadly by examining the entire list in a dialog box and then deselecting the recipients that you do not want to include in the mail merge.

You can also apply a filtering rule that automatically deselects certain recipients. For example, if you have an international list of recipients, you might want to filter the list to include only those recipients from a particular country.

Filter the Recipient List

Filter the Recipient List to Exclude Certain Records

1 Perform the steps in the previous sections.

2 Click the **Mailings** tab.

3 Click **Edit Recipient List**.

Ⓐ You can also click **Edit recipient list** in the task pane.

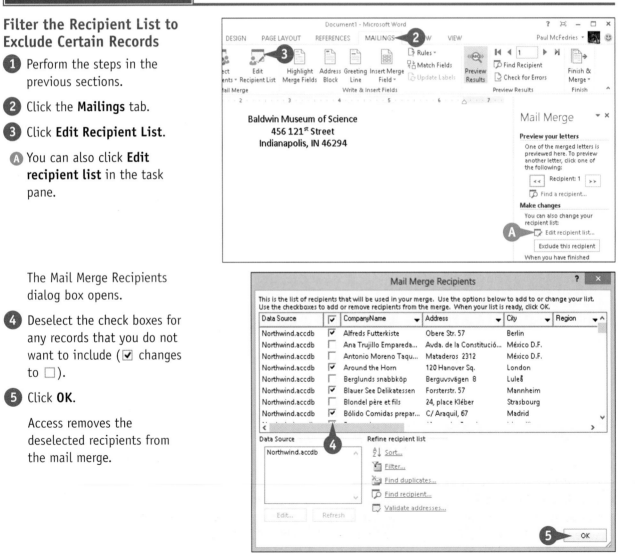

The Mail Merge Recipients dialog box opens.

4 Deselect the check boxes for any records that you do not want to include (☑ changes to ☐).

5 Click **OK**.

Access removes the deselected recipients from the mail merge.

Filter the Recipient List Based on Criteria

1 Perform the steps in the previous sections and then click **Edit Recipient List** on the **Mailings** tab.

2 In the Mail Merge Recipients dialog box, click **Filter**.

The Filter and Sort dialog box opens.

3 Click the **Filter Records** tab.

4 Click the **Field** ⌄ and click the field that you want to use.

5 Click the **Comparison** ⌄ and click an operator.

6 Type a comparison value.

B You can choose additional criteria on subsequent lines.

C You can click this ⌄ and click **And** to require all criteria for a record to be included; click **Or** to allow records that meet any of the criteria.

7 Click **OK**.

D The recipient list changes to show only records that match your criteria.

8 Click **OK**.

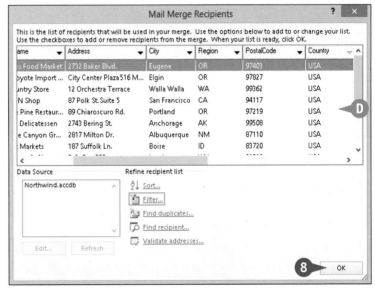

TIPS

How do I clear a filter?	Can I filter based on whether a particular field is blank or nonblank?
To clear the filter, click **Filter** again in the Mail Merge Recipients dialog box (which reopens the Filter and Sort dialog box) and then click **Clear All**.	Yes. In the Mail Merge Recipients dialog box, click the heading above the column by which you want to filter and then choose **(Blanks)** or **(Nonblanks)** from the menu that appears.

Sort the Recipient List

You might want the mail merge results to print in a certain order. For example, you might want them to be sorted by zip code, as is required for some mass-mailing services, or you might want them sorted by the recipient's last name to make it easier to file copies of the letters.

Whatever the reason, you can use the Mail Merge Recipients dialog box to sort the recipients based on any field in the table. You can sort the field in ascending or descending order.

Sort the Recipient List

1 Perform the steps in the previous sections.

2 Click the **Mailings** tab.

3 Click **Edit Recipient List**.

Ⓐ You can also click **Edit recipient list** in the task pane.

The Mail Merge Recipients dialog box opens.

4 Click the heading of the field by which you want to sort.

Word sorts the list by that field.

If you want to sort in reverse order, click the column heading again.

5 Click **OK**.

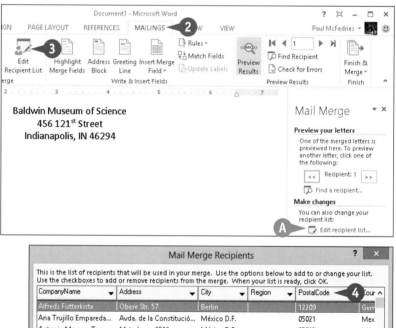

Merge to a New Document

Instead of merging directly to a printer, as described in the next section, you might prefer to merge to a new Word document. This means that instead of printing the letters, Word creates a new document and uses it to store all the letters.

This is useful if you do not have the printer available that you want to use. Similarly, you might need someone else to approve the letters before you send them. Either way, you can first merge them to a document and then print the letters later.

Merge to a New Document

1 Perform the steps in the previous sections.

2 Click the **Mailings** tab.

3 Click **Finish & Merge**.

4 Click **Edit Individual Documents**.

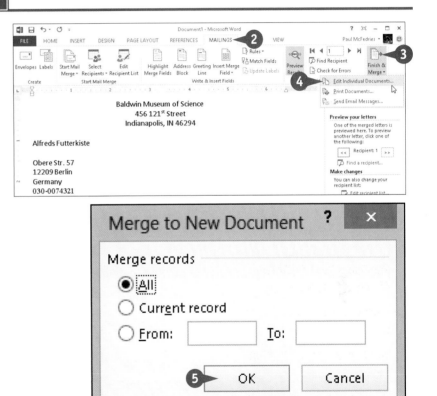

The Merge to New Document dialog box opens.

5 Click **OK**.

The letters appear in a new Word document. You can save it, print it, or discard it by closing it without saving your changes. You can also make changes to individual letters before printing.

Merge Directly to a Printer

If you have entered your merge field codes, filtered the records as needed, and previewed the merge results, you can be confident that the results of your merge are complete and accurate. In that case, you might want to merge directly to your printer. This is the easiest and quickest way to perform a merge, especially for a previously created merge that you are simply reprinting.

Windows uses whatever printer you set as the default unless you specify a different printer.

Merge Directly to a Printer

1 Perform the steps in the previous sections.

2 Click the **Mailings** tab.

3 Click **Finish & Merge**.

4 Click **Print Documents**.

The Merge to Printer dialog box opens.

5 Click **OK**.

The Print dialog box opens.

6 Change any print settings if needed.

Ⓐ You can change the printer here.

7 Click **OK**.

Word sends the letters to the printer.

Save the Merge for Later Use

aving the main document — that is, the merge document you have created in this chapter — is different from saving the results of a merge. When you save the main document, you can rerun the merge later. This might be useful if the records are likely to change. For example, you could have a mail merge for your Christmas letter and then rerun it every year based on your database of friends.

Save the Merge for Later Use

1 Perform the steps in the previous sections.

2 Click **File**.

The File options appear.

3 Click **Save As**.

You can also click the Save button (⊞) on the Quick Access Toolbar or press Ctrl + S.

4 Click **Computer**.

5 Click **Browse**.

The Save As dialog box opens.

6 Select a location.

7 Edit the filename as needed.

8 Click **Save**.

Word saves the file.

CHAPTER 15

Working with External Data

Access offers many powerful features for working with outside data. You can import data into Access from a variety of sources, including Excel, Outlook, other Access databases, text files, web pages, and XML files. You can also export Access data to other formats, including an Excel worksheet, a web page, and a text file.

Import an Excel Worksheet

You can import data from an Excel worksheet into Access to create a new table. This new table becomes a part of the Access database; it does not retain any ties to Excel.

For the best results, the Excel data should be database-oriented. That is, the data should be in a row-and-column format, with headings at the top of each column and sets of related data in each row. When the data is imported into Access, the column headings become the field names in the new table, and the rows become the records. Excel data that includes formulas and functions does not import well.

Import an Excel Worksheet

1. Click the **External Data** tab.

2. In the Import & Link group, click **Excel**.

   The Get External Data – Excel Spreadsheet dialog box opens.

3. In the **File name** field, type the path and filename for the Excel file.

A. You can click **Browse** to browse for the file if you prefer.

4. Click **Import the source data into a new table in the current database** (○ changes to ◉).

5. Click **OK**.

   The Import Spreadsheet Wizard opens.

6. Click **Show Worksheets** (○ changes to ◉).

7. Click the sheet that you want to import.

B. A preview of the data on that sheet appears.

8. Click **Next**.

9. If Excel displays a warning about field names, click **OK**.

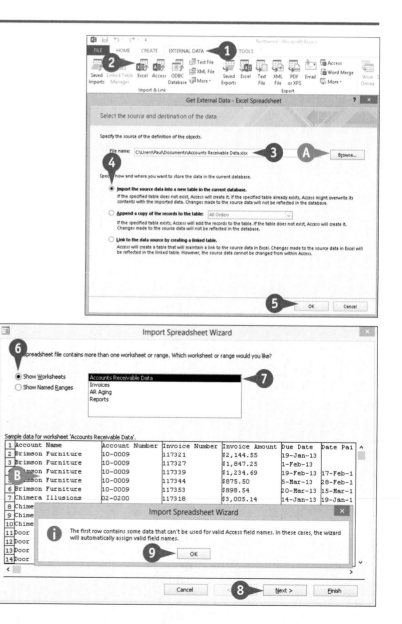

The column headings page of the wizard appears.

10 If the first row contains column headings, click **First Row Contains Column Headings** if it is not already selected (☐ changes to ☑).

11 Click **Next**.

The field options page appears.

12 Use the **Field Name** text box to edit the field name for the first field.

13 Click the **Data Type** ☑ and then click the data type that you want.

TIPS

How should I prepare the Excel worksheet before importing it?

For Excel data to import correctly into Access, it must be set up to mimic a datasheet in Access. Follow these guidelines in Excel:

- Place the field names in row 1.

- Remove any blank rows or titles above the field names.

- Place each record in a separate row, starting immediately below the row containing the field names.

- Do not include any formulas or functions. Omit cells containing them from the range to import or convert them to values.

Can I import only part of a worksheet?

Yes. In step **6**, you can alternatively click **Show Named Ranges** (○ changes to ●) and then click the named range that you want to import. However, you must set up the range in Excel first. To create a named range in Excel, follow these steps:

1 Select the range.

2 Click here and type a name for the range.

3 Press Enter.

Import an Excel Worksheet (continued)

The Import Spreadsheet Wizard asks you about several setup options that you would ordinarily configure when creating a new table, such as whether fields should be indexed and whether duplicates are okay.

The Import Spreadsheet Wizard also gives you the opportunity to set a primary key and to name the table. In each case, you can proceed just as though you were creating an Access table from scratch.

Import an Excel Worksheet (continued)

14 Click the **Indexed** ☑ and then choose whether the field should be indexed and whether duplicates are okay.

Ⓐ You can click **Do not import field (Skip)** (☐ changes to ☑) to exclude a field from being imported.

15 Click the next column and then repeat steps **12** to **14**.

16 When you have set up all the fields, click **Next**.

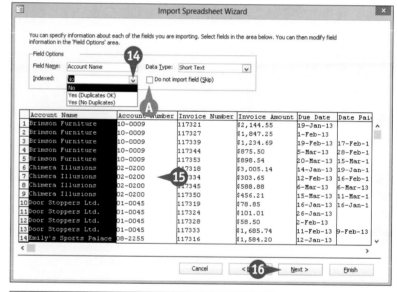

The primary key page appears.

17 If the imported data contains a field that you want to use as the primary key, click **Choose my own primary key**, click ☑, and choose that field.

Ⓑ You can click **Let Access add primary key** to allow the wizard to create a new field to be used as a primary key.

Ⓒ You can click **No primary key** to decline to use a primary key in the table.

18 Click **Next**.

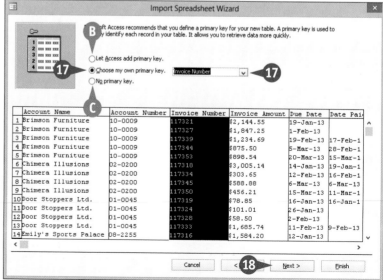

The table name page appears.

19 Type the name for the table.

Note: The default name is the name of the tab from the worksheet.

20 Click **Finish**.

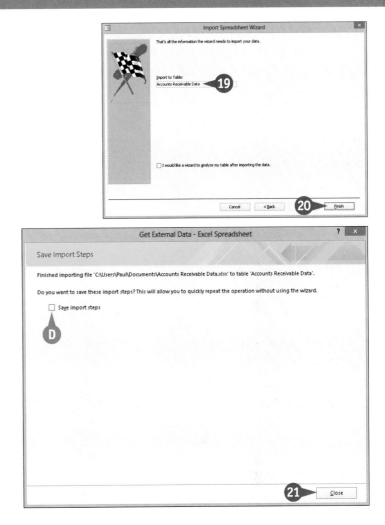

You are returned to the Get External Data – Excel Spreadsheet dialog box.

D You can save the import steps by clicking **Save import steps** (☐ changes to ☑).

Note: You will learn more about saving import steps later in this chapter.

21 Click **Close**.

Access imports the Excel data as a new table in the Objects list.

TIPS

Should I allow the wizard to create a primary key field?

It depends on whether you already have a field in the data that contains unique entries for each record and that will always contain unique entries. If you do, make that one the primary key. However, if you do not have any fields that fit that description, you should allow the wizard to create one for you.

Should I save the import specifications?

If you plan on doing this same import again later, then yes. For example, suppose that you have a table that a colleague maintains in Excel, and every month, you have to use it in Access. You could save the import settings to make it easier to import that file in the future. An even better approach, though, would be to link to the worksheet, as covered in the following section, "Link to an Excel Worksheet."

Link to an Excel Worksheet

If you frequently need to reimport the same data from Excel, you can save time and effort by linking to that worksheet instead of repeatedly reimporting it.

When you set up a link to an Excel worksheet, the data is always up to date. Each time that you use Access to open the linked worksheet, Access refreshes the link to the data. This means, however, that the Excel file must always be in its original location or an error will occur.

Link to an Excel Worksheet

1 Click the **External Data** tab.

2 In the Import & Link group, click **Excel**.

The Get External Data – Excel Spreadsheet dialog box opens.

3 In the **File name** field, type the path and filename for the Excel file.

A You can click **Browse** to browse for the file if you prefer.

4 Click **Link to the data source by creating a linked table** (○ changes to ◉).

5 Click **OK**.

The Link Spreadsheet Wizard opens.

6 Click **Show Worksheets** (○ changes to ◉).

7 Click the sheet to which you want to link.

B A preview of the data on that sheet appears.

8 Click **Next**.

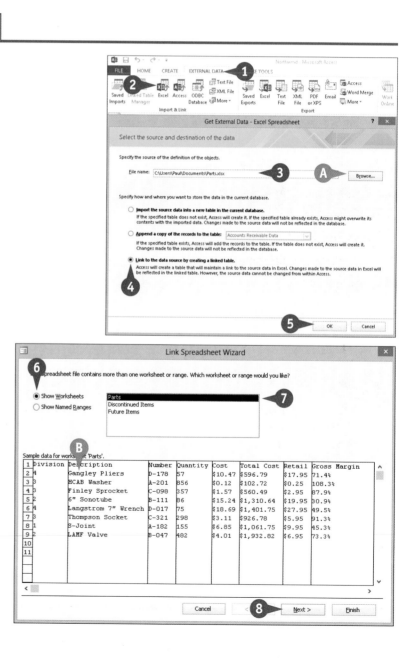

280

The column headings page of the wizard appears.

9 If the first row contains column headings, click **First Row Contains Column Headings** (☐ changes to ☑).

10 Click **Next**.

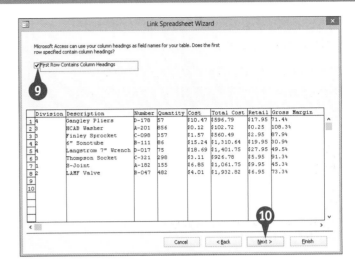

The table name page appears.

11 Type a name for the linked table.

Note: This will be the name that appears in the list of tables.

12 Click **Finish**.

A confirmation dialog box appears.

13 Click **OK**.

The linked table appears in the Objects list in the Tables category.

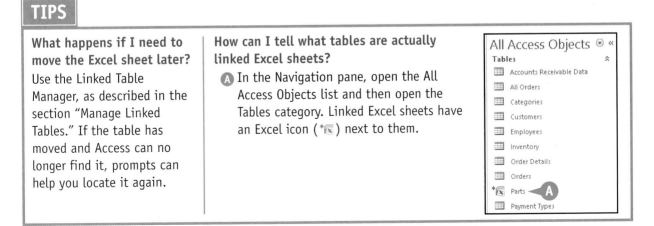

What happens if I need to move the Excel sheet later?
Use the Linked Table Manager, as described in the section "Manage Linked Tables." If the table has moved and Access can no longer find it, prompts can help you locate it again.

How can I tell what tables are actually linked Excel sheets?
Ⓐ In the Navigation pane, open the All Access Objects list and then open the Tables category. Linked Excel sheets have an Excel icon (⁺🅧) next to them.

All Access Objects ⊙ «
Tables ⌃
▦ Accounts Receivable Data
▦ All Orders
▦ Categories
▦ Customers
▦ Employees
▦ Inventory
▦ Order Details
▦ Orders
⁺🅧 Parts ⟵Ⓐ
▦ Payment Types

Link to an Outlook Folder

If you use Microsoft Outlook as your main contact management program, there may be times when you want to use the Outlook Contacts list as a data source in Access. For example, if you store your customer information in Outlook, you may want to link certain orders or invoices to customers there. You can do this by using Access to set up a link to an Outlook folder. As when you create a link to an Excel worksheet, a link to an Outlook folder creates a new Access table that always contains up-to-date information from Outlook.

Link to an Outlook Folder

① Click the **External Data** tab.

② In the Import & Link group, click **More**.

③ Click **Outlook Folder**.

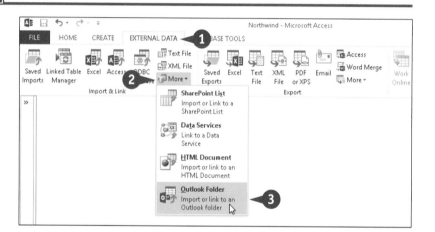

The Get External Data – Outlook Folder dialog box opens.

④ Click **Link to the data source by creating a linked table** (○ changes to ◉).

⑤ Click **OK**.

The Import Exchange/
Outlook Wizard opens.

6 Click ⊞ to expand the
available categories and then
click the Outlook folder that
you want.

7 Click **Next**.

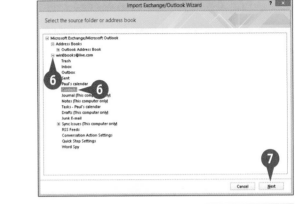

The table name page appears.

8 If needed, change the default
name for the linked table.

9 Click **Finish**.

A dialog box opens, saying
that linking to the table is
finished.

10 Click **OK**.

The link is complete, and the
new linked table appears in
the Tables category of the
Objects list.

**Can I import the data from Outlook
rather than linking it?**
Yes. It works very much like importing data
from Excel. In step 4, click **Import the
source data into a new table in the
current database** (○ changes to ◉). Keep
in mind, however, that if you import data,
any future changes you make to the data in
Outlook will not be reflected in Access.

**What are the Address Books listed in the Outlook folders
list in step 6?**
Outlook has an Address Book utility that interfaces with your
Contacts list and also optionally interfaces with other data
sources, such as an employee directory on a file server or a
mobile address book from a handheld device. You can link to
one of these sources instead of Contacts if you prefer. Be
cautious, though, about linking to an address book stored on
a mobile device that might not always be available.

Manage Linked Tables

One of the biggest advantages of setting up a table that is linked to an Excel worksheet or an Outlook folder is that Access automatically displays the most recent data when you open the linked table. That is fine if you just have one or two linked tables, but if your database has a large number of linked tables, it can be time-consuming to open each one just to make sure that you have the latest data. A better way to update multiple linked tables at once without having to open each one is to use the Linked Table Manager.

Manage Linked Tables

1 Click the **External Data** tab.

2 In the Import & Link group, click **Linked Table Manager**.

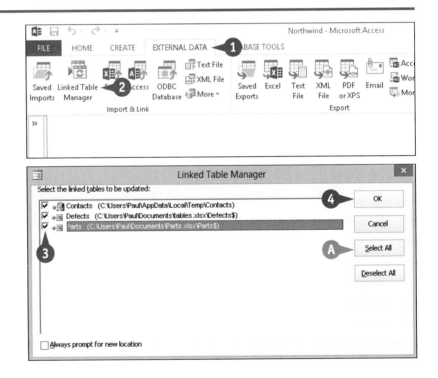

The Linked Table Manager opens.

3 Click the check box for each linked table that you want to update (☐ changes to ☑).

Ⓐ You can also click **Select All**.

4 Click **OK**.

If a linked table cannot be located, a Select New Location dialog box opens.

If Access finds the linked table, you can skip to step **8**.

5 Select the new location of the file.

6 Click the file.

7 Click **Open**.

You may have to repeat steps **5** to **7** for additional tables.

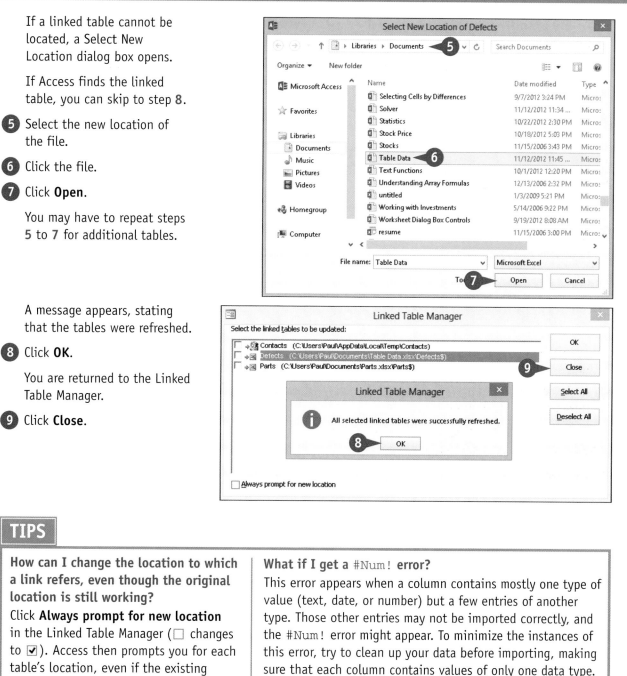

A message appears, stating that the tables were refreshed.

8 Click **OK**.

You are returned to the Linked Table Manager.

9 Click **Close**.

TIPS

How can I change the location to which a link refers, even though the original location is still working?

Click **Always prompt for new location** in the Linked Table Manager (□ changes to ☑). Access then prompts you for each table's location, even if the existing location is still working.

What if I get a #Num! **error?**

This error appears when a column contains mostly one type of value (text, date, or number) but a few entries of another type. Those other entries may not be imported correctly, and the #Num! error might appear. To minimize the instances of this error, try to clean up your data before importing, making sure that each column contains values of only one data type. Formatting the columns in the Excel file with a particular numeric type also helps.

Import a Table from Another Access Database

You may find that another Access database has data that you require in the current Access database. For example, the other database might have a table that contains information that would be useful in your current database. In that case, you can import the table from the other database into the current database.

You can also import other Access database objects, including queries, forms, and reports, but the destination database must have the needed tables and queries on which they are based.

Import a Table from Another Access Database

1 Click the **External Data** tab.

2 In the Import & Link group, click **Access**.

The Get External Data – Access Database dialog box opens.

3 In the **File name** field, type the path and filename for the Access file.

Ⓐ You can click **Browse** to browse for the file if you prefer.

4 Click **Import tables, queries, forms, reports, macros, and modules into the current database** (○ changes to ●).

5 Click **OK**.

The Import Objects dialog box opens.

6 Click **Options**.

The Import options appear at the bottom of the dialog box.

7 Click the tables that you want to import.

Ⓑ For each table or query, you can optionally click **Definition only** (○ changes to ●) to import only the table structure, not the data.

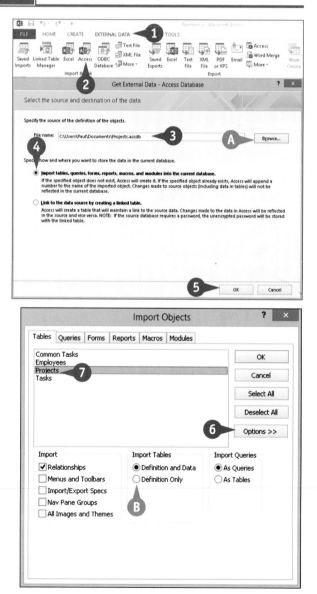

286

8 Click the **Queries** tab.

9 Click any queries that you want to import.

10 If you selected any queries, click how you want them to be imported.

C You can click other tabs and select any other objects that you want.

11 Click **OK**.

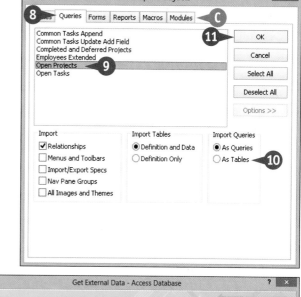

The Save Import Steps screen appears.

D You can save the import steps by clicking **Save import steps** (☐ changes to ☑).

Note: You will learn more about saving import steps later in this chapter.

12 Click **Close**.

Access imports the objects into the database.

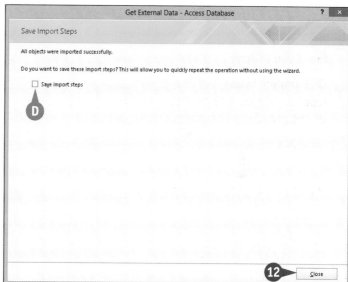

TIPS

What is the difference between importing a query as a table and importing it as a query?
Importing a query as a table creates a new table with a datasheet that includes the query's results. Any records or fields the query definition excludes are excluded. Importing a query as a query imports just the query definition. The database must have a table of the same name as the one the query uses, with compatible fields.

Can I link to content from another Access database?
Yes. In the Get External Data – Access Database dialog box, click **Link to the data source by creating a linked table** (○ changes to ●).

Import Data from a Delimited Text File

Nowadays, most data resides in some kind of special format: database object, XML file, Excel workbook, and so on. However, it is still relatively common to find data stored in simple text files because text is a universal format that users can work with on any system and in a wide variety of programs. You can analyze the data contained in certain text files by importing the data into an Access table.

Note, however, that you cannot import just any text file into Access. Instead, you can only import *delimited* or *fixed-width* text files. See the first Tip in this section to learn more.

Import Data from a Delimited Text File

1. Click the **External Data** tab.

2. Click **Text File**.

   The Get External Data – Text File dialog box opens.

3. In the **File name** field, type the path and filename of the text file.

   Ⓐ You can click **Browse** to browse for the file.

4. Click **Import the source data into a new table in the current database** (○ changes to ◉).

5. Click **OK**.

   The Import Text Wizard opens.

6. Click **Delimited** (○ changes to ◉).

   Ⓑ If you are importing a fixed-width text file, click **Fixed Width** (○ changes to ◉) instead.

   Note: Because fixed-width text files are relatively rare, they are not covered in this section.

7. Click **Next**.

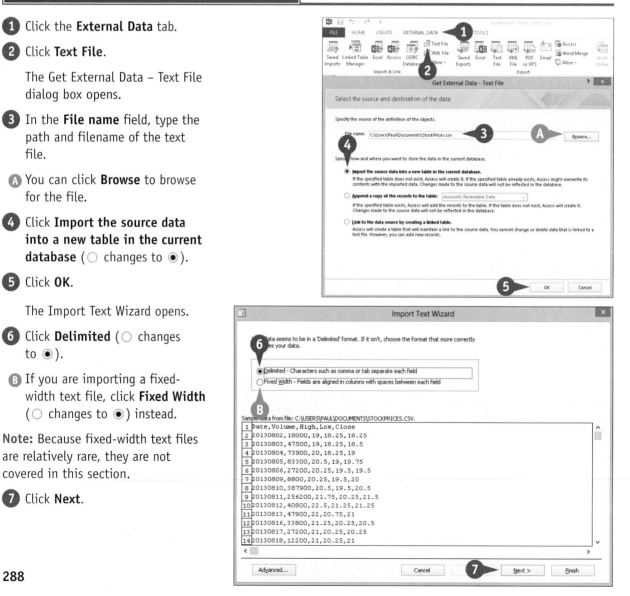

The delimiter character page of the wizard appears.

8 Click the delimiter used in the file (○ changes to ◉).

C You know that you have chosen the correct delimiter when the data appears in orderly rows and columns in the sample area.

9 Click **First Row Contains Field Names** (☐ changes to ☑) if the first row contains the field names.

10 Click **Next**.

The field options page appears.

11 Click a field to select it.

12 Change the field name if needed.

Note: If the first row does not contain field names, field names are generic and should be changed in step **12**.

13 Click the **Data Type** ⌄ and click the data type if needed.

14 Repeat steps **11** to **13** for each field that you want to change.

TIP

What are delimited and fixed-width text files?

A *delimited* text file uses a text structure in which each item on a line of text is separated by a character called a *delimiter*. The most common text delimiter is the comma (,). A delimited text file is imported into Access by treating each line of text as a record and each item between the delimiter as a field.

A *fixed-width* text file uses a text structure in which all the items on a line of text use a set amount of space — say, 10 characters or 20 characters — and these fixed widths are the same on every line of text. A fixed-width text file is imported into Access by treating each line of text as a record and each fixed-width item as a field.

continued ▶

xcept for the beginning part of the process, the steps for importing data from a delimited text file are nearly identical to those for importing data from an Excel file, as described earlier in the "Import an Excel Worksheet" section. That is, you can choose which fields if any should be indexed; you can choose to skip certain fields that you do not need; and you can specify a primary key or let Access create one for you. In each case, you can proceed just as though you were creating an Access table from scratch.

Import Data from a Delimited Text File (continued)

15 Click the **Indexed** ⌄ and click the indexing setting if needed.

Ⓐ If you choose **Yes (No Duplicates)**, make sure that each record has a unique entry for this field; otherwise, an error will occur at import.

Ⓑ You can click **Do not import field (Skip)** (☐ changes to ☑) to skip a field.

16 Repeat step **15** for each field.

17 Click **Next**.

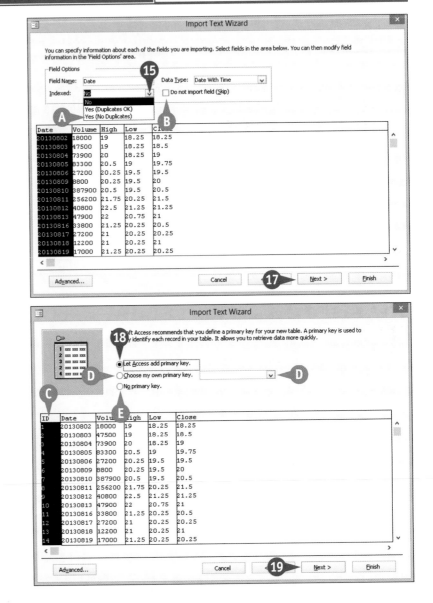

The primary key page appears.

18 Click **Let Access add primary key** (○ changes to ●).

Ⓒ Access adds an ID field as the primary key.

Ⓓ You can also click **Choose my own primary key** (○ changes to ●) and then choose a field from the drop-down menu.

Ⓔ You can also click **No primary key** (○ changes to ●).

19 Click **Next**.

The table name page appears.

20 Type the name to use for the imported table.

21 Click **Finish**.

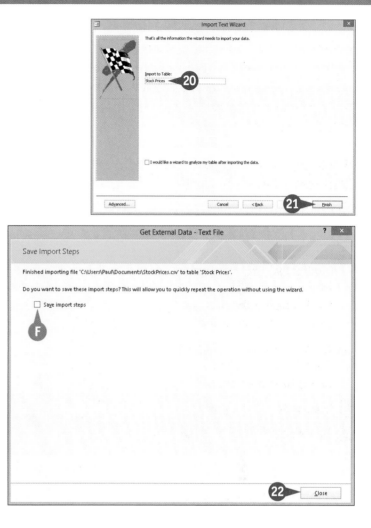

The Save Import Steps screen appears.

F You can click **Save import steps** (☐ changes to ☑) to save the import, as described later in this chapter.

22 Click **Close**.

Access imports the data into a new table with the name that you specified.

TIPS

My text file includes dates such as 20130823 (for August 23, 2013). Will this data import correctly?

Not unless you tell Access that the date field uses this specific date format. Before you click **Next** in step **17**, click **Advanced** to open the Import Specification dialog box. Click the **Date Order** ⌄ and then click **YMD** for Year Month Day order. Delete the character in the **Date Delimited** text box and then click **OK**.

Do I have to specify field names in order to import data if the data file does not already have field names in the first row?

No. But generic field names will be used (Field1, Field2) in the imported table. You can then use the Table Design view to modify the field names. Make sure that you change the field names to names that are more meaningful before you start using the imported table as the basis for other objects such as queries, forms, and reports.

Import Data from a Web Page

ata is often available on web pages. Although this data is usually text, some web page data comes as either a table (a rectangular array of rows and columns) or as preformatted text (text that has been structured with a predefined spacing used to organize data into columns with fixed widths).

Both types are suitable for import into Access so that you can perform more extensive data analysis. To import web page data, the file must reside on your computer or on your network.

Import Data from a Web Page

1 Click the **External Data** tab.

2 In the Import & Link group, click **More**.

3 Click **HTML Document**.

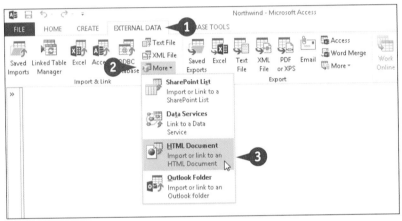

The Get External Data - HTML Document dialog box appears.

4 In the **File name** field, type the path and filename of the web page file.

Ⓐ You can click **Browse** to browse for the file.

5 Click **Import the source data into a new table in the current database** (○ changes to ◉).

6 Click **OK**.

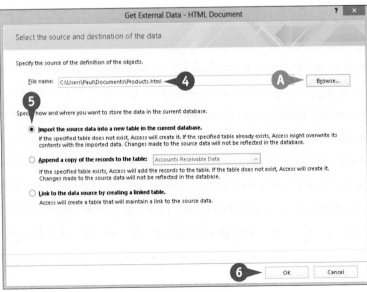

The Import HTML Wizard appears.

⑦ If your web page data contains column headings, click **First Row Contains Column Headings** (□ changes to ☑).

⑧ Click **Next**.

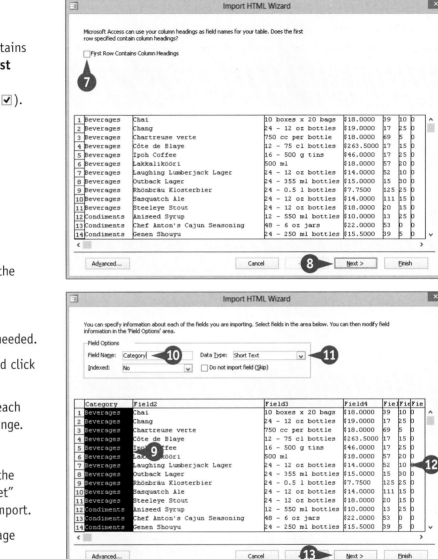

The field options page of the wizard appears.

⑨ Click a field.

⑩ Change the field name if needed.

⑪ Click the **Data Type** ☑ and click the data type if needed.

⑫ Repeat steps **9** to **11** for each field that you want to change.

⑬ Click **Next**.

⑭ Follow steps **17** to **21** in the "Import an Excel Worksheet" section to complete the import.

Access imports the web page data to a table.

TIP

How can I append records to an existing table from a web page?
On the initial Get External Data – HTML Document screen, click **Append a copy of the records to the table** (○ changes to ⦿) and then click the ☑ to select the table to which you want the web page data appended. For this to work, the table must have the same fields, with the same field types, as the data you are importing.

⦿ Append a copy of the records to the table:	Products	☑

If the specified table exists, Access will add the records to the table. If the table does not exist, Access will create it.
Changes made to the source data will not be reflected in the database.

Import Data from an XML File

You can analyze data that currently resides in XML format by importing that data into Access and then manipulating and analyzing the resulting table.

XML (extensible markup language) is a standard that enables the management and sharing of structured data using simple text files. These XML files organize data using *tags,* among other elements, that specify the equivalent of a table name and field names. Because XML is just text, if you want to perform data analysis on the XML file, you must import the XML file into an Access table.

Import Data from an XML File

1 Click the **External Data** tab.

2 In the Import & Link group, click **XML File**.

The Get External Data - XML File dialog box appears.

3 In the **File name** field, type the path and filename of the XML file.

Ⓐ You can click **Browse** to browse for the file.

4 Click **OK**.

The Import XML dialog box appears.

5 Click **Structure and Data** (◯ changes to ◉).

6 Click **OK**.

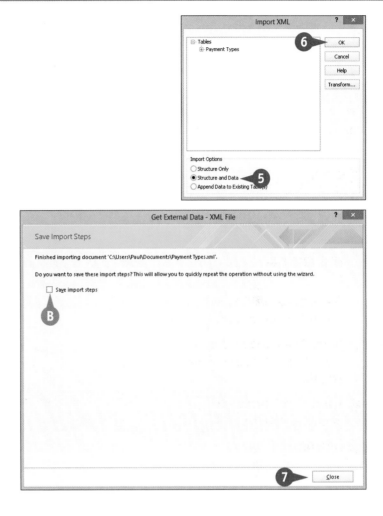

The Save Import Steps screen appears.

Ⓑ You can click **Save import steps** (☐ changes to ☑) to save the import, as described later in the chapter.

7 Click **Close**.

Access imports the XML data into a new table.

TIPS

What does an XML file look like?

An XML file is a text file that uses a specific structure. Here is a simple XML example that constitutes a single record in a table named *Products:*

```
<Products>
<ProductName>Chai</ProductName>
<CompanyName>Exotic Liquids</CompanyName>
<ContactName>Charlotte Cooper</ContactName>
</Products>
```

Can I add the XML data to an existing table rather than create a new table?

Yes. To do so, in the Import XML dialog box, click **Append Data to Existing Table(s)** (◯ changes to ◉).

Export Data to Excel

The section "Import an Excel Worksheet," earlier in this chapter, shows how to import data from Excel to an Access table. You can also perform the opposite task: export data from Access to Excel.

When you export Access data to Excel, Access creates a new Excel workbook file. As part of the export process, you can choose the format of that file. This depends on whether you will be sharing the workbook with other people. In most cases, the Excel Workbook format is best. However, you can also choose a format that is compatible with Excel versions prior to Excel 2007.

Export Data to Excel

1 Click the table that you want to export.

2 Click the **External Data** tab.

3 In the Export group, click **Excel**.

The Export – Excel Spreadsheet dialog box opens.

4 In the **File name** field, type the destination path and filename for the file to be exported.

Ⓐ You can click **Browse** to locate a file or folder if you prefer.

5 Click the **File format** and click the Excel format.

Ⓑ You can click **Export data with formatting and layout** (☐ changes to ☑) to export formatting and layout as well as data.

6 Click **OK**.

The Save Export Steps page appears.

Ⓒ You can optionally click **Save export steps** (☐ changes to ☑) to save these export steps for later use.

7 Click **Close**.

Access completes the export.

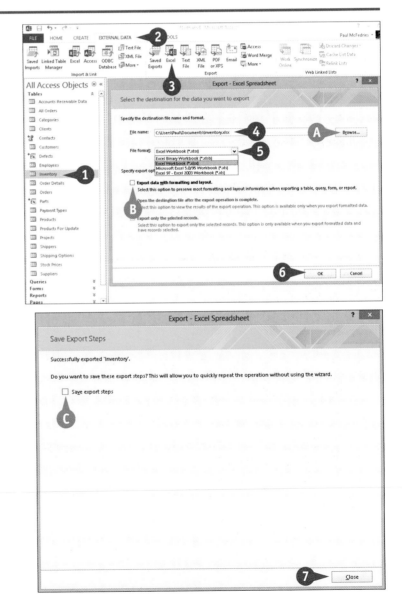

Export Data As HTML

One way to share data with others is to export it to a web page — that is, to the HTML format. *HTML* is short for *hypertext markup language,* the standard language used to create web pages. You normally need to know the HTML code to create a web page from scratch, but Access makes it easy to export your data to an HTML file that is ready to share on the web.

There are more complex ways of making Access data available online, but for simple sharing in which the data is static, exporting to an HTML page is the easiest method.

Export Data As HTML

1 Click the table to be exported.

2 Click the **External Data** tab.

3 In the Export group, click **More**.

4 Click **HTML Document**.

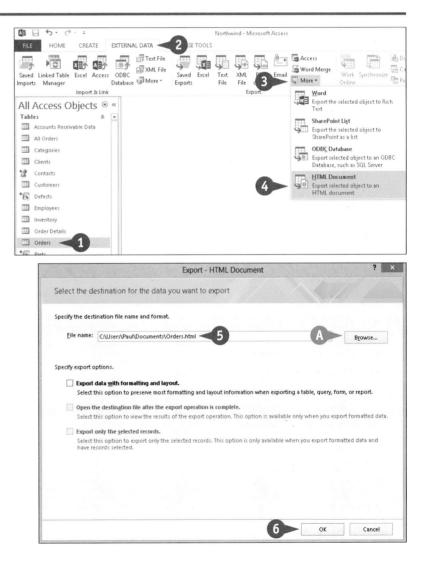

The Export – HTML Document dialog box opens.

5 In the **File name** field, type the destination path and filename for the file to be exported.

Ⓐ You can click **Browse** to locate a file or folder if you prefer.

6 Click **OK**.

The Save Export Steps dialog box opens.

7 Click **Close**.

Access completes the export.

Export Data to a Plain Text File

You may come across situations in which exporting Access data to an Excel workbook or a web page is not possible because the person you want to share the data with cannot use those exported files. For example, the other person might be using a database program that does not accept Excel or any of the other formats available to you. In such cases, exporting your Access data to a plain text file may be your only option.

Plain text exports can be delimited by characters such as commas or tabs or, less frequently, set to be fixed-width.

Export Data to a Plain Text File

1 Click the table to be exported.

2 Click the **External Data** tab.

3 In the Export group, click **Text File**.

The Export – Text File dialog box opens.

4 In the **File name** field, type the destination path and filename for the file to be exported.

Ⓐ You can click **Browse** to locate a file or folder if you prefer.

5 Click **OK**.

The Export Text Wizard opens.

6 Click **Delimited** (○ changes to ◉).

Note: It is unusual to do a Fixed Width export; most database programs can import delimited data.

7 Click **Next**.

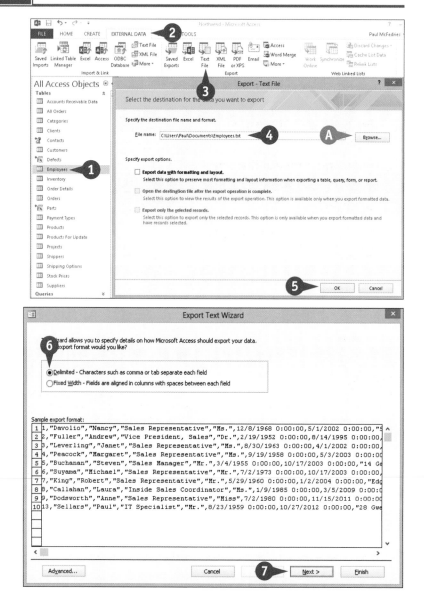

The delimiter character page of the wizard appears.

⑧ Click the delimiter that you want to use (○ changes to ●).

⑨ Click **Include Field Names on First Row** (□ changes to ☑) if you want to include the field names on the first row.

⑩ Click **Next**.

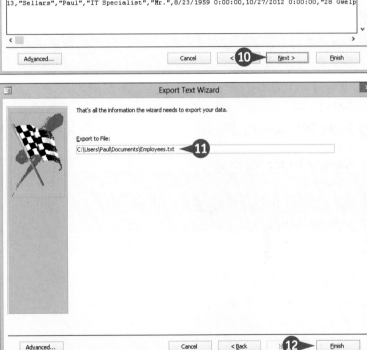

The final page of the wizard appears.

⑪ Confirm the path and filename for the file you want to export.

⑫ Click **Finish**.

The Save Export Steps dialog box opens.

⑬ Click **Close**.

Access completes the export.

When should I use the Export Data with Formatting and Layout option?
Use this when you want to include helper characters in certain types of data, such as parentheses and dashes in phone numbers or dashes in a nine-digit zip code. If you choose this option, the rest of the steps in the process are different (just follow the prompts), and the result is a fixed-width file rather than a delimited one.

How can I change field names as I export?
After step **5**, click **Advanced** to open the Export Specification dialog box. From there, you can change field names, change the delimiter character, and more. To change one of the field names, double-click it in the **Field Information** area and then type a new name.

Save Import or Export Specifications

The last step of every import or export process is a dialog box in which you can optionally click a check box to save the import or export steps. In this section, you see what happens when you do so.

If you often perform a particular import or export operation, it can be time-consuming to repeat those steps over and over. You can reduce time and effort by saving the steps. This enables you to perform the import or export operation in the future with just a few mouse clicks, as described in the next section, "Using Saved Import or Export Specifications."

Save Import or Export Specifications

1 Perform an import or export, as shown earlier in this chapter.

2 On the Save Export (or Import) Steps screen of the operation, click **Save export steps** (or **Save import steps**) (☐ changes to ☑).

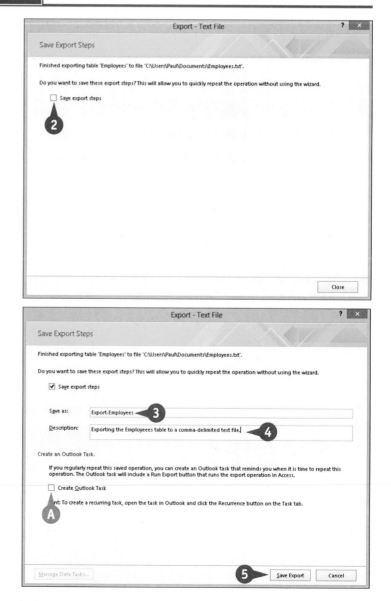

Additional text boxes appear in the dialog box.

3 Type a name for the saved settings.

4 Type a description.

A You can click **Create Outlook Task** (☐ changes to ☑) to create an Outlook task to remind you of this activity.

5 Click **Save Export** (or **Save Import**).

Access saves the operation's steps.

If you chose to create an Outlook task, the task opens in Outlook.

Using Saved Import or Export Specifications

After you have saved an import or export specification, as described in the previous section, "Save Import or Export Specifications," you can easily recall it. This enables you to run the entire import or export operation with just a few mouse clicks.

This saves you a great deal of time because saved settings perform an import or export by using the same source data and destination location that you specified when you originally ran the import or export. The saved steps also include all the same settings, file formats, and other specifications that you chose in the original import or export.

Using Saved Import or Export Specifications

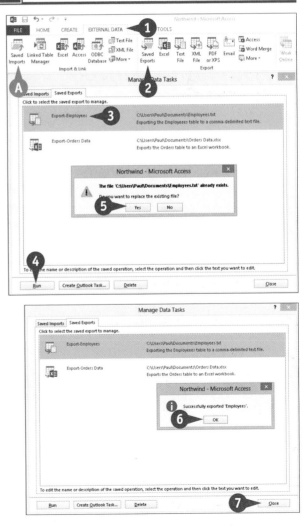

1 Click the **External Data** tab.

2 Click **Saved Exports**.

A For an import, you would click **Saved Imports**.

The Manage Data Tasks dialog box opens.

3 Click the export or import that you want to use.

4 Click **Run**.

The export or import is run.

If the file still exists from a previous export or import, a warning appears.

5 Click **Yes** to replace the previously exported or imported file.

A message appears, saying that the file has been exported or imported.

6 Click **OK**.

7 Click **Close**.

Note: The saved settings are saved in the Documents folder for the current user.

Analyze Access Data Using an Excel PivotTable

Access tables can contain thousands of records. Analyzing that much data can be a nightmare without the right kinds of tools. You have seen that Access offers some analysis tools such as grouping and sorting, but its selection of data analysis features is limited. However, Excel offers a powerful data analysis tool called a *PivotTable*. This tool enables you to summarize thousands of records in a concise tabular format. You can then manipulate the layout of — or *pivot* — the table to see different views of your data. If you have exported Access data to Excel, you can create a PivotTable from that data.

Analyze Access Data Using an Excel PivotTable

1 In Excel, open the workbook that contains the exported Access data.

2 Click a cell within the range that you want to use as the source data.

3 Click the **Insert** tab.

4 Click **PivotTable**.

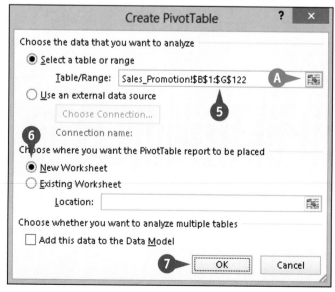

The Create PivotTable dialog box appears.

5 Make sure that the displayed range address is correct.

A If the range address is incorrect, click here and then click and drag with your mouse to select the range.

6 Click **New Worksheet** (○ changes to ◉).

7 Click **OK**.

B Excel creates a blank PivotTable.

C Excel displays the PivotTable Fields list.

8 Click and drag a field and drop it inside the ROWS box.

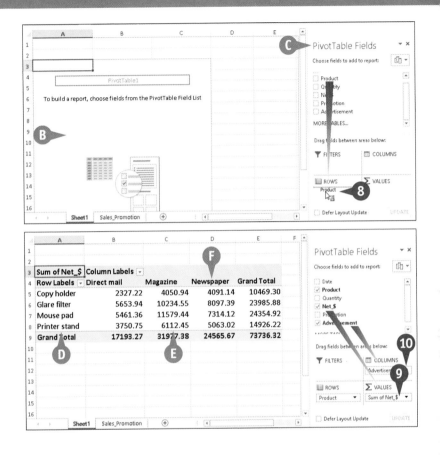

D Excel adds the field's unique values to the PivotTable's row area.

9 Click and drag a numeric field and drop it inside the VALUES box.

E Excel sums the numeric values based on the row values.

10 Click and drag a field and drop it in the COLUMNS box.

F Excel adds the field's unique values to the PivotTable's column area.

TIPS

Are there faster ways to build a PivotTable?
Yes. In the PivotTable Fields list, if you click a check box for a text or date field (☐ changes to ☑), Excel adds the field to the ROWS area; if you click a check box for a numeric field (☐ changes to ☑), Excel adds the field to the VALUES area. You can also right-click a field and then click the area that you want to use.

What is the FILTERS box used for?
You use it to add a filter field to the PivotTable, which enables you to display a subset of the data that consists of one or more unique values from the filter field. For more details, see the "Apply a PivotTable Filter" section later in this chapter.

Add Multiple Fields to a PivotTable Area

Y ou can add multiple fields to any of the PivotTable areas. This is a powerful technique that enables you to perform further analysis of your data by viewing it differently.

For example, suppose that you are analyzing the results of a sales campaign that ran different promotions in several types of advertisements. A basic PivotTable might show you the sales for each Product (the row field) according to the Advertisement used (the column field). You might also be interested in seeing, for each product, the breakdown in sales for each promotion. You can do that by adding the Promotion field to the ROWS area.

Add Multiple Fields to a PivotTable Area

Add a Field to the ROWS Area

1 Click a cell within the PivotTable.

2 Click the check box of the text or date field that you want to add (☐ changes to ☑).

A Excel adds the field to the ROWS box.

B Excel adds the field's unique values to the PivotTable's row area.

Add a Field to the ROWS or COLUMNS Area

1 Click a cell within the PivotTable.

2 In the PivotTable Fields list, click and drag the field that you want to add and drop the field in either the ROWS box or the COLUMNS box.

C Excel adds the field to the ROWS or COLUMNS box.

D Excel adds the field's unique values to the PivotTable's row or column area.

	Direct mail	Magazine	Newspaper	Grand Total
Sum of Net_$	Column Labels			
Row Labels	Direct mail	Magazine	Newspaper	Grand Total
Copy holder	2327.22	4050.94	4091.14	10469.30
Glare filter	5653.94	10234.55	8097.39	23985.88
Mouse pad	5461.36	11579.44	7314.12	24354.92
Printer stand	3750.75	6112.45	5063.02	14926.22
Grand Total	17193.27	31977.38	24565.67	73736.32

Sum of Net_$	Column Labels		Direct mail Total	Magazine
	Direct mail			
Row Labels	1 Free with 10	Extra Discount		1 Free with 1
Copy holder	1196.58	1130.64	2327.22	2610.
Glare filter	3293.40	2360.54	5653.94	5224.
Mouse pad	2991.45	2469.91	5461.36	6464.
Printer stand	2070.81	1679.94	3750.75	3148.
Grand Total	9552.24	7641.03	17193.27	17448.

TIP

Can I add multiple fields to the data area?

Yes. Adding multiple fields to the data area enables you to see multiple summaries for enhancing your analysis. For example, suppose that you are analyzing the results of a sales campaign that ran different promotions in several types of advertisements. A basic PivotTable might show you the sum of the Quantity sold (the data field) for each Product (the row field) according to the Advertisement in which the customer reported seeing the campaign (the column field). You might also be interested in seeing, for each product and advertisement, the net dollar amount sold. You can do that by adding the Net_$ field to the data area.

Move a Field to a Different PivotTable Area

A PivotTable is not a static collection of worksheet cells. You can move a PivotTable's fields from one area of the PivotTable to another. This enables you to view your data from different perspectives, which can greatly enhance the analysis of the data. Moving a field within a PivotTable is called *pivoting* the data.

The most common way to pivot the data is to move fields between the ROWS and COLUMNS areas. However, you can also pivot data by moving a row or column field to the FILTERS area.

Move a Field to a Different PivotTable Area

Move a Field between the ROWS and COLUMNS Areas

1 Click a cell within the PivotTable.

2 Click and drag a COLUMNS field button and drop it within the ROWS box.

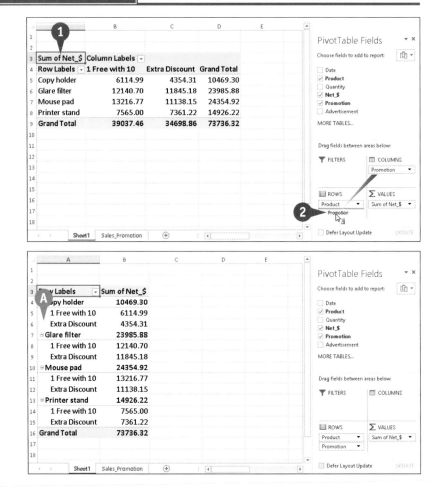

Ⓐ Excel displays the field's values within the row area.

You can also drag a field button from the ROWS box area and drop it within the COLUMNS box.

Move a Row or Column Field to the FILTERS Area

1 Click a cell within the PivotTable.

2 Click and drag a field from the ROWS box and drop it within the FILTERS box.

B Excel moves the field button to the report filter.

You can also drag a field button from the COLUMNS box and drop it within the FILTERS box.

TIP

Can I move a field to the PivotTable's data area?
Yes, you can move any row, column, or filter field to the PivotTable's data area. This may seem strange because row, column, and page fields are almost always text values, and the default data area calculation is Sum. How can you sum text values? You cannot, of course. Instead, Excel's default PivotTable summary calculation for text values is Count. So, for example, if you drag the Promotion field and drop it inside the data area, Excel creates a second data field named Count of Promotion.

Group PivotTable Values

To make a PivotTable with a large number of row or column items easier to work with, you can group the items together. For example, you could group months into quarters, thus reducing the number of items from twelve to four. Similarly, a report that lists dozens of countries could group those countries by continent, thus reducing the number of items to four or five, depending on where the countries are located. Finally, if you use a numeric field in the ROWS or COLUMNS area, you may have hundreds of items, one for each numeric value. You can improve the report by creating just a few numeric ranges.

Group PivotTable Values

1 Click any item in the numeric field that you want to group.

2 Click the **Analyze** tab.

3 Click **Group**.

4 Click **Group Field**.

The Grouping dialog box appears.

5 Type the starting numeric value.

A Click these check boxes
(☐ changes to ☑) to have
Excel extract the minimum and
maximum values of the numeric
items and place those values in
the text boxes.

6 Type the ending numeric value.

7 Type the size that you want to
use for each grouping.

8 Click **OK**.

B Excel groups the numeric values.

Grouping ? ✕

A

☐ <u>S</u>tarting at: 0 **5**

☐ <u>E</u>nding at: 2200 **6**

<u>B</u>y: 200 **7**

8 OK   Cancel

Sum of Quantity	Column Labels		
Row Labels	1 Free with 10	Extra Discount	Grand Total
0-200	186.00	203.00	389.00
200-400	429.00	430.00	859.00
400-600	638.00	619.00	1257.00
600-800	363.00	286.00	649.00
800-1000	440.00	791.00	1231.00
1000-1200	473.00	632.00	1105.00
1200-1400	429.00	293.00	722.00
1400-1600	473.00	120.00	593.00
1600-1800	110.00	254.00	364.00
1800-2000	132.00	274.00	406.00
2000-2200	275.00		275.00
Grand Total	3948.00	3902.00	7850.00

TIPS

How do I group date and time values?
Click any item in the date field that you want to group. Click the **Analyze** tab, click **Group**, and then click **Group Field**. In the Grouping dialog box, type the starting date or time and the ending date or time. In the **By** list, click the type of grouping that you want, such as **Months** or **Quarters**. Click **OK**.

How do I group text values?
You must create custom groups. For example, to group by continent, you could create custom groups named *North America, South America, Europe,* and so on. Begin by selecting the items that you want to include in a group. Click the **Analyze** tab, click **Group**, and then click **Group Selection**. Click the group label, type a new name for the group, and then press Enter. Repeat for each custom group that you want to create.

Apply a PivotTable Filter

By default, each PivotTable displays a summary for all the records in your source data. This is usually what you want to see. However, there may be situations in which you need to focus more closely on some aspect of the data. You can focus on a specific item from one of the source data fields by taking advantage of the PivotTable's filter field.

For example, suppose you are dealing with a PivotTable that summarizes data from a sales promotion by showing the net amount sold by product and promotion. To break down this summary by Advertisement, you could add that field to the filter area.

Apply a PivotTable Filter

Apply a Report filter

1 Add a field to the FILTERS box.

2 Click ▾ in the filter field.

Excel displays a list of the report filter field values.

3 Click the item that you want to use as a filter.

A If you want to display data for two or more report filters, click **Select Multiple Items** (☐ changes to ☑) and then repeat step **3** to select the other filters.

4 Click **OK**.

ⓑ Excel filters the PivotTable to show only the data for the item that you selected.

Remove the Filter

1 Click 🔽 in the report filter field.

Excel displays a list of the report filter field values.

2 Click **All**.

3 Click **OK**.

Excel removes the filter from the PivotTable.

Can I add multiple fields to the filter area?

Yes. This enables you to apply multiple filters to the data. For example, suppose you have a PivotTable that summarizes sales promotion data by showing the total amount sold for each product, and that you have a filter field with Advertisement data that enables you to isolate the sales by product for a specific type of advertising used in the promotion. You could extend your analysis to look at the advertisement-specific sales by product for individual promotions.

To do this, add the Promotion field as a second field in the FILTERS area and then use the steps in this section to choose a specific advertisement and a specific promotion. It does not matter which order the fields appear in the filter because the filtering comes out the same in the end.

CHAPTER 16

Maintaining a Database

Access provides several tools for performing maintenance and administrative functions on a database. You can switch between file formats and back up, repair, and compact a database. You can also create an easy-to-use Switchboard system that makes your database more accessible to beginners.

Set a Trusted Location

M acro security is quite stringent in Access 2013, which is not surprising given the number of macro-based viruses and other malware that have appeared in the past few years. A *trusted location* is a folder that Access assumes contains only trustworthy documents, so it automatically enables any macros contained in those documents. When you open a file from an untrusted location, security warnings appear. One way to avoid this problem is to save your Access database files in a trusted location. Before you can do this, you must set a trusted location.

Set a Trusted Location

1 Click **File**.

The File menu appears.

2 Click **Options**.

The Access Options dialog box opens.

3 Click **Trust Center**.

4 Click **Trust Center Settings**.

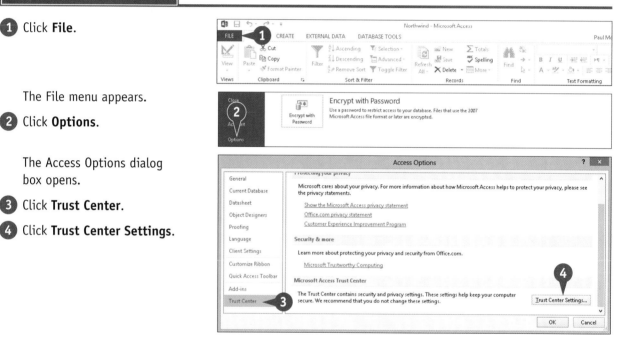

The Trust Center dialog box opens.

5 Click **Trusted Locations**.

6 Click **Add new location**.

The Microsoft Office Trusted Location dialog box opens.

7 Type the path that you want to set to be trusted.

A You can also click **Browse** to locate the path.

B You can click **Subfolders of this location are also trusted** (☐ changes to ☑) to also trust subfolders of this location.

8 Click **OK**.

The location is added to the Trusted Locations list.

9 Click **OK**.

10 Click **OK**.

Files from the location that you specified will now be trusted.

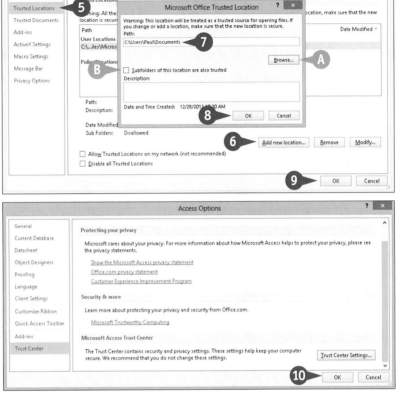

TIPS

Can I choose a network folder as a trusted location?
Yes. On the Trust Center's Trusted Locations tab, click **Allow Trusted Locations on my network** (☐ changes to ☑). You can then select a shared network folder as a trusted location. The check box includes the "(not recommended)" text because you probably do not have control over what files other users put in those folders.

Is there a quick way to turn off location-based trusting?
Yes. On the Trust Center's Trusted Locations tab, click **Disable all Trusted Locations** (☐ changes to ☑). This option temporarily turns off all location-based trusting. It is quicker and easier than removing each trusted location from the list and then adding it to the list again later.

☑ Allow Trusted Locations on my network (not recommended)

☐ Disable all Trusted Locations

Save in an Earlier Version Format

The file format used in Access 2007 through Access 2013 is not backward-compatible with earlier versions of Access. This means that if someone is using an earlier version of Access, that person cannot open any of your Access database files that use the current file format. Therefore, if you need to share a database file with someone who uses an earlier version of Access, you must save the file in that earlier format.

If you will be sharing the file on an ongoing basis with others who use Access 2003 and earlier, you must continue using the database in that format.

Save in an Earlier Version Format

1 Click **File**.

The File menu appears.

2 Click **Save As**.

3 Click **Save Database As**.

4 Click the older format that you want to use.

Note: Certain database features make it impossible to save the file in an earlier version, such as multivalued fields. If you have any such features in your database, an error will appear letting you know. At that point, you can edit the database to remove those features, or you can decide not to save in the older format.

5 Click **Save As**.

The Save As dialog box opens.

6 If needed, choose a different save location.

7 Type a filename.

8 Click **Save**.

The file is saved in the older format to the location that you specified.

316

Convert to the Access 2007-2013 Format

If you have databases created in early versions of Access, you can choose to update them to the Access 2007-2013 file format, which is called Access Database. (Access 2007, 2010, and 2013 use the same format.) Doing so offers several advantages, including the ability to use multivalued fields, calculated columns, and other features.

Note, however, that after you convert the database file to the latest format, you will not be able to use the file in earlier versions of Access.

Convert to the Access 2007-2013 Format

1 Click **File**.

The File menu appears.

2 Click **Save As**.

3 Click **Save Database As**.

4 Click **Access Database**.

5 Click **Save As**.

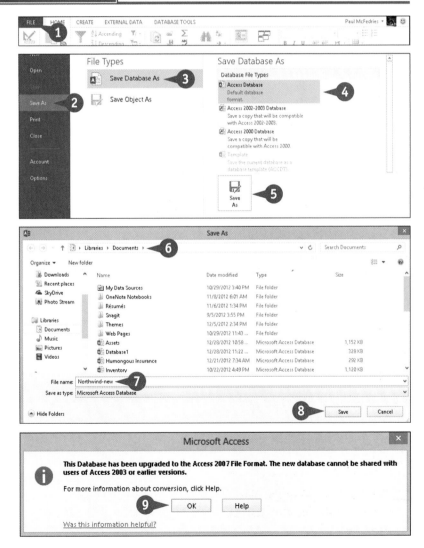

The Save As dialog box opens.

6 Change the save location if needed.

7 Type a different filename if needed.

8 Click **Save**.

A confirmation box appears.

9 Click **OK**.

The database file remains open but is now in the latest Access format.

Back Up a Database

Computer problems are an inevitable fact of life. One of these days, your system will crash, or your hard drive will become corrupted. These and similar glitches can cause problems for your database file, which could become unreadable. Therefore, it is a good idea to back up your database files periodically to ensure that your data is safe.

Backing up a database is similar to saving a copy of it; the main difference is that by default, the current date is appended to the filename.

Back Up a Database

1 Click **File**.

The File menu appears.

2 Click **Save As**.

3 Click **Save Database As**.

4 Click **Back Up Database**.

5 Click **Save As**.

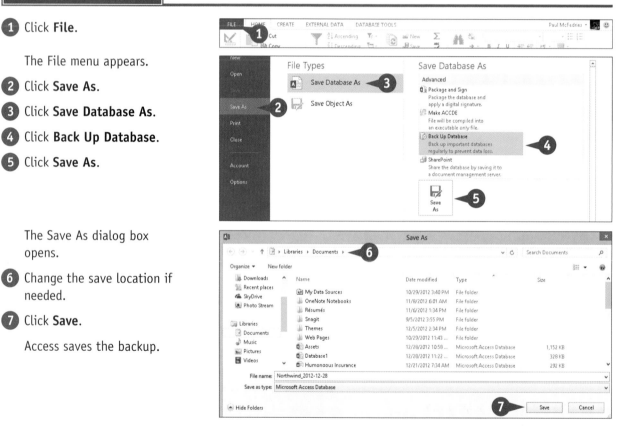

The Save As dialog box opens.

6 Change the save location if needed.

7 Click **Save**.

Access saves the backup.

Analyze Database Performance

Access databases generally perform queries, sorts, groupings, and other dynamic tasks quickly. However, as your tables grow larger, as the relationships between those tables grow more complex, and as your queries grow more sophisticated, you might notice that Access takes more time to perform certain tasks. In that case, you can run the Performance Analyzer tool, which analyzes your database objects and then offers suggestions to improve their performance.

Analyze Database Performance

① Click the **Database Tools** tab.

② Click **Analyze Performance**.

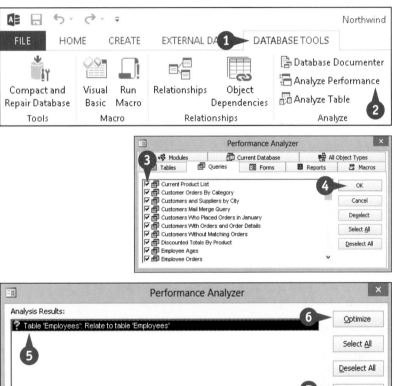

The Performance Analyzer dialog box opens.

③ On each tab, click the check box next to all the objects that you want to analyze.

④ Click **OK**.

Access displays the results of the analysis.

⑤ If Access displays a suggested fix, click the suggestion.

⑥ Click **Optimize**.

Access applies the suggestion to your database.

⑦ Click **Close**.

The report appears in Print Preview. From there, you can save it and print it.

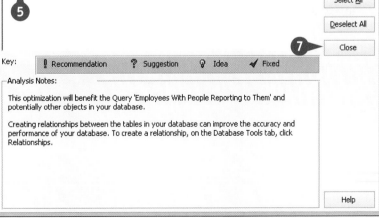

319

Compact and Repair a Database

When you delete objects from an Access database, Access ensures that the deletion happens quickly by simply creating blank space in the file where the object used to reside. This leaves your database file the same size. Compacting a database reduces the file size by eliminating wasted blank space. You can optionally set up the database to compact itself automatically each time you close it.

Repairing a database checks it for storage errors and corrects any that it finds. Compacting and repairing are actually two separate functions, but they are performed by using the same command.

Compact and Repair a Database

Compact and Repair

1 Click **File**.

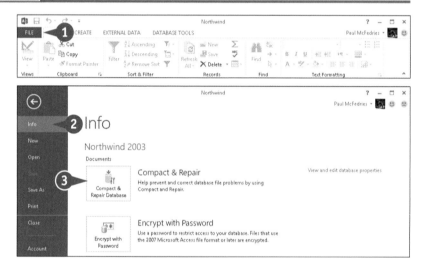

The File menu appears.

2 Click **Info**.

3 Click **Compact & Repair Database**.

Access compacts and repairs the database. No additional prompts appear.

Automatically Compact on Close

1 Click **File**.

The File menu appears.

2 Click **Options**.

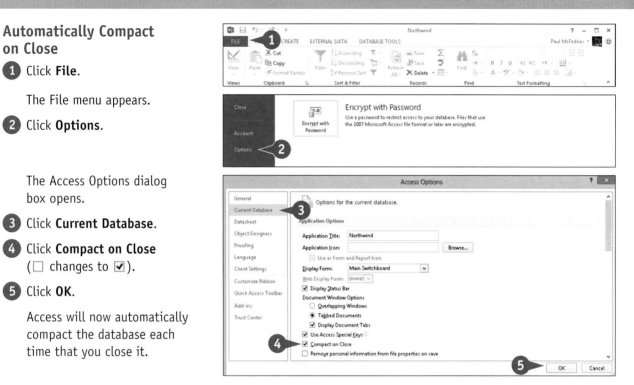

The Access Options dialog box opens.

3 Click **Current Database**.

4 Click **Compact on Close**
(□ changes to ☑).

5 Click **OK**.

Access will now automatically compact the database each time that you close it.

TIPS

What does compacting do?

Compacting a database removes any blank space that it contains so that it takes up less space on disk. When you delete records, for example, the space that they occupied in the database remains as blank space until you compact the database.

What does repairing do?

Repairing fixes any logical or linkage problems in the database — anything that may cause the database not to open properly or any of its objects not to perform as expected. Periodic repairing of a database file can ensure that small problems do not escalate into large ones.

Password-Protect a Database

Most databases contain nonsensitive data that requires no extra security precautions. However, you might be dealing with a database that does contain sensitive, private, or secret data. In that case, you can assign a password to the database so that only authorized users can open it.

Before you can set or change a password for the database, however, you must open it for exclusive use. This prevents others from using the database at the same time you are trying to put a password on it.

Password-Protect a Database

Open a Database for Exclusive Use

1 Click **File**.

The File menu appears.

2 Click **Close**.

Access closes the database.

3 Click **Open Other Files** (not shown).

4 Click **Computer**.

5 Click **Browse**.

The Open dialog box opens.

6 Click the database that you want to open.

7 Click this 🔽 and then click **Open Exclusive**.

Access opens the database for exclusive use.

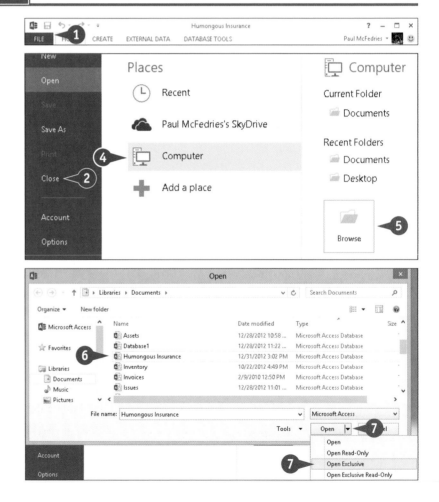

Password-Protect the Database

1 Click **File**.

The File menu appears.

2 Click **Info**.

3 Click **Encrypt with Password**.

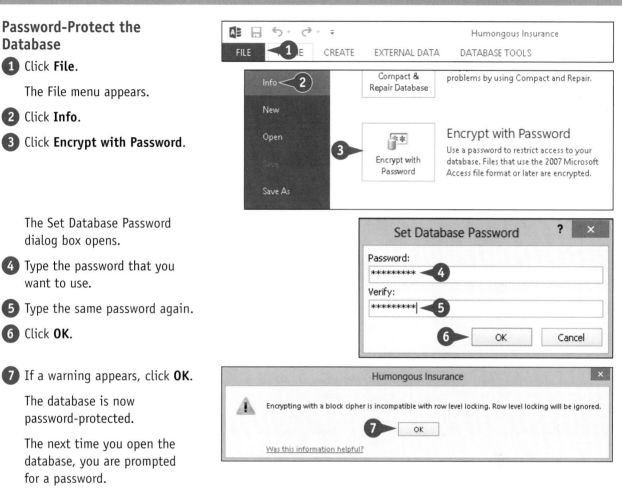

The Set Database Password dialog box opens.

4 Type the password that you want to use.

5 Type the same password again.

6 Click **OK**.

7 If a warning appears, click **OK**.

The database is now password-protected.

The next time you open the database, you are prompted for a password.

TIPS

How does password protection actually work?
When you set the password, Access jumbles the database into an unreadable format using a process called *encryption* to ensure that it cannot be browsed from outside of Access. When you enter the password, Access *decrypts* the file to make it readable again.

How do I unset (remove) a password?

1 Open the database for exclusive use.

2 Click **File**.

3 Click **Decrypt Database**.

4 Type the password.

5 Click **OK**.

Note: You cannot unset the password if you do not know it.

Create a Switchboard

Adatabase with many objects can be intimidating for an end user to navigate. Many of the people who may use and benefit from your database may not have the same level of computer expertise as you and may find it easier to work with a simpler interface. You can create your own navigation forms one by one by creating and linking forms together, but there is an easier way: the Switchboard feature. A switchboard automatically creates and links the forms to provide an easy-to-navigate user interface.

Create a Switchboard

Add the Switchboard Manager to the Quick Access Toolbar

1. Click the Customize Quick Access Toolbar button ( ).

2. Click **More Commands**.

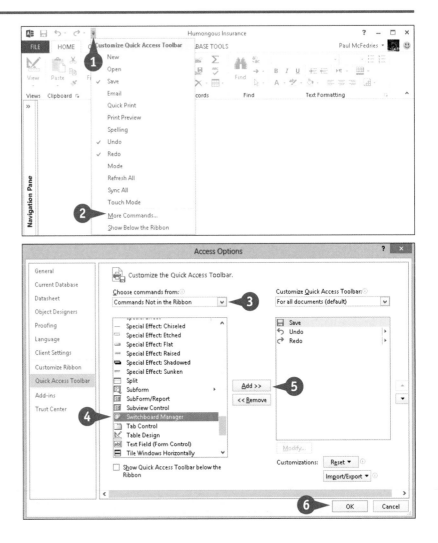

The Access Options dialog box opens and displays the Quick Access Toolbar tab.

3. Click the **Choose commands from** and click **Commands Not in the Ribbon**.

4. Click **Switchboard Manager**.

5. Click **Add**.

6. Click **OK**.

The Switchboard Manager button is added to the Quick Access Toolbar.

Start a New Switchboard

1 Click the Switchboard Manager (🖳) button on the Quick Access Toolbar.

A message appears that the Switchboard Manager was unable to find a valid switchboard and asks if you want to create one.

2 Click **Yes**.

Ⓐ The Switchboard Manager opens with a default switchboard page created.

You can now create additional switchboard pages and add items to each page.

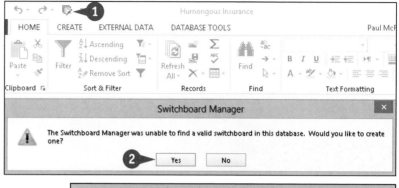

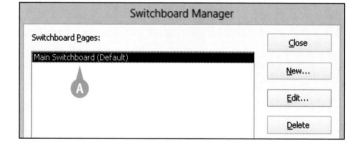

TIP

Can I format the switchboard?

Yes. The switchboard is a form and can be formatted like other forms.

Ⓐ After closing the Switchboard Manager, you can open the Switchboard form in the Design view and change the fonts, background, and other attributes. However, you should avoid making layout changes to the form or deleting the placeholders on it.

Ⓑ The Switchboard form pulls its data from a table called *Switchboard Items,* and if you delete the ItemText placeholder on the form, it loses its connection to the data it needs.

Ⓒ You can open the Switchboard Items table in the Datasheet view, the same as other tables. Examining that table can provide a behind-the-scenes view of how the switchboard works.

SwitchboardID ▾	ItemNumber ▾	ItemText ▾	Command ▾	Argument ▾
1	0	Main Switchboard		Default
1	1	Open Customers Form	2	Customers
2	0	Forms Page	0	
3	0	Reports Page	0	
✱	0			

continued ▶

Create a Switchboard (continued)

The basic switchboard consists of a single page. You may want to create additional pages and link them to the main page rather than place all your commands on that single main page. For example, on the main page, you might have links for Forms and Reports, and then you might create two separate pages: Forms Page and Reports Page. On each of those pages, you would then create links that open various forms and reports, respectively.

Create a Switchboard (continued)

Add a Switchboard Page

1 In the Switchboard Manager, click **New**.

The Create New dialog box opens.

2 Type the name for the new page.

3 Click **OK**.

Leave the Switchboard Manager open for further customization in the following subsection.

Add Commands to a Switchboard Page

1 In the Switchboard Manager, click the page that you want to edit.

2 Click **Edit**.

The Edit Switchboard Page dialog box opens.

3 Click **New**.

The Edit Switchboard Item dialog box opens.

④ Type the text that should appear for that item on the form.

⑤ Click the **Command** ☑ and click an action for the item.

⑥ Click this ☑ and click the item that the command will affect.

Note: The name of this command changes depending on what you chose in step **5**.

⑦ Click **OK**.

⑧ Repeat steps **3** to **7** to create more commands as needed.

⑨ Click **Close** to close the Edit Switchboard Page dialog box.

Your edits to the page are saved.

You can close the Switchboard Manager window or leave it open for further editing.

Edit Switchboard Item

Text: Go to Forms Page ◄ 4

7 ► OK

Command: Go to Switchboard 5 ☑ Cancel

Switchboard: Forms Page 6 ☑

Edit Switchboard Page

Switchboard Name: 9 Close

Main Switchboard

Items on this Switchboard: New...

Go to Forms Page

Edit...

Delete

Move Up

Move Down

TIPS

How do I create items that open forms or reports?
Follow the steps in the subsection "Add Commands to a Switchboard Page." For a form, in step **5**, choose either **Open Form in Add Mode** (opens the form with a new record started, for data entry) or **Open Form in Edit Mode** (opens the form with an existing record displayed). Then, choose the form name in step **6**. For a report, in step **5**, choose **Open Report** and then choose the report in step **6**.

Edit Switchboard Item

Text: Open Customers Form OK

Command: Open Form in Add Mode ☑ Cancel

Form: Customers ☑

How do I return to the main switchboard from one of the other pages?
Create an item on each switchboard page called *Go to Main Switchboard* and set its command to **Go to Switchboard** (step **5**). Set the switchboard you want to go to as the **Main Switchboard** (step **6**).

Edit Switchboard Item

Text: Go to Main Switchboard OK

Command: Go to Switchboard ☑ Cancel

Switchboard: Main Switchboard ☑

Set Switchboard Startup Options

The switchboard is most useful when it is set to appear automatically every time the database opens. That way, the user does not need to understand how to open a form by using the Navigation pane; the form simply appears.

You may also want to make the switchboard a pop-up form in a window rather than a tabbed form (the default). Users are more likely to be familiar with windows than with tabbed pages, so the windowed style may make them feel more comfortable.

Set Switchboard Startup Options

Set the Switchboard to Open Automatically at Startup

1 Click **File**.

The File menu appears.

2 Click **Options**.

The Access Options dialog box opens.

3 Click **Current Database**.

4 Click the **Display Form** ⌄ and then click **Switchboard**.

5 Click **OK**.

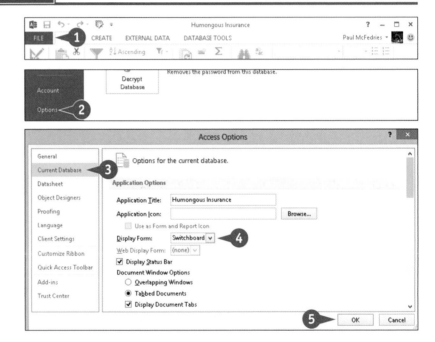

A message appears that you must close and reopen the database for the change to take effect.

6 Click **OK**.

The Switchboard form is now set to display automatically the next time you open the database.

Set the Switchboard to Open As a Floating Pane

1 Right-click the Switchboard form and then click **Design View**.

The form opens in the Design view.

2 Click the **Design** tab.

3 Click **Property Sheet**.

The Property Sheet opens.

4 Click the **All** tab.

5 Set the **Pop Up** setting to **Yes**.

6 Click 💾 to save the form.

7 Click **View** to preview the form.

The form appears as a pop-up window.

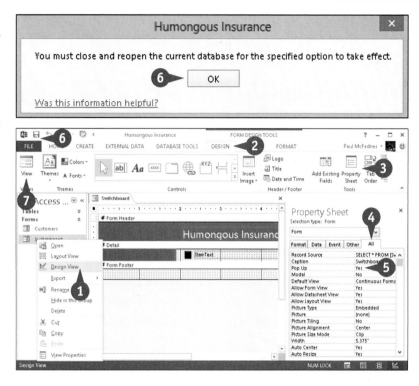

TIPS

The Switchboard window has a lot of empty space at the bottom. How can I make it appear smaller?

This happens because by default, the Switchboard form is set to display as continuous forms. On the Property Sheet in the Design view, set the **Default View** property to **Single Form**.

After I put the form in the pop-up mode, how can I get back to the Design view to edit it some more?

Right-click the Switchboard form in the Navigation pane and then choose **Design View** from the shortcut menu.

Index

Symbols and Numerics

H

I

J-K

L

Office **InDesign** **Facebook**

THE WAY YOU WANT TO LEARN.

HTML **Photoshop**

DigitalClassroom.com

Flexible, fast, and fun, DigitalClassroom.com lets you choose when, where, and how to learn new skills. This subscription-based online learning environment is accessible anytime from your desktop, laptop, tablet, or smartphone. It's easy, efficient learning — on *your* schedule.

- Learn web design and development, Office applications, and new technologies from more than 2,500 video tutorials, e-books, and lesson files
- Master software from Adobe, Apple, and Microsoft
- Interact with other students in forums and groups led by industry pros

Learn more! Sample DigitalClassroom.com for free, now!

We're social. Connect with us!

facebook.com/digitalclassroom
@digitalclassrm